C000091586

Meanings as Species

MARK RICHARD is a Professor of Philosophy at Harvard University. He is the author of *Propositional Attitudes: An Essay on Thoughts and How We Ascribe Them* (Cambridge, 1990), *When Truth Gives Out* (Oxford, 2008), *Context and the Attitudes: Meaning in Context, Volume 1* (Oxford, 2013), and *Truth and Truth Bearers: Meaning in Context, Volume 2* (Oxford, 2015).

Meanings as Species

Mark Richard

OXFORD
UNIVERSITY PRESS

OXFORD
UNIVERSITY PRESS

Great Clarendon Street, Oxford, OX2 6DP,
United Kingdom

Oxford University Press is a department of the University of Oxford.
It furthers the University's objective of excellence in research, scholarship,
and education by publishing worldwide. Oxford is a registered trade mark of
Oxford University Press in the UK and in certain other countries

First published 2019
First published in paperback 2021

Published in the United States of America by Oxford University Press
198 Madison Avenue, New York, NY 10016, United States of America

British Library Cataloguing in Publication Data
Data available

Library of Congress Cataloging in Publication Data
Data available

ISBN 978-0-19-884281-1 (Hbk.)
ISBN 978-0-19-284837-6 (Pbk.)

Contents

Acknowledgments

The beginning and end of Chapter 3 appear in slightly different form as 'Analysis, Concepts, and Intuitions' in *Analytic Philosophy* 55 (2014); some of the material in the middle of that chapter appears as 'How Do Slurs Mean?' in David Sosa, editor, *Bad Words* (Oxford University Press, 2018). Sections of 4 and 6 of Chapter 6 appear, again in different form, as 'The A-Project and the B-Project' in Burgess, Cappelen, and Plunkett, editors, *Conceptual Engineering* (Oxford University Press, 2019). Early parts of Chapter 5 are adapted from the Introduction to my *Meaning in Context, Volume I* (Oxford University Press, 2013). I thank the publishers for permission to use this material.

I've been thinking about the topics discussed in this book since 2010, when it occurred to me while teaching a seminar on social construction that the sort of account of meaning developed here was just what the social constructionist ordered. In the interim I've read bits of what follows in many venues in the last few years. Thanks for questions, comments, and good-natured skepticism from both students in various seminars and audiences at the University of London, the University of Bonn, the University of St. Andrews, Tufts University, the University of Konstanz, the University of Groningen, Dartmouth University, Rutgers University, the University of Connecticut, the University of Palermo, the University of Oslo, Cambridge University, the University of Leeds, the Argentine Society for Analytic Philosophy, and the University of Miami. Members of these audiences who asked particularly useful questions are mentioned in notes. I'm indebted to Herman Cappelen for inviting me many times to Oslo to present early versions of this material. Three readers for the Press gave me detailed and useful comments; thanks to them as well.

My debt in what follows to the writings of Dan Dennett, Hilary Putnam, W.V. Quine, and Bob Stalnaker is too obvious not to mention.

Finally and as always, thanks to Max, Eleanor, Anneliese, and Michael for being such great kids-who-are-now-adults. And, of course, to my muse, Nancy.

Introduction

I start with what for me is a puzzle. An analytic sentence is a sentence one can see to be true simply by understanding it (and, perhaps, using a little logic). The hoary example is the sentence 'all bachelors are unmarried': to understand the sentence one must understand the word 'bachelor', knowing that it means unmarried man; so to understand the sentence is not just to know that it says that all bachelors are unmarried but to know that it says something that comes to no more and no less than that all unmarried men are unmarried. But any rational animal who can think the thought that all unmarried men are unmarried knows it.

I accept Quine's observation in 'Two Dogmas of Empiricism' that no sentence, not even 'all bachelors are unmarried', is beyond rational revision. I take it to imply that there are not and could not be analytic sentences. But I take seriously the worry Paul Grice and Peter Strawson expressed about Quine's position. Quine's view, they pointed out, seems to lead to the conclusion that there is no sense to be made of the idea that expressions can be synonymous, which in turn suggests that talk of meaning is senseless. Thus the puzzle: Can we agree with Quine that there are no analyticities without saying that talk about the meaning of the word 'bachelor' is senseless?

Quine's remarks at the end of 'Two Dogmas' suggest a certain picture of our way of being in the linguistic world. At any time, the way we use our words gives them a particular role in inference: for example, our current way of using 'bachelor' gives a double thumbs-up to the inference *Paul is married; so Paul is not a bachelor*. Our linguistic activity also embodies presuppositions about the world and assumptions about how others will use their words when they speak. The inferential role and presuppositions accompanying our words determine how we use our language as a tool for inquiry and communication. But the inferential roles and presuppositions that determine use are fluid and dynamic. How we should proceed in the face of 'recalcitrant experience' isn't determined at the outset, and we can change course—change the presuppositions and inferential role that accompany our words—when it seems apt. So there are no epistemically fixed points in the history of inquiry. Quine's fundamental worry about analyticity, I think, was that whatever an analytic sentence is supposed to be, it would have to be a fixed point in inquiry.

Now in this picture there is something that plays the role of the meaning of a term—its inferential role and the firmly held presuppositions about use and the world that are associated with it. But this meaning is inherently dynamic. It's not a fixed Fregean sense or

Platonic universal, but a constantly evolving set of hypotheses, inferential dispositions, and expectations about the world and the speech of others.

There is also something that potentially functions as a criterion of 'sameness of meaning'. Changes in inferential role or in presuppositions that result in fluid conversation being stymied or in the role of a sentence in inquiry being radically revised can be sensibly called changes in meaning. If, of a sudden, the noun 'duck' takes on the role of the noun 'cookie'—well, that would be a change of meaning. But the statement-sized alterations that Quine had in mind in 'Two Dogmas'—dropping, say, the belief that ducks are birds while preserving the thought that ducks are fuzzy-feeling aquatic things given to airborne migration—those sorts of changes needn't upset the apple carts of inquiry and conversation. On this picture, 'meaning identity' is not unlike artifact identity. A change in a few of the planks and nails that constitute Theseus' ship doesn't make the ship disappear; a sudden, wholesale replacement of the wooden parts with aluminum ones does.

Returning to the puzzle we began with: There are no analyticities because nothing plays the role in inquiry and communication that something would have to play to count as analytic. That doesn't mean that there isn't a phenomenon that deserves to be called 'meaning'. But it's an inherently dynamic one, and sameness of meaning is a lot like sameness of ship. At the end of the day, many of our ordinary and theoretical judgments of sameness of meaning—both diachronic and synchronic—are judgments of similarity that we frame in the language of identity. Nothing wrong with a little idealization so long as we are aware that we are idealizing.

*

For the moment, let us not quibble with those who are internalists about language. Let us, that is, allow that languages are (in part, at least) psychological structures which, molded by the idiosyncratic histories of speakers in acquiring their tongues, invariably vary in details of pronunciation, syntax, and meaning; each speaker thus speaks her own language. That granted, when speakers are in actual and potential communication there is typically an enormous amount of similarity in their languages. Communication and language acquisition conspire to insure this: enough evidence that others use a word in ways different than I tends ceteris paribus to reproduce the others' usage in my idiolect. The linguistic sins of the father tend to be visited on the dialect of the daughter.

Speakers in actual and potential communication have similar idiolects; they tend to associate very similar inferential roles and presuppositions with their words. Of course, for all the similarity there is diversity, not only in presuppositions but in phonology, morphology, syntax, and so on. Linguistic individuals interact, and these interactions produce changes in the idiolects of the interactors. These changes are typically ones in which the language of one speaker comes more or less permanently to resemble the language of those with whom he interacts. These changes—that is, the properties acquired because of linguistic interaction—can be and often are transmitted down the road to others. Some such changes spread aggressively across a population whose members communicate with one another; others fizzle or even disappear; yet others (think of slang) persist in a minority equilibrium. Over time enough changes in the linguistic behavior of a linguistic lineage may lead to linguistic behavior that is radically different than the behavior from which it descended.

To me—and, I hasten to say, to many linguists, as my analogy is hardly novel—it is striking how much this resembles the biological world. There we find populations of individuals who are very similar—they have similar genomes. The members of a population interact with another—I believe 'hook up' is the biological term—with the interactions resulting in individuals who tend to resemble the interactors. Over time, individuals who make up a population lineage may, as changes in transmitted properties become fixed in the population, become so different from their ancestors that we say they are of a different species.

What follows investigates whether linguistic entities—in particular, word meanings—are well understood when we think of them as being like those segments of population lineages that we label species. I think we gain a certain amount of illumination if we combine the idea that meanings are species-like with the picture of meaning that a little while back I ascribed to Quine.

*

If meanings are species-like, what exactly are they? What, for example, is the meaning of 'cousin'?

When a speaker speaks, she makes presuppositions that she expects her audience will recognize as made, ones she expects the audience will have ready for use in making sense of what she says. Some such presuppositions are tied to particular words and accompany their use. When we speak of cousins using 'cousin', we expect to be recognized as talking about parents' siblings' progeny; we expect the audience can access the idea, that this is what cousins are, in interpretation. For some such presuppositions, it will be common ground in a linguistic community that speakers make them and expect that to be recognized by their audience. I call these sorts of presuppositions interpretive common ground—ICG for short. It is, for example, ICG among English speakers that 'cousin' is a term for cousins, and cousins are parents' siblings' progeny; speakers presuppose this and expect the presupposition to be recognized and used in interpretation; everybody is cognizant of this. I say the meaning of lexical items is, to a first approximation, ICG in the sense just sketched.

You should say: What do you mean by 'meaning'? I could mean something like the determinant of reference and truth conditions, something like what David Kaplan calls character. Or I could mean something that can be asserted, believed, and so on, something associated with a sentence's use by convention and context, or more idiosyncratically by a speaker. Or I could mean meaning in the sense of that with which one must be in cognitive contact in order to qualify as a competent speaker in a population.

I mean the last. ICG is relevant to reference and truth, but reference and truth can't be read off it, if only because what's common ground is often erroneous. There is, I think, a sense of 'what is said' in which what is said by a sentence is determined by the ICG of its phrases and their referential semantic values; there are other senses of 'what is said' in which ICG (and reference) does not determine what is said. ICG is meaning as the anchor of linguistic competence; it is what knits us together as beings who share a language and thus can communicate.

ICG is pretty clearly a species-like phenomenon. Pick a herd of individuals in actual and potential communication with each other, a herd whose communication is intuitively a matter of their sharing a common tongue. Pick a word—that is, a particular morphology and phonology married to a syntactic role—that is part of the common tongue. Let's say we picked the English speakers of Newton Highlands MA in 1962 and the word 'marry'. Members of the herd assume that everyone knows that when people use 'marry', they make certain presuppositions which they expect their audience to recognize as being made and to invoke if necessary in interpretation. Members of the herd, for example, assume it's commonly known that when a speaker uses 'marry' she assumes that the word picks out a relation that can only hold between a man and a woman; the herd knows that (all know that) speakers expect the audience to recognize this. Each member of the herd has a 'lexical entry' for 'marry' that is in part constituted by those presuppositions she takes to be commonly made by users of the word. There will be a good deal of similarity from one entry to another, as speakers tend to cotton on pretty quickly to what all assume all assume. But just as there is variation among the genomes of individual speakers, so will there be variation across the flock about what is commonly presupposed by users of 'marry': Just as some of us have green eyes and others blue, some of us think that people think marriage between second cousins is forbidden, while others think this is not what people think. Just as genomes in a population lineage display allelic variation, so do lexical entries. And over time the contours of such variation may shift as a result of speakers' interactions with one another and with the social environment, as the usefulness of an assumption about a word for understanding its use shifts. The presupposition that people think that (people think that) same-gendered marriage is impossible, for example, has gone by the wayside.

*

The task of the first three chapters of this book is to set out in some detail the two ideas I've been pointing at. Those chapters argue that we should honor Quine's insights about analyticity and synonymy, not by abandoning the notion of meaning, but by seeing meaning as a dynamic, population-level phenomenon. And they set out the idea that what I've called interpretive common ground is an important kind of meaning: it has some call to be said what we are trying to articulate when we engage in philosophical analysis; it is meaning in the sense of what anchors linguistic competence. To be a competent speaker of a group's language, I argue, is in part to 'have the right relation' to the ICG of the words the group shares.

Chapter 1 shows how Quine's remarks about meaning and analyticity strongly suggest a picture of meaning on which the biological analogy is apt. There has been and continues to be pertinacious resistance among philosophers to Quine's conclusions in 'Two Dogmas', and Chapter 2 discusses some notable responses to Quine—for example, the complaint that Quine couldn't be right because, well, obviously we could simply stipulate that a novel expression is to mean what an existent phrase does, as well as the idea that broadly Bayesian accounts of rational credence supply all we need to define what it is for a speaker's uses of an expression to mean the same thing from one time to another. Chapter 3 begins with a discussion of the idea that much of what's called philosophical analysis is a sort of conceptual (or meaning) analysis. Developing this idea quickly leads to a picture of (one kind of) linguistic meaning as ICG. It takes a fair amount of work—all of it great fun, I assure you—to develop this picture; if you are skeptical of the theoretical utility of the idea of meaning-cum-ICG on the basis of the five paragraphs devoted to it above, I pray you hold your skepticism in abeyance until you've finished Chapter 3.

Species can and usually do evolve without ceasing to be. But evolution can and does lead to the existence of new species, the death of old. It is a nice question as to what the conditions, interestingly necessary or sufficient, are for a species to come or cease to be. If meanings are species-like, there is a question *aussi belle* as to when linguistic evolution leads to a linguistic form's having a new meaning. Chapter 4 takes up, but doesn't pretend to solve, this question. It makes a proposal about the sorts of synchronic relations speakers need to stand in order for it to be apt to say that they share a language, and thus for their words to share a meaning. But answering the question, What makes my contemporaries speakers of my tongue?, isn't answering the question, What makes future speakers who use the sentences of my tongue mean what I mean with those sentences?

One approach to this question asks under what conditions it is apt to say that in five (or ten or ten to ten to the ten) minutes, a use of a sentence will say the same as its current use. The not unreasonable thought behind this approach is that since a sentence's meaning is an important determinant of what it can be used to say, switches in saying power tend to indicate mutation of meaning. Since it's natural to think that what an utterance says is in part determined by the reference of its parts and the truth conditions of the whole, this thought leads to the thought that preservation of reference is necessary for sameness of meaning. Chapter 4's midsection is devoted to developing the beginnings of an account of the conditions under which one can reasonably ascribe same saying across days, decades, or centuries. It takes seriously the idea that there is a certain amount of indeterminacy in what we use our words to talk about—not the wild indeterminacy that says that 'sad' and 'silly' might reasonably be said to have sets of numbers as extensions, but a more tempered indeterminacy thesis that acknowledges that, absent interpretive interests and intent, there is just no saying whether 'water' as used by George II was true of samples of D_2O. This means that same saying is to a certain extent a matter of interpretation. And so insofar as a sentence's continuing to mean what it does is tied to its continuing to be a vehicle for saying what it presently does, whether a word preserves its meaning across time is to some extent a matter of interpretation.

I said that it was not unreasonable to think that because sentence meaning is coupled with what sentences say, shifts in saying power are indicators of changes of meaning. As I noted, one might go on to say that since what is said determines truth conditions, shifts in truth conditions must produce shifts in meaning. It is a short road from this conclusion to what Chapter 4 calls referentialism, the view that that within a linguistic community, diachronic constancy of a sentence's character is necessary and sufficient for it to preserve its meaning. If by 'meaning' one means something like 'determinant of reference and truth', referentialism is obvious enough. But if one means something along the lines of 'cognitive anchor of linguistic competence', referentialism is much less obvious. Chapter 4 ends with a frankly skeptical discussion of referentialism about meaning-cum-anchor-of-competence.

I observed above that it's natural to think that there must be a close connection between what a sentence means, what it is used to say, and the cognitive structures which realize a belief ascribable with the sentence. But just as I don't think there is a one-size-fits-all-theoretical-needs notion of sentence meaning, so I don't think there is a distinguished notion of what is ('strictly and literally') said by a sentence.

It is reasonable to think that if we fix a group of speakers in actual and potential communication—be it all the English speakers in zip code 79104, the students in and teacher of this year's iteration of Philosophy 147, or me and my wife—a sentence will have a 'default interpretation' relative to the group, one constructed from its semantic values and the ICG of its words in the group. Such a default interpretation is the starting point for interpretation, a reification of what someone from the group will have in mind when she begins interpreting the sentence's use.[1] Chapter 3 argues that this is one thing that might be identified as 'what is said' by a sentence S's use. But there are many other candidates for this role. There is, for example, what the clause S contributes to determining the truth conditions of things like *Jill said that S* or *Jack's pretty sure that T*. It strikes me as wildly implausible that in making such ascriptions we are very often to be understood as saying that Jack or Jill stands in an interesting relationship to a default interpretation of S as we and our audience use it. When I say, for example, that the Sumerians thought that Venus is a star, I am not suggesting that they made the sorts of presuppositions we make about Venus and the stars.

Chapter 5 spells out in some detail what I think is going on when we ascribe beliefs, sayings, and the like. It seems to me that what we do is to use our words as a representation—a 'translation', if you will—of a state or an utterance of the subject of the ascription. The correctness of an ascription like *Jill thought Jack was at the top of the hill* turns on whether its content sentence—the bit after 'that'—is an adequate representation of one of Jill's belief states, with standards of adequacy varying with the interests and intent of the speaker. I argue that, contrary to what you might think, thinking of ascription of belief and the like in this way doesn't make it difficult to understand how

---

[1] This way of putting things ignores contextual variability due to such things as demonstratives, gradable adjectives, and so on.

computers or non-human animals like wolves and wildebeests can have beliefs and make presuppositions (and so are in principle and practice able to mean things by behavior in the same sense in which our linguistic behavior does). The chapter argues against the idea that there is a close tie between some sort of (not merely referential) meaning of a sentence S and what we are saying about someone when we say that she said or believes or only just realized that S. It closes by using the account of attitudes and attitude ascription it sets out to defend some of the conclusions of Chapter 4 about meaning persistence.

My thought in this book is that we gain a certain amount of insight into language if we think of meaning as analogous to the population-level processes studied by biologists. But just how much is meaning change like biological evolution? Is it really a matter of something well described in terms of fitness and selection? This is the topic of Chapter 6, which suggests that some but not all of the processes that drive meaning change look to be like evolution via natural selection. That chapter ends with some discussion of interventions in the process of linguistic evolution, focused on Sally Haslanger's idea of ameliorative philosophical analysis. One of the conclusions of this discussion is that thinking of meaning in the way developed in previous chapters makes the project of ameliorative analysis—as well as many of the projects clustered under the title 'conceptual engineering'—appear much more sensible than it is otherwise likely to seem.

1

Quine and the Species Problem

One way to think about meanings has them static and unchanging, neither physical nor mental, abstract denizens of a 'third realm'. This is more or less how Frege seemed to think of them. This, it seems to me, is a bad way to think about meaning.

Meaning is something our words, sentences, and (some of our) token mental states have. What each of our linguistic and mental states means is determined by a very large array of factors indeed: inferential relations, including tendencies to make inductive and abductive inferences; patterns of application and what contributes to determining them (e.g., prototype structures); tendencies to defer to others about matters of application; environmental and social relations; and so on. These determinants are not static: patterns of application change, prototypes evolve, we come to defer less (or more) to others, etc., etc. One could say that while the determinants of meaning shift, a meaning itself can't change: like the number six or the Platonic form of Harmony, the meaning of 'marriage', the concept marriage, stays as it is, unchanging forever. One could say this, but it seems about as attractive as saying that the objects evolutionary biology studies—species, clades, and the like—do not change over time: species, like the number nine and the Platonic form of Justice, stay ever the same, even as the determinants of what species a population realizes shift. *Quatsch.*

I have tried to cast my point in a way that is neutral as to whether the linguistic bearers of meaning are words and sentences of idiolects (the idiosyncratic language of a single individual) or words and phrases of public, shared languages. Of course, insofar as meanings are publicly shared, things passed on from mothers to daughters, the biological analogy just drawn is even stronger.

My goal in this and the following chapters is to convince you that there is indeed a rather strong analogy between biological entities (species, clades, population lineages) and linguistic and semantic entities (words, meanings, concepts, languages). This chapter makes a modest beginning on this. Its first sections review some obvious facts about language communities and speakers, some elementary facts about the ways biology thinks about species, and points out that there is indeed a prima facie case for thinking that things like word meanings are analogous to species. The chapter's later sections argue that if we take the analogy at face value, we can embrace Quine's conclusion in 'Two Dogmas of Empiricism'—that there is no theoretically interesting notion of analytic truth, no sort of synonymy that can do epistemological work—while still thinking that the notion of meaning can carry a real theoretical load.

1. Private Language, Public Language

I assume that underlying each speaker's linguistic ability is an internalized grammar. Such grammars are collections of mental representations that realize rules and procedures; these rules and procedures determine what the sentences of the speaker's language are. Grammars involve a lexicon, a 'mental dictionary', that records broadly syntactic information about (basic) words—their syntactic category, phonetics, orthography, argument structure, ways in which they are abnormal or otherwise marked, and so on. Lexical entries are somehow interpreted—they are not senseless signs but have meanings that contribute to determining the meanings of the sentences in which they occur.

It is natural to think that lexical entries will change over time, if only because language is something that is learned over time. Children acquire a word and then expend a fair amount of effort to make their lexical entry similar in various ways to those of speakers in their surround: they refine and correct their pronunciation (*smellow* becomes *marshmallow*) and morphology (*goed* becomes *went*); they correct over- and under-extensions of predicates. It would be a strange theory indeed that insisted that every such change was the substitution of one vocabulary item for a new one.

Some, in an orgy of internalist fastidiousness, foreswear identifying the languages or even the words used by different individuals. They hold that the proper objects of linguistic study are individual grammars—the idiolects—of individual speakers. They say public languages are myths, since individual idiolects vary between parents and children, sibling and sibling; there is thus not a single set of sentences that constitutes the sentences of 'the' language spoken by the members of a single family, much less such a thing as 'the' grammar or 'the' language they speak.

Idiolects do indeed vary from individual to individual, and we can grant that it is more than just a rarity for parent and child or sibling and sibling to literally share an idiolect. That admitted, there is surely something significantly amiss in the idea that linguistics, thought of as the study of human language, is only concerned with individual idiolects. Languages, after all, are vehicles of communication. And it is hard to see how they could be vehicles of communication within a population—a family, a fourth-grade class, the readers of *The New York Times*—unless there were mechanisms in place that coordinated the different idiolects in the group so that what a speaker utters is reliably identifiable and thus understandable at some level quite independently of the identity of the speaker and the interpreter, independently of the particulars of contexts of use and interpretation.[1] Whatever differences there may be between Mom's, Dad's, Brother's, and Sister's grammars, there is surely a coordination between their lexicons that links individual entries for the noun 'stranger': Dad uses his 'stranger' entry, S_D, to interpret the words that are generated by Mom's, Brother's, and Sister's

---

[1] The sort of understanding I have in mind is *not* identifying 'what is said' by an utterance but what we would pre-theoretically call 'knowing what sentence was uttered', something that is normally necessary but usually not sufficient for 'knowing what was said'.

'stranger' entries S_M, S_B, and S_S; each of the other three use these entries to interpret the tokens generated by the others' entries. Each interprets the others as producing the same word, and the word each interprets the others producing is the word the others interpret him as producing. Something similar is true of larger phrases, of course.

Part of what makes the child's grammar a language is that it is a medium for communicating with those who are linguistically connected via this sort of coordination with the child; part of the study of language is the study of such linguistic connection, of what underlies, reinforces, and disrupts it, of how it evolves over time. If this is correct, then perhaps there is, internalist objections notwithstanding, something to the idea of a public language. Suppose, for example, that there is a more or less determinate, more or less robust relation *lexical entry e is at time t coordinated with lexical entry e'* that connects the entries in different speakers' lexicons, a relation that (more or less) reflects when speakers do and do not understand one another: save in exceptional circumstances, I interpret your utterance of a word correctly just in case the entry your utterance tokens is coordinated with the entry I use to interpret it. If this relation is (more or less) an equivalence relation, we might understand talk about common vocabulary as shorthand for talk about relations of lexical coordination. And if such coordination projects up from the lexicon to more complex phrases so that it determines a ragged equivalence relation on phrases in different individual grammars, we might be able to understand talk about common languages as shorthand for talk about this sort of coordination. Whether it's reasonable to think that something resembling the everyday notions of (public language) word and phrase can be so constructed is an issue to which I will eventually return.[2]

2. Species and Meanings

There are analogies between biological objects—population lineages, species, genomes, and such—and various linguistic objects—languages, vocabularies, individual words, their meanings, and the like. (Public language word) meanings being a kind of concept, it will be no surprise that these analogies extend to concepts. The analogies are useful because they suggest useful ways to think about linguistic and conceptual continuity. In particular, they help us see how it might be that while Quine was substantially correct in his pessimism about analyticity and conceptual truth, he was—or at least might have been—wrong to conclude that something like the ordinary notion of meaning is unable to do serious theoretical work.

Before looking at analogies, let's review some facts about species and speciation. The currently dominant accounts of species take them to be parts of population lineages—parts, that is, of sequences of populations related by descent and ancestry. Not just any such sequence is a species—we're conspecific with our grandparents but we aren't conspecific with every ancestor of the chimpanzee, though there is a tree of descent (a phylogeny) that has the chimps and us descending from common ancestors. There is

---

[2] More on the notion of coordination in Chapter 4.

considerable controversy as to what 'the right' species concept is; the species problem is the puzzle of whether there is a notion of species that can do the theoretical work demanded by talk of species in various branches of biology—systematics, evolutionary biology, ecology, population genetics, and so on.

There seem to be something in the neighborhood of two dozen characterizations of species knocking about, and little sign of a great synthesis that would significantly narrow this number.[3] Some take species to be something like populations distinguished from others by certain evolved features—a new species arises when a particular set of distinguishing features arises (eleven-toed, tripedal, blue feathers...); the species is the sequence of populations with these features descending from the founding population. Others take them to be populations united by one or another (usually relational) property: the ability to interbreed, geographical or ecological range, fecundity of offspring, etc. Even if—and it remains very much an 'if' in evolutionary theory—speciation is usually relatively abrupt in geological terms, the fact remains that, looking at a population generation by generation, it can be difficult or impossible to say in a principled way where one species leaves off and a new one begins.[4]

While there's a good deal of variation across species concepts, there's also some unity. On most accounts, species are certain population lineages whose stages[5] (i) tend to reproduce themselves in ways that preserve certain kinds of synchronic cohesion in the succeeding population, and (ii) are subject to diachronic change over generations of reproduction that can result in 'diachronic lack of cohesion' between stages of the lineage in which the species occurs. They are lineages which (at each time at which some population realizes the lineage) are unified—there is enough commonality in the genomes of a species' individuals that we can speak of a common genetic structure with common, functionally defined areas. But they are also diverse: variants of genes (alleles, in biospeak) occur at particular loci in the genome across the population; while every (normal) individual has a version of some trait (eye color, height as an adult, etc.), the form of a trait's realization varies across the population. As one population descends from another, new forms arise and spread through the population; some traits whose past realizations varied across the population see a particular realization become fixed in successor populations. Enough 'diachronic lack of cohesion'—enough difference between one segment of a lineage and a later segment—implies that speciation has occurred. What varies across species concepts is (in good part) the sort of cohesion needed for a population in a particular temporal interval to form a stage of a species. On some accounts, it is morphological traits originating in some ancestor that separate

---

[3] Richards (2010) cites Mayden (1997) as claiming that there are more than twenty species concepts in use among biologists. Both Richards (2010) and Hull (1997) give useful discussions for philosophers of the range of species concepts.

[4] There are notions of species that come close to untying the idea of a species from the idea of descent, with species defined in more or less observable terms. That said, it is not clear that anyone, not even Aristotle or Linnaeus, really had a totally ahistorical notion of biological species. Again, see Richards (2010) for an illuminating discussion.

[5] Think of the stages of species as the populations that constitute them at particular times. The use of 'stage' here is not an attempt to suggest that species or languages are 'four-dimensional objects'.

the species from all others; on other accounts, it is the potential to interbreed; on others, it is a matter of being part of a single gene pool; on others, something else.

There are some who are skeptical that species 'reflect an important ontological divide in nature' (Ereshefsky 1999, 286). Some claim that the soritical way in which evolution occurs makes species non-starters as serious theoretical entities. On one version of this view, what is biologically real are lines of descent in which populations diverge in ways passed on by descent, ways driven toward fixation by selection; species are nothing more than a gerrymandered and incomplete way the folk and the biologist have of describing parts of this reality in which they are interested.

It is striking how much of all this seems to be reflected in the linguistic world.[6] Think of a population that we would describe as sharing a common language—the residents of Long Island, say, who are in the habit of using English to talk to each other. The grammars that describe the idiolects these people speak are united. They share large swatches of vocabulary and a grammatical template (for example, all these idiolects are Subject/Verb/Object languages, not Verb/Subject/Object languages). But there is also diversity in the community: there is individual variation in morphology, orthography, and conceptual structure in individual realizations of the lexicon; the grammars differ on some rules, morphology varies, and so on. As in the biological case, the (lexical and grammatical) unity that underlies variation in such a population is critical for its (linguistic) perpetuation: one generation typically transmits the lexicon and grammatical template that unifies its linguistic community to the next, (more or less) insuring that the next generation can communicate with one another (and with the previous one).

Of course languages, lexicons, and individual words—like species—evolve. As one population 'reproduces' its language in the next, new words arise, old words have their meanings changed, phonology shifts, grammatical rules may be modified, and so on.[7] As is the case with species, some of this evolution will be quite gradual: successive generations are able to fluently communicate with one another, just as successive generations in a population lineage are (counterfactually and in principle) able to interbreed, have fertile progeny, share a system for recognizing mates, etc. As is the case with species, even when abutting generations enjoy the sort of cohesion that would drive the observer to classify them as speakers of a single language, the soritical ways of linguistic change, given enough time, will lead to a diachronic lack of cohesion so great that no one will say that ancestor and descendent populations speak the same language, even though the languages they use are related by descent.[8]

---

[6] A good discussion that recognizes the possibility of an analogy between population genetics and linguistic descent is Lightfoot (1999).

[7] There are of course major disanalogies between biological and linguistic evolution. For example: Linguistic evolution is in good part Lamarckian, with 'acquired traits' often becoming fixed in a language. Even granting that there are some Lamarckian processes in biological evolution, they are presumably nowhere near as important biologically as they are linguistically.

[8] The same sort of thing can occur synchronically in both the linguistic case and the biological one. So-called ring species are made up of populations that abut one another, with the abutters being able to interbreed and produce fertile progeny, although the populations at the ends of the ring are unable to. And

There are those who are skeptical of the reality—or at least the theoretical interest—of public languages, shared vocabularies, and word meanings. Some point to the soritical way languages change across geographic regions or times; some object that if there's no learnable grammar, there's no natural language, but there is no reason to think that a grammar that would generate just the sentences that 'speakers of English' would recognize (under idealization removing finite limits on processing) as sentences of English.[9] It is plausible that the worry that there is 'no important ontological divide' between public languages as the folk and philosophers think of them and more encompassing linguistic taxa is at least as well grounded as the worry that there is no important ontological divide between species and other segments of population lineages.

3. Quine's Argument in 'Two Dogmas'

Some of Quine's worries about the notion of meaning—in particular, the skepticism he voices in 'Two Dogmas of Empiricism' (Quine 1951)—can be seen as kindred to the skepticism of those who think there is no principled distinction between species and other phylogenies. Quine made at least two important points about analyticity and conceptual change in 'Two Dogmas'. One was about rational constancy in belief: Quine argued that one could rationally continue to accept a sentence or statement 'come what may'. He was led to this conclusion by reflecting on how observation impacts theory. One can, and science often enough does, hold on to a hypothesis in the face of evidence that it makes incorrect predictions by discounting that evidence. As Quine put it, 'our statements about the external world face the tribunal of sense experience not individually but only as a corporate body' (Quine 1951, 41). If one accepts this, it is natural to think that evidential connections are not essential to the meaning of a sentence: if I can rationally continue to accept the statement made by a sentence no matter how the evidence goes, then revising a sentence's evidential connections doesn't—or at least needn't—change the sentence's meaning.

Quine's second point was that no sentence or statement was immune to rational revision. At any time, we accept certain claims—they make up our 'total theory'—and we take the field of claims to stand in broadly logical and evidential relations to one another and to experience. But there is nothing sacrosanct or meaning-constitutive about these relations: considerations of, for example, theoretical economy or unification could in principle lead us to revise logical laws, but it would be a mistake to see this as simply 'changing the meaning' of the logical particles. Theory revision is not in and of itself meaning change.

Of course one could, out of love for the sound of the sentence S, tenaciously accept it come what may by redefining its words; one might, for a lark, redefine 'or' to mean 'and'

---

more or less gradual variation in dialects across a region can produce incomprehension between speakers on the edges.

[9] Both of these complaints can be found in Chomsky (1980).

and consequently revise one's opinion about the truth of 'Bob is here or Bob is not here'. Some qualification is needed in Quine's claims, presumably something like this: one may rationally accept any sentence come what may/revise whether one accepts any sentence without there being good reason to say that one means something different by the sentence than what one formerly did.

It would, of course, be useful to have some sort of a story about when one does or does not have good reason to say that a sentence has changed its meaning. Quine doesn't provide one, but one can imagine what one might say on his behalf. At any time, the way we use our words gives them a particular inferential role. Our linguistic activity embodies presuppositions about the world as well as assumptions about how others will use their words when they speak. The inferential role and presuppositions accompanying our words determine how we use our language as a tool for inquiry and communication.

In order for there to be reason to say that a sentence has changed its meaning in virtue of some change in use or a user's mental states, there has to be a 'lack of cohesion' between how things were before the change and how things are afterwards. Changes in inferential role or in presuppositions that result in fluid conversation being stymied or in the role of a sentence in inquiry being radically revised can be sensibly called a change in meaning.

Suppose a change in a speaker's use of a sentence (or in the mental states reasonably held to contribute to one's understanding of the sentence) doesn't cause (actual or potential) interruption in the fluidity of communication—the change in the speaker's use, that is, does not result in a loss of the feeling-of-understanding-without-need-of-correction-or-reinterpretation on the part of audiences when the speaker uses the word. Suppose further that it has a relatively minimal effect on the role of the sentence in inquiry and on the mass of mental states that contribute to linguistic understanding. Then the change doesn't give one good reason to think that the sentence means something other than it did before the change; one has good reason, simply given the change, to think its meaning is constant.

This is not an unreasonable criterion. If we accept it, it seems we can spin Putnamian stories that show that putatively analytic sentences—'cats are animals', 'pencils are inanimate objects'—can be rejected without the rejection occasioning a change in meaning (Putnam 1975, 1986). After all, if we did find ourselves in a Putnamian scenario—cats turn out to be robots from Mars, pencils turn out to be disguised worms—we would naturally describe them as scenarios in which . . . cats turn out to be robots from Mars, pencils turn out to be disguised worms. We would feel our use 'cats are (not) animals', 'pencils are (yuck) worms' after our discovery cohesive with our use before. We would find the suggestion that we had 'changed the meaning' of our words at best odd.

I cast Quine's point as an epistemological one: any statement-sized change in what one accepts may occur without one's having reason to say that one has changed the meaning of some word (used in making the statement). How do we get from the epistemological point to the claim that Quine is often thought to have argued for—that the relevant changes aren't changes in meaning?

It is Quinean at least in spirit to argue so. What determines the meaning of a word or sentence is relatively 'big'. Meaning is determined by inferential relations, including tendencies to make various sorts of inductive and abductive inferences, patterns of application and things that contribute to determining them (e.g., prototype structures), tendencies to defer to others about matters of application, environmental relations, and so on. But the sorts of statement-sized changes that Quine has in mind in 'Two Dogmas' are for the most part relatively 'small'. Even rejecting the claim that cats are animals needn't have all that much of an impact on how one uses the terms in 'cats are animals', or on whether others understand you. It needn't have all that much of an impact in that it may leave a great deal of what is meaning-determinative for one's words or concepts—inferential relations, inductive patterns, patterns of application and deference, environmental relations, and so on—more or less unchanged. But whether it is correct for x to say that her words mean the same as y's, or that she and y share such and such concepts, is determined by the extent of overlap between what is meaning-determinative for x and y's words or concepts. Since it would generally be absurd for x to say, when there is only a small failure of overlap between x's words or concepts and y's—a small failure that doesn't in any way impede fluid communication—that x and y don't mean the same things by their words or that they fail to share (the relevant) concepts, we may conclude that a person who rejects putatively analytic statements like the statement that cats are animals does not thereby change the meanings of the words in the sentence.

I think this sort of argument—I'll call such an argument a *gradualist argument*—is basically on target. What follows are some comments on it, along with some comparisons with the case of biological entities like species.

(a) I understand Quine's claims to have a modal element: no statement is immune to revision in the sense that there are (possible) situations in which one could reject the statement without thereby changing the meanings of the words one uses to make it. To say this is not to say that in every situation in which one rejects the statement the meanings of the relevant words remain constant. Dramatic examples are the most obvious here. Suppose all at once I decide that cats are not animals because I have been misidentifying them, foolishly deferring to my parents and others about which things in the environment are cats: actually, I decide, cats are ubiquitous, as ubiquitous as protons. If I really accept this, I am not using 'cat' to talk about cats (or anything else); if this madness is unaccompanied by some concepts coming to play a role more or less like the role my cat concept used to play for me, I have lost that concept.

It seems to me that similar things should be acknowledged about speciation. No small genomic, phenotypical, geographical, or ecological change in a population is intrinsically, of necessity speciating. Which is not to say that there might not be reasons to point to a particular change (or relatively small group of changes) or a particular event as one that marks a species boundary. Geographic isolation which halts the flow of genes between subpopulations and leads to evolutionary divergence is a natural place to draw a species boundary. But this is very much a contingent, historical matter. It is not the event of separation itself that causes speciation. Suppose P actually splits into subpopulations P1 and P2 at t, and this leads to speciation. If P had split into P1 and P2 at t but shortly thereafter its member populations were reunited (a defect in the dam that separated the populations causes the dam to collapse, say), no speciation would have occurred. Much the same could be said about genetic, phenotypical, and ecological changes: whether a particular such change marks a good boundary to draw a line and say that the line non-arbitrarily marks where speciation has occurred is very much a matter of the historical context in which the change occurs; it is not, unless the change is massive, intrinsic to the change itself.

(b) A familiar idea from the literature on vagueness is that when a predicate's range of application generates sorites series, the predicate's application will vary with the context. Confronted with a sequence of patches that very gradually change from orange to yellow and asked to judge of each patch in succession whether it is orange, yellow, or some intermediate category ('not sure', 'indeterminate', whatever), an observer will start judging patches orange and at some point begin judging them yellow; when the switch occurs, she will then be inclined to reverse her judgment on the immediately preceding patches. ('Yes, I know I said that one before was indeterminate, but if this one's yellow, then that one's yellow, and this one is yellow.') Given that there is a close tie between the judgments of the competent user of an observational predicate like 'yellow' and its correct application—the applications the competent user is prepared to stick by are ceteris paribus correct—this strongly suggests that in the course of evaluating the patches in the series, the application conditions of 'orange' and 'yellow' as the speaker uses them change.[10]

It is obvious that in such cases the speaker does not undergo conceptual change—she does not lose one concept of yellow and acquire a new one—or begin using a word with a new meaning which just happens to be spelled like her old word 'yellow'. True, we *might* mark this sort of contextual change of use by saying, 'well, at that point [when the speaker reverses judgment about earlier cases that she did not judge yellow] she meant something else by "yellow" than before'. Pre-theoretical talk about meaning is a pretty blunt instrument, and we do tend to label shifts in correct application as a 'change in meaning'.[11] But even those who are inclined to say this recognize its awkwardness in this sort of case, and allow that in an (in *the*) important sense the woman does not change what she means by 'yellow' as she revises judgment about the cases in the series.

---

[10] This sort of point was first emphasized in Raffman (1994). It has been endorsed and developed in various ways by Graff (2000) and Soames (1999), among others. The point is orthogonal to the question of whether the relevant predicates are bivalent.

[11] A good deal of care is required to state this correctly. Chapter 4 takes up relations between various notions of meaning and reference.

If we agree with this story about the color concepts, we will say that they have a limited 'perspectival relativity': within a certain (somewhat vaguely delineated) area, users of those concepts have a certain amount of leeway as to what is and what is not their correct application. This perspectival relativity doesn't render the concepts 'defective'. For most of the everyday, non-technical jobs we call upon these concepts to perform, their contextual shiftiness is irrelevant; when it matters, we can work around it via stipulations. Ditto for other soritical concepts that may have contextually shifting extensions. A term or concept may be soritical and consequently have shifting boundaries while still being perfectly useful for certain practical or theoretical purposes.

We should apply this moral quite generally to our concepts of particular species, languages, word meanings, and concepts. The concept yellow has a certain limited perspectival relativity. It is a 'rule of proper usage' of the concept *yellow* that if x is observed in favorable circumstances and competently judged yellow, then x and whatever is indistinguishable from it color-wise is yellow.[12] Something similar is true of species concepts like *Fulvous Whistling-Duck*, language concepts such as *American English*, and concept concepts like *the concept book*. If the community of biologists competently judges (knowing all the relevant facts) that a certain population P is a single species and that populations 'next to it' in the population lineage(s) in which P occurs are conspecific, those judgments are acceptable and may be counted as correct. If a linguistic population is able to converse fluidly with the linguistic population that spawned it and with the linguistic population it spawns, its judgment that it speaks the same language as those neighboring it in its linguistic lineage is generally correct. If a population makes a small adjustment in what is meaning-determinative for a word— where dropping the claim that some cats are animals in a Putnam scenario is small in the relevant sense—but does not feel that it has done anything more than correct an erroneous belief, their judgment that they 'still mean the same thing' with the relevant word is ceteris paribus correct.

Note that holding this does not imply that the relevant notion is of no theoretical utility. Species are fuzzy around the edges. Those 'in the thick of evolution' might permissibly—and thus correctly—apply a species concept to temporally nearby populations in ways that someone who could survey the course of history could reasonably criticize. This does not show that the notion of a species is unfit to carry explanatory weight in various fields in biology. Ditto for the various linguistic notions.

(c) One might worry that the gradualist argument, like many a sorites argument, proves too much.[13] The argument comes perilously close to suggesting (for example) that meaning is indefinitely plastic. We can, after all, imagine a soritical shift in the various factors that determine a word's meaning: on Monday we replace a prototype that guides the user in applying the term; on Tuesday another; and so on through the

---

[12] Competence requires that in favorable circumstances one's judgments do not stray *too* far from paradigm examples.

[13] The worry is suggested by comments by Alex Byrne about a kindred argument.

week, until the word has an entirely new prototype structure. The next week we chip away at inferential relations, dropping one one day, adding one the next. And so on and so on, until over the course of time a word that began with the meaning *female fox* ends up with the meaning *clairvoyant*. One of the premises in the argument above suggests that, so long as each change is 'little', no change can be said to change the word's meaning. But that's absurd. A word that means *female fox* does not mean what a word that means *clairvoyant* means.[14]

In point of fact, the argument implies no such thing. Its crucial step is the claim that it would be absurd—and thus incorrect—for a user x of a word w to say of a speaker y's word w' that w and w' meant different things, given that the meaning determinants of w and w' differed only marginally. This is a claim about what someone in a particular situation, someone who had a particular perspective on words w and w', would be licensed to say about them. It does not follow from the fact that someone in one situation is licensed to say such and such that a person in a quite different situation is licensed to say that thing, any more than it follows from the fact that a sorites series could in principle be constructed from red to blue that everything in the series is red. And in any case, Quine's most significant point is a modal, historical point: any 'small' change in meaning can occur without the linguistic equivalent of speciation occurring. It is not just the fact that meaning may change in soritical ways that underlies 'Two Dogmas', but the fact that even claims that (occurring as they do in dictionaries) are said to be definitional typically make relatively small contributions to meaning.[15]

That said, I think Quine himself might have been tempted by a soritical argument to the conclusion that the notion of meaning is incoherent, or at least of no theoretical utility. Suppose you think that (i) sameness of meaning is a matter of being able to 'convey a thought', and conveying a thought is a matter of mutual understanding. Then, you might conclude, (ii) when we speak of sameness of meaning, we must allow that small differences in the use of an expression that do not (and would not, no matter how long the conversation went on) impede communication or understanding do not require one to say that users mean different things by the expression. Suppose you add to this something along the lines of (iii) judgments about meaning purport to be judgments about objective facts, and thus their correctness can neither be a subjective matter nor vary with the situation of she who judges. Then you have the makings of an argument to the incoherence or at least theoretical uselessness (due to subjectivity) of the concept of meaning.

There's plenty of evidence in Quine's writings that he endorsed (i) and (ii).[16] I imagine that back when Quine flourished—a time when almost everyone thought that demonstratives, indexicals, and other bits of context sensitivity in natural language

---

[14] My intention is that this paragraph should call to mind Putnam (1986)'s example of clairvoyant foxes.

[15] The argument here turns on delicate issues about when it is apt to report someone as having said such and such. The discussion of attitude ascription in Chapters 4 and 5 underwrites the assumptions about same saying that are necessary to make the argument valid.

[16] I read the early pages of Quine (1969b, 1969c) as implying (i) and (ii).

were 'imperfections' and relativism was considered about as acceptable as bestiality in a rush-hour subway car—something like (iii) would have gone without saying. Myself, I don't endorse this argument.

4. Of What Interest Is the Notion of Analyticity?

Does the gradualist argument show that there are no analyticities whatsoever? Arguably not. In this section, I will discuss some putative examples of analyticity that supposedly aren't shown to be non-analytic by the gradualist argument. I am more interested in what the examples might tell us about the notions of meaning and meaning change than whether they show that there are some analytic sentences.

There are some cases in which a relatively simple formula tells us all there is to be told about the determination of a term's reference. Hilary Putnam (1962) once pointed to sentences in which words like 'hunter', 'baker', and 'runner' occur, as bearers of something like analyticity. These words are compounds of verbs and the affix '-er'. There are relatively few things that affixing '-er' to an activity verb does. One thing it can do is form a noun that picks out things that are (or are capable of being) agents of the activity the verb picks out. When the affix is so used, there seems to be nothing else to say about the meaning of the result of combining it with a verb. And as a consequence, there seems to be something special about the sentence, 'A hunter is something that hunts' something that distinguishes it from putative analyticities like 'bachelors are unmarried': given how the compound 'hunter' is constructed, it would seem to be impossible to make head or tail of what someone meant who denied the sentence was true and insisted that they weren't indulging in one or another trope—metaphor or irony or covert homophony. It's easy to see why: in this case, there is only one determinant of the meaning of the form -er, a determinant that links the meaning of V+er to the meaning of V in a way that makes the sentence true. So someone who utters, 'Some hunters aren't things that are capable of hunting' is either confused or is attaching a meaning to the form that has no overlap whatsoever with the meaning we attach to it. Something similar is true, I think, of argument structure. If someone were to tell me that donating was like running—one can donate without there being anything donated; nor does one need to direct a donation to a particular agency, cause, person, whatever—I wouldn't know what to make of his performance.

Something similar is arguably true of certain context-sensitive terms—'I' and 'yesterday', for example. These are words that have something along the lines of an algorithm attached to them—tokens of 'I' refer to their producer; tokens of 'yesterday' refer to the day before their production; tokens of 'today' refer to the day of their production—which one has to have mastered in order to understand or competently use them. And there is pretty much nothing else that determines the meaning of these words. So there is call to say that a sentence like *yesterday is the day before today* is in some important sense analytic: knowledge of what it means suffices to provide conclusive justification for believing that a token of it is true-as-tokened. Something similar is arguably true of determiners. The question is: what should we make of this?

Broadly speaking, there are two ways in which one might characterize analyticity: as some sort of 'truth in virtue of meaning', or as truth deducible from what one must know in order to understand the sentence. The first road to characterizing the notion has been much poo-pooed since Quine observed that a sentence can't be true simply in virtue of what it means: a sentence's truth depends on how the world is, even if those facts which determine its truth couldn't help but obtain. Gillian Russell (2008)—in some ways following Putnam's footsteps—argues that Quine's observation doesn't show that there isn't a useful notion of analyticity-as-truth-in-virtue-of-meaning. According to Russell, associated with an extension-bearing item like a simple predicate or name is a 'reference determiner'. In the case of names and natural-kind terms, the reference determiner is typically the content of a description (perhaps contextually sensitive) that, relative to a 'context of introduction', determines an extension. For example, the reference determiner for 'water' is (we may assume) something like the content of 'the liquid that for the most part makes up oceans, rivers, rain, and comes out of the tap'; the reference determiner for a 'purely descriptive predicate' like 'bachelor' is a set of properties true of just those objects that are unmarried and male. The reference determiner for a simple indexical is the sort of rule that David Kaplan called a character, a rule like *In any context of use, a use of 'today' refers to the day in which that context occurs.*[17]

The reference determiner of a term . . . well, it determines its reference. The reference determiner for 'water', relative to the actual introduction of the word, determines H_2O. We can, of course, ask what reference a reference determiner would determine in various counterfactual circumstances. Relative to Twin Earth, the reference determiner of 'water' determines XYZ. The reference determiner for 'sister', on the other hand, determines the property of being a female sibling relative to any context of introduction. Reference determiners often stand in various structural relations. In particular, one reference determiner may 'contain' another (in which case, if the determined are predicates, whatever the first applies to, the second must apply to). So it goes, on Russell's view, with the reference determiners for 'sister' and 'female'. Reference determiners may also stand in a relation of 'exclusion', as do, for example, those for 'color' and 'monarchy'. Analyticity, Russell says, is a matter of 'truth in virtue of reference determiners'. For example, a sentence of the form *all As are Bs* will be analytic provided that the reference determiner for A includes that for B; *no As are Bs* is analytic if the

---

[17] Russell (2008), 59ff. Note that the reference determiner for an expression is a very different thing from the 'content' of the expression, where an expression's content is its contribution to 'what is said' by the sentence (or, if you prefer, its contribution to determining the semantic value of complement clauses in which the expression occurs). Russell takes the content of 'Hesperus' to be the content of 'Phosphorus' to be the planet Venus. But the expressions have different reference determiners—the first has something like the property of being the twinkling heavenly body visible from location l at time t as its reference determiner; the other has a different property as reference determiner.

predicates' reference determiners exclude one another. Given that the reference determiner of an expression is part of its meaning, the use of such a sentence is guaranteed to be true no matter how the world turns out to be, and so is in a straightforward sense determined to be true by its meaning alone.[18]

Let us grant for the moment that something along these lines provides a coherent notion of analyticity. Of how much theoretical interest is it? Russell's discussion explicitly invokes Locke and Kant's discussions of trivial and analytic truths, discussions that (seem to) take talk of one meaning or concept being a part of or contained in another quite literally. She leaves the notion of containment as a primitive—we are told that containment involves the sort of entailment relation noted above, but not much else. Insofar as reference determiners are sets of properties or properties 'strung together' by operations that are metaphysical analogs to conjunction or quantifying predicates together, the idea of containment makes a certain amount of sense.

But it is pretty implausible that the determination of the reference of natural-language vocabulary is on the whole well conceptualized in this way. Take 'water' as an example. There has been rather fierce debate as to whether coffee, tea, Pepsi, or the contents of the Cuyahoga River are water: some philosophers claim that they all are, since they are all (basically nothing but) samples of H_2O; there is not insubstantial evidence that English speakers think that the first three are not, and the last one is, though the percentage of H_2O in the latter is probably considerably less than in normal samples of the first three. Insofar as the use of speakers is not just relevant but partially determinative of what their words refer to, the idea that there is some thing—a property or condition—associated with a word like 'water' that 'determines' its reference seems completely wrong; it's a philosopher's fantasy. It might be that in some cases we can reverse engineer from use to a property that picks out a predicate's extension, but that's what we are doing: reverse engineering, not discovering the thing that determined the extension in the first place.

Suppose for a second that the only 'job' concepts and meaningful terms had was to contribute to representations of the passing scene, and the only—or at least the primary—dimension on which such representations were to be evaluated was in terms of their accuracy and truth. Under that supposition, there is a natural criterion for conceptual continuity and meaning change: when and only when there is a shift in a concept or representation's contribution to truth conditions—to reference, extension, or possible worlds intension—do we have conceptual discontinuity or change of meaning. Russell's account of analyticity could be seen as motivated by a sophisticated epicycle on this idea: Given that the job of a concept or word meaning is to supply a representation, and that representations are first and foremost things with truth conditions, conceptual or meaning constancy is a matter of constancy in what determines what a term contributes

---

[18] Russell offers several notions of analyticity; what I have to say about this one applies, I think, to all of them. I should point out that Russell says some things that seem to conflict about whether reference determiners are 'part of meaning'.

to truth conditions; analyticity is a matter of grasping this last enabling one to see that true use is guaranteed.[19]

The primary problem with this view is that it is absurd to suppose that many concepts and meanings have relatively segregated compartments where their 'reference determiner' is stored. Concepts and conceptual structures stand in inferential relations; they involve our ways of characteristically interacting with what we take the concept to pick out, as well as our affect toward such objects, our expectations, stereotypes, and bits and pieces of our Weltanschauung. (I think phenomenologists like Heidegger and Hilary Putnam have said something like this.) They are partially constituted by masses of subpersonal psychology—prototype structures, to mention but one such bit of the subpersonal. It is not that these things are irrelevant to reference—change them enough, at least in the right social context, and a change in reference may occur. But they all contribute to a greater or lesser extent to reference, and it is just not plausible to think there are many concepts for which some small subset of these aspects of 'use' are 'the reference determiners'.

A change in the only rule that governs the meaning of a morphological transformation; a change of a verb from ditransitive to intransitive—these changes, qua changes in meaning, are profound. They are, it's tempting to say, as profound as the sort of morphological change that occurred when dinosaurs with hollow bones evolved from ones with solid ones. The linguistic changes, were they to occur, would mark a discontinuity as semantically profound as those that clearly mark speciation are biologically profound. If one likes the label 'analytic'—myself, I think we're better off scuttling it—one might reasonably say that sentences underwritten by these sorts of morphological or thematic facts are analytic.

Whether we stick with this sort of terminology or not, we should agree that Quine is correct to think that the notion of analyticity is of little to no use in the study of language. But it certainly doesn't follow from this that the notion of meaning can't bear any explanatory load, any more than it follows from the fact—biological species do not have essences; none of the small changes that might lead, when summed over time, to speciation are themselves intrinsically changes that separate one species from another—that the notion of species cannot bear any explanatory weight. The notions of word meaning, concept, and (public) language are no worse off because of Quine's and allied arguments and observations than is the notion of species because of Darwinian arguments and observations that speciation is a historical process and that it is folly to think that species have anything like essences.

This doesn't mean that all is rosy with the notion of meaning. Darwin himself seemed at times skeptical about the reality of species:

I look at the term species, as one arbitrarily given for the sake of convenience to a set of individuals closely resembling each other, and that it does not essentially differ from the term variety,

---

[19] I don't know whether this is how Russell herself conceptualizes her view.

which is given to less distinct and more fluctuating forms. The term variety, again, in comparison with mere individual differences, is also applied arbitrarily, and for mere convenience sake.

(Darwin 2003, 52)

The question to ask, about both the notion of a species and notions like the notions of word meaning, concept, and language, is whether they can be elaborated in a theoretically useful way. I will take up the linguistic half of this question starting in Chapter 3. Those of you who agree that there's no hope for a theoretically useful notion of analyticity should feel invited to go directly to that chapter.

But not everyone, I know, is yet convinced that the notion of analyticity is best forgotten. Because of this, the next chapter is to devoted to winning more converts to my low-church Quineanism.

2

Internalism to the Rescue?

If meanings are interestingly like species, meanings are multitudes and what my words mean isn't up to me: what 'rescue' means as I use it supervenes not just on my use but on the uses of those around me, before me, and those to come. I imagine someone might grant the coherence, even the usefulness for some purposes, of such a notion of meaning while insisting that meaning is, au fond, determined by the individual. Of course, this someone says, we can sum the meanings each individual assigns to 'rescue', then factor out those bits that aren't recognized by all or most as being commonly shared, and arrive at something that is public and, being something that speakers share and need to track in order to understand one another, is a kind of meaning with theoretical utility. But such a thing is arrived at by performing arithmetic on the meanings individuals assign to their words; it is these that are ur-meanings.

I don't deny that one finds things that can reasonably be labeled 'meanings' at the level of the individual. I don't deny that these things are of theoretical interest. I do deny that internalist theorizing about meaning provides a way to resuscitate the notion of analyticity. I also think that on a tenable internalist picture meanings turn out to be a lot like diachronic ensembles of mental states related by analogs of descent—they turn out to be analogous to species.

A complete case for these claims is a book-length enterprise; this is not that book. But I think we learn useful things if we consider the merits and demerits of internalist ideas about meaning; this chapter takes up two ideas of this sort. The chapter's first half discusses a popular response to 'Two Dogmas'—that even Quine admits that we can create synonymy, and thus analyticity, through stipulation. The response is particularly attractive to those who lean internalist—if I am the master of my linguistic domain, then surely I can stipulate what my words mean. But there are a number of problems with the idea that stipulation can fix synonymy. For one thing, I am multitudes in the sense that there are many components of my mentality that contribute to determining what my words mean. Of many of these—prototype structures, to name but one—I have no conscious control and little or no direct access. I can of course stipulate that by 'gronk' I mean 'to behave in public like a fraternity bro'; and that will give 'gronk' a meaning. But since (for example) the stipulation does not insure—indeed, obviously does not make it the case—that the simple phrase is associated with the same prototype structure as the complex phrase, the stipulation does not insure/make it the case that the two phrases are synonymous. A second problem is that the multitudes that I am and the mental structures they determine are things that endure through time. To make the stipulation about 'gronk' is to bring a word into the linguistic world, something whose meaning is realized by—indeed, for an internalist is to be identified with—a mental structure that persists through changes, including changes that may annul some of what was achieved in the initial stipulation. Even if we are internalists, we need to recognize that a word's meaning is determined by something which has the sort of historical structure of a population lineage: the successors of today's lexical entry for 'gronk' carry on, preserving the meaning of the word even when they modify or discard elements of the stipulation that brought that meaning into existence. So, at any rate, I'll argue.

This chapter's second half takes up an internalist response to Quine due to David Chalmers. Chalmers suggests that we think of conceptual constancy in the intrapersonal case in Bayesian terms. What it is, speaking roughly, for the meaning of 'Mary owns a Ford' as I use it to be constant from one time to the next is for it to be the case that, for any sentence S, the credence I give to 'Mary has a Ford' given S remains pretty much the same from the first time to the second. On this account we replace talk of identity of sentence meaning across time with talk of similarity. Analyticity (in some sense) is possible so long as one's conditional credences remain constant; that said, it is unlikely, as conditional credence is bound to fluctuate. Chalmers' proposal is worth serious consideration. But even from an internalist perspective I think it's unacceptable. The proposal gets the relationship between meaning and subjective credence backwards, and it involves a picture of what it is to rationally revise one's beliefs that is, well, just plain wrong. So, at any rate, I'll argue.

1. Inter-Speaker Synonymy

I take the interesting notion of analyticity to be an epistemic one. A sentence is analytically true provided that one who understands it—and thus knows what it means—is thereby in a position to know of any use of the sentence that it is true, and to know the truth the sentence expresses. (Compare Boghossian (1997), 334.) I have allowed that something like analyticity occurs with sentences like *Hunters are capable of hunting* or *tomorrow is the day after today*. This is likely to spark the response that if these sentences are analytic, many sentences are or could be analytic.

Here is an argument that there at least could be many such sentences. Suppose that I understand English. Then, we may assume, I know, simply in virtue of understanding the language that sentences of the form *all As are Bs* are true just in case whatever A is true of is something of which B is true. Likewise, we may assume, I know, simply in virtue of my understanding the language, that if n is a noun and a is an (intersective) adjective, then *a n* is true of something just in case a is true of it and n is true of it. Now surely I can take two words I already understand—'blue' and 'car', say—and define a word in terms of them. I can, for example, introduce the word 'bluecar', stipulating that it is to mean, by definition, blue car. Surely if I do this, then I know, in virtue of my understanding of English and my understanding of my meaning-fixing stipulation, that, since 'bluecar' is true of something only if 'blue' and 'car' are true of it, the sentence 'all bluecars are blue' is true. And in virtue of my understanding the words in question, I know that the sentence says that all bluecars are blue. Analyticity regained.[1]

This is a patently invalid argument. A sentence is analytic, remember, provided that anyone who understands it can determine, simply in virtue of what gave her the understanding, that the sentence is true. Our little argument observes that if one learns what 'all bluecars are blue' means in a particular way—by stipulating the meaning of 'bluecar' to be that of 'blue car'—one is thereby in a position to know that the sentence is true. It doesn't follow that every way of coming to understand the sentence is one which would put one in a position to know that all bluecars are blue. And there seems little hope of our establishing, as a lemma to the argument, that the only way of coming to understand the sentence involves becoming privy to the stipulation, or to its (putative) upshot, that 'blue car' and 'bluecar' are synonymous. Someone could acquire the term 'bluecar' by listening to and watching me, never bothering to ask me what its definition was. Would such a person have to think that 'bluecar' and 'blue car' are synonymous, or at least be disposed to believe this if asked? Perhaps they would believe, or at least be disposed to the belief, that all bluecars are blue—it would, after all, be a natural induction to make, assuming that I never misapply the term (which I might, of course, if the light is often bad or I sometimes apply the term on the basis of a fleeting glance). But to believe this is not to believe that 'bluecar' and 'blue car' are synonymous. We all believe that 'water' is a term we use to corral samples of H_2O, and thus that all samples of water are samples of H_2O. But we don't think that 'water' and 'H_2O' are synonymous.

Indeed, there is no reason to think that someone who learns 'bluecar' in this way even needs to believe, much less know, that it is coextensive with 'blue car'. If the learner uses 'bluecar' in a way that projectibly tends to be in accord with my usage, that seems sufficient for understanding it. But that does not insure knowledge of co-extensiveness. It does not even insure belief—the learner might be brought up short by the question of whether bluecars are invariably blue.

Perhaps it will be said that in the present case the language learner and I don't mean exactly the same thing by 'bluecar'. I stipulated that the word was to be defined by (and thus synonymous with) 'blue car'; the learner did not. So there is a meaning-fixing property my 'bluecar' has that his 'bluecar' lacks. So let it be granted that his version of 'all bluecars are blue' is not analytic. That does not mean my version is not. And after all, I am surely the master of my linguistic domain. 'bluecar' lacked a meaning until I gave it one, and didn't I indeed give it a meaning? Didn't I give it the meaning of 'blue car'? What could stop me from doing this?

---

[1] There are some steps left out here, needed to establish that I can know that *any* use of the sentence is true. Let's not be fussy.

Alas, this response is no better than the original argument. Let it be granted that when I defined 'bluecar' I made it synonymous with 'blue car'. Why are we supposed to think that in the present case the word and the phrase are not synonymous in the idiolect of the language learner? Presumably because he understands both and does not, or at least need not given his understanding, think them synonymous. But now we need to have some reason for thinking that someone who understands synonyms must know, or be in a position to know (simply in virtue of whatever brought him to understand the phrases), that the synonyms are synonyms. Prima facie, there's no reason to think this. For prima facie, no matter what word we might consider, there will be more than one way to come to understand it, just as there is more than one way to come to understand 'bluecar' and thus learn what it means. One might acquire a word by being given an explanation of its use in words one already understands. But there will, of course, often be many ways in which this might be done. Or one might acquire a word by observing how it is used. And again, there may be very different sorts of observations that might be sufficient to induce understanding.

We need an argument for the claim that different ways of coming to understand a word—ways which in any intuitive sense each suffice for coming to use the word with the same meaning as others do—cannot result in one's meaning with one's use of the word what others mean with it. We need such an argument especially for the case in which, upon learning a word from me, you are able as a result to correctly interpret my utterances of the word by using it and I am able to interpret your uses of the word with my uses—the case, that is, in which, once you acquire 'bluecar' from me, you know, when I utter 'John has a bluecar', that I said that John has a bluecar, and I know, when you utter 'June has a bluecar', that you said that June has a bluecar.

2. Synonymy in an Idiolect

One might try to generate the needed argument as follows. Analyticity is a property of sentences-in-a-particular-language. Languages are to be individuated (in part) in terms of what one needs to know in order to understand them. Now we can and do impose different standards in different contexts, for different purposes, on what counts as understanding an utterance. In particular, one might claim, we distinguish 'public conditions' for understanding another person's utterance—those conditions that are necessary for everyday conversational understanding—from more stringent conditions for understanding, conditions required when one has carefully stipulated the properties of an idiolect or a particular artificial language. Thus, we might say that utterances are typically utterances in several languages at once, utterances in both a public language and in a particular idiolect.

If one accepts all this, one might argue so. Let us grant that we speak a common language, and that there is no particular way in which its terms must be acquired. But the sentences we utter are not only sentences of a public language. We each speak our own idiolect, related to but not identical to the public language; we have authority over our idiolects in a way in which we do not have authority over the public language. 'bluecar' as I use it—at least when I use it in public after having introduced it in some publicly accessible way—has a public language meaning. But it also has the meaning that I originally gave it, when I fixed 'bluecar' to mean what I meant with 'blue car'.

'bluecar', as I use it, has two meanings, for when I use it, I speak two languages. Its idiolectical meaning need not be its public language meaning. Conceding for argument's sake that analyticity is absent from, even impossible in, the common language is not conceding that it is absent from, or even could be absent from, the idiolects of which the common language is (so to speak) the lowest common denominator. To speak my idiolect, one must fix the meaning of 'bluecar' as I did. But if one does that, then one is in a position, simply in virtue of being a speaker of my language, to know that 'bluecar' is only true of that of which 'blue' is true.

Someone who so argues is liable to be unimpressed with certain applications of the gradualist argument. Yes, of course, she may say, a version of the gradualist argument (on which over time people come to think that, well, perhaps a few bluecars aren't blue) shows that the public language sentence 'Bluecars are blue' is not analytic. But how could such an argument show that 'bluecars are blue' isn't analytic in my idiolect? My idiolect at the time 'bluecar' becomes a part of it is in part defined by the fact that I introduced 'bluecar' as meaning 'blue car'. Either I continue to be aware of this and embrace the stipulation, or I don't. If I do, then, well, I will continue to know that 'all bluecars are blue' is true. If not—because, say, I have forgotten this—I have forgotten part of what I need to know to speak the language I spoke at the time I introduced 'bluecar'. If not—because I remember my stipulation but have decided to abandon it—then the facts that determine what the word means have changed. In sum: the gradualist argument does not show—indeed, nothing Quine says shows—that it is impossible to stipulate that in my language a novel expression is to have exactly the meaning of some already meaningful phrase. So nothing Quine says suggests that synonymy—indeed, synonymy of which, since I am its origin, I have a priori knowledge—within my idiolect is impossible. And so nothing that Quine says even begins to suggest that analyticity—or a priori knowledge, for that matter—is impossible.[2] I can't help but think that something like this argument underlies much of the resistance to Quine's writings on analyticity.

It will eventually be useful to have a regimentation of this argument in front of us:

1. We can add phrases to our language and assign them meanings.
2. If we can assign phrases meanings, we can assign a novel phrase the same meaning as one already in use.
3. If we do this, sentences which differ only by uses of the two phrases will have the same meaning.

---

[2] One could read Boghossian's (1997) discussion of Quine on stipulation as suggesting an argument like this.

4. If sentences have the same meaning, bi-conditionals in which they sit to the left and to the right are analytic.
5. So, it is possible for there to be (many, many pretty interesting) analytic sentences in our language.
6. If a sentence of our language is analytic, the proposition it expresses is a priori for us.
7. So, it is possible for there to be (many, many pretty interesting) claims that are a priori for us.

The argument relies on (a) the analyticity of logical truth, (b) the idea that we have, in principle at least, stipulative control over what our words mean, and (c) the thought that given (a) and (b), we are in a position via stipulation to create analyticity and thereby to gain a priori knowledge. In what follows I'm primarily concerned with (b) and (c). But I will eventually observe that if what I say is correct, there are grounds for rejecting (a) as well.

3. Truth by Convention

It is illuminating at this point to turn to Quine's article 'Carnap and Logical Truth'. There Quine allows that truth can be created by stipulation or definition. He takes explicit definition of novel notation to be 'convention in a properly narrow sense of the word' (Quine 1960b, 118). In the case of set theory we can understand the adoption of, say, the axioms of separation and foundation as a sort of '[l]egislative postulation [that] institutes truth by convention' (Quine 1960b, 118). The thought is in part like Carnap's thoughts about linguistic frameworks: When set theorists first decide to use epsilon in accord with foundation and separation, that decision is responsible for those axioms expressing truths when set theorists theorize. One thinks that if Quine is good with this, then he should be good with the thought that, were it the case that a physicist or group thereof had at a certain point said

V.   Let's use 'force' to mean 'the product of a body's mass and its acceleration'

that would have made

V'.   A body's force is equal to the product of its mass and its acceleration

true by definition or convention.

For Carnap, as I understand him, such stipulation gives Foundation, Separation, and V' special epistemological status. Quine will have none of this:

[Conventionality] is a [property of] particular acts of definition, and not germane to the definition as an enduring channel of intertranslation ... conventionality is a passing trait, significant at the moving front of science but useless in classifying the sentences behind the lines. It is a trait of events and not of sentences.   (Quine 1960b, 119)

The idea, I take it, is that of course we can decide to speak or theorize in a certain way, and in cases like the above, at the time of stipulation that (and that alone) explains why speaking in that way is correct. But it simply doesn't follow that we are bound to the decision or that we could not down the road come to think that we should modify our stipulation—perhaps, for example, we should replace foundation with the claim that a set that does not contain every set has a least element. Once the act of stipulation has occurred, sentences implicated in the stipulation become part of whatever theoretical enterprise we were engaged in when we had occasion to stipulate. They do not have a distinguished status because of the way they were introduced to the enterprise. What their use says has no claim to be said to be known more securely or with more certainty than any other claim involved in the enterprise.

Now a fan of the argument in the last section will likely say that if this is what Quine has in mind, then he is admitting that a priori knowledge is possible: If (at the time of stipulation) stipulation and stipulation alone explains why uttering V' is correct, shouldn't my understanding of V' along with my recognizing the stipulation suffice for knowing what V' says? If so, I have created analyticity. And because neither of these states of mine are ones that provide evidence of truth, that knowledge is a priori. Perhaps this isn't the most exciting bit of knowledge to ever come down the pike; but it actually has a certain substance: to know it is to know that there is something, force, that a thing might have and that it is the product of two other properties of that thing, its mass and its acceleration.

I expect Quine would be underwhelmed by this argument because of the thought in the last cited passage: the status of V' is transitory and has no epistemological significance, because we are free to eschew our stipulation should we see it as a poor choice in the context of later theory. But of course the fan of the argument above will reject this response, saying that all the fact that we can abandon a stipulation such as V shows is that we are free to stop using 'force' to mean what V makes it mean. It doesn't show that we don't, so long as we stick to our stipulation, know a priori that force is mass times acceleration.

It's not all that easy to fashion a response likely to change minds to this objection using only what Quine bequeathed us. But there is a compelling response.

4. Stipulating Meaning

We are granting the fan of analyticity the right to be internalist about idiolects. We have promised not to deny that each of us speaks his own idiosyncratic idiolect, the properties of which are determined by the owner, comprehension of which requires mastery of the way the owner has fixed the meaning of its terms. I think that even such heavy-duty internalism can't save analyticity.

To see why, return to my introduction of 'bluecar' by saying to myself, 'I'll use "bluecar" to refer to [all and only] blue cars'. Would this guarantee that the two phrases had the same meaning in my idiolect?

Consider a somewhat more empirical question. Before I introduced 'bluecar' I somehow mentally represented the meaning of 'blue car', that representation presumably involving my mental representations of the meanings of 'blue' and 'car'. After I introduce 'bluecar', I mentally represent its meaning as well as the meaning of 'blue car'. How is the representation of the meaning of 'bluecar' likely to be related to my representation of the meaning of 'blue car'? Are they likely to be identical, at least modulo the fact that one is connected to 'blue car', the other to 'bluecar'? Or might they be significantly different? How you answer is likely to depend on where your theoretical allegiances in cognitive psychology lie. So let us review in Cliff's Notes fashion some recent theories of conceptual representation.[3]

Before 1970, the dominant picture in cognitive psychology seems to have been a broadly empiricist one, on which some concepts are without definitions (they are associated with some perceptual mechanism which determines their application), and the rest are represented via definitions that can in principle be reduced to combinations of undefined concepts. This picture provided no explanation of a variety of data—for example, the fact that people have robust tendencies to rank instances of concepts as more or less typical. As a result, cognitive psychologists have proposed and tried to test novel accounts of conceptual representation. Among these are views on which

concepts are representations involving one or more prototypes (which one can think of as sets of features) along with a similarity measure that relates potential category members to prototypes;

concepts are representations involving sets of exemplars (which one can think of as token memories of encountered instances) along with an algorithm which determines classification in terms of relations to exemplars;

concepts are representations involving certain quasi-propositional bits of theory—for example, schemas for inductive inference and scripts that organize expectations about objects or events—that help constitute and organize an individual's beliefs about a domain.

It would be understating things to say that there is no consensus about whether one of these views provides even the beginnings of an adequate model of conceptual representation. Each is successful in explaining some observations about categorization; each fails to account for significant data. Two things, however, are clear. First off, we just don't know a priori how our concepts are represented. Second of all, what we do know makes it at least reasonable to think that when I introduce 'bluecar' as a term for blue cars, my mental representations of the meanings of 'blue car' and 'bluecar' need not be even close to the same.

Consider what is sometimes described in the literature as the intransitivity of concept containment (Hampton 1982; Murphy 2002). People will happily tell you that all seats are furniture, that car seats are seats, and that car seats are not furniture.

---

[3] Useful introductory discussions include Machery (2009), Margolis and Laurence (1999), and Murphy (2002). Margolis and Laurence (1999) gives a useful, if somewhat dated, discussion of explanatory strengths and weaknesses of the views mentioned below.

This behavior is explained on the assumptions that (a) conceptual structure is responsible for categorization and assessment of *As are Bs* claims, and (b) the ways the concepts seat, furniture, and car seat are represented involve a prototype or an exemplar structure—or, more probably, both. These assumptions make it reasonable to suppose that prototypes (or exemplars) contribute to typicality effects and the assessment of *As are Bs* claims. Concentrate, for brevity, on the assumption that concepts typically have a prototype structure. The natural elaboration of this will take the prototype to be a (possibly weighted) set of features which encode information about typical members of the concept; assessment of *As are Bs* claims will involve comparison of the prototypes for the concepts A and B. Typicality ratings of furniture, seats, and car seats in turn make it plausible that the prototype for car seat is not a function, simple or otherwise, of the prototypes for seat and furniture. And this gives the beginning of an explanation of the rather startling intransitivity phenomenon.

What does all this tell us about 'bluecar' and 'blue car'? Well, it certainly tells us that we can have strong intuitions—that words are 'connected by meaning', that certain sentences in which those words occur are therefore 'true in virtue of meaning'—that are not reflected at the level at which meaning is represented. The intuitions—that the sentences 'car seats are seats' and 'seats are furniture' are 'true in virtue of meaning', that when sentences of the forms *As are Bs* and *Bs are Cs* are true, then so is *As are Cs*—are about as strong, I think, as the intuition that 'bachelors are unmarried' and 'vixens are foxes' are so. It would appear that the representation(-cum-prototype) we have of the meaning of 'car seat' is not derived in any straightforward way from those for 'car' and 'seat'. Indeed, there is no reason to think that the representation that would be generated in the course of processing the phrase 'seat that is for a car' (or any other definition of 'car seat') would be very much like that attached to the expression 'car seat'.[4] And why should we think that things must be different for 'bluecar' and 'blue car'? Do we know a priori that when we introduce 'bluecar' as a term for blue cars, we do not immediately assign to the phrase a prototype? Surely not; we know a posteriori that a reasonable hypothesis about concept formation is that in the course of concept formation prototype structures are assigned to perceptually applied concepts. Do we know a priori that if 'bluecar' has a prototype associated with it, it will be the same as that associated with 'blue car'? Not only do we not know this a priori, we have reason, given phenomena like conceptual intransitivity, to think that this may often not be the case.

How so? Well, prototype assignment is not a procedure that transfers prototype information from a phrase or a collection of phrases to a new phrase by a mechanical, much less compositional process. The phrase 'car seat', one thinks, was introduced when someone wanted a quick way to refer to seats for children in cars. This sort of introduction is an awful lot like an introduction by the stipulation, 'Hey, let's use "car

---

[4] I take it that 'car seat', though written as two words, has the status in most of our lexicons of a single term—it's as much of a word as (say) 'manslaughter'. There are various syntactic tests which suggest that this is the right thing to say.

seat" for "seat for a child that is in a car" '. But the prototype for 'car seat' isn't generated from the prototypes for the vocabulary in 'seat for a child that is in a car'. Rather, the prototype for 'car seat' is sui generis, something that is as much a function of the cognitive history and interests of the introducer as anything else.

Introducing a new term is something a particular person does in a particular situation. The introducer has a particular cognitive history, an idiosyncratic collection of experience, information, and expertise. When I introduced 'bluecar' I had a particular history of seeing blue cars, one that made blue cars like my old blue Honda Accord particularly salient to me. When I made my stipulation, I did not pick out a prototype to associate with the term. Rather, my language faculty conspired with my experience, encyclopedic knowledge, and so forth to do this. I no more choose the non-consciously accessible properties of novel terms I introduce than I choose the locus in the brain where those properties are recorded.

Now, the prototype or exemplar structure associated with a concept or word is surely relevant to its (referential) semantics. It contributes to the determination of what the concept or word is true of, even if we cannot read the semantics off of the prototype (since many other things contribute to semantics). So even if, when speaking of concepts and meanings, we confine what constitutes a concept/meaning to those things that contribute to its (referential) semantics, prototypes contribute to constituting concepts and meanings—they are, if you like, 'parts' of concepts and meanings. If we identify concepts (or meanings) when and only when they have the same 'parts and structure', the upshot is that the fact that I introduced 'bluecar' by saying, 'By "bluecar" I mean "blue car"' really doesn't give us any good reason to think that the phrases express the same concept or have the same meaning in my idiolect. Indeed, given the ways in which prototypes vary, there are good reasons to think that 'bluecar' and 'blue car' are not synonymous in my idiolect.

Let me try to make the point in a slightly different way. Consider inference. It is a cognitive process of which, like stipulation, we are (often enough, at least) consciously aware. I become aware that a particular thing X has properties F, G, and H. I ask myself: what is more likely, that X has property J or that X has property K? I consider the matter for a bit and conclude that it's more likely that X is a J than a K. I take myself to have good reason for my belief—at the least, if you asked me why I thought this, I could and would tell you a story about how being an FGH makes a thing (more) likely to be a J than a K.

It should be obvious to anyone who knows the work of Kahneman, Tversky, and many others that often enough my belief that my judgment is reasonable is simply mistaken.[5] Told that Linda was politically active in college, a frequent contributor to Planned Parenthood, and unmarried, people will say that it is more likely that she is a feminist bank teller than a bank teller. The explanation Kahneman and collaborators offer of this is that in making the relevant sorts of judgments we—without being

---

[5] For a readable summary see Kahneman (2013).

conscious of it—rely on various heuristics that sometimes but not invariably lead to good inferences. Sometimes when we try to make something happen mentally (we put some premises into the inference hopper and consciously tamp them down), what we want to happen happens (an inference occurs), but processes of which we are not aware do things we did not intend which affect the result.

I am suggesting that there is reason to think that stipulation is like this. We stipulate that A is to mean what B does, hoping that this will introduce a new word. This does succeed in introducing a new word; it does succeed in introducing a word whose semantic properties are related to those of the 'meaning-fixing' expression B. What it need not do is introduce a word whose semantic properties are identical with those of B.

I have been complaining that introducing a word via stipulation is no guarantee of sameness of meaning between prior and novel phrases. I have complained as well that our epistemological relation to the stipulated word's meaning does not enable us to know any synonymy that might have been created. We don't know of such synonymy—we certainly don't know of it a priori—because there are reasons, ones not defeated by anything we know a priori or otherwise, to think that synonymy may not have been achieved. This doesn't quite show that 'all bluecars are blue' fails to be analytic in the case at hand, since it is consistent with all I've said that even if 'bluecar' and 'blue car' have different meanings, what we know about those meanings suffices for knowing that all bluecars are blue. But it is hard to see why we would think this. 'Part of the meaning' of 'bluecar' is its associated prototype structure. The latter makes a contribution to determining what the term is true of. We are in the dark about whether the prototypes for the two phrases are the same. So we are in the dark about whether the two expressions have the same reference: the fact that we stipulated that they do does not mean that they do.

5. What Constitutes What My Words Mean?

Quine appeared willing to concede that at the moment of stipulation 'bluecar' and 'blue car' or 'force' and 'mass times acceleration' could be said to be synonymous, but he saw no reason to think this transitory synonymy to be of any significance. Suppose we were to concede for argument's sake that the stipulation does make it apt, at the time it occurs, to say that the terms share a meaning. What follows?

Observe that the stipulation, whatever else it does, creates a new word. Indeed, insofar as concepts are mental particulars with semantic properties, the stipulation introduces a new concept, albeit one which at birth is very much like the concept associated with 'blue car'.[6] Should we say that meaning of 'bluecar' or the concept it expresses are completely determined by the stipulative act?

---

[6] Relevant to this claim is the fact that if the stipulation actually were to be made, one of the things that would happen is that a new locus for storing information (with such information available for such tasks as categorization during perception) is created.

Surely not. The concept *bluecar* is something we expect to be modified but not extinguished by learning and experience. There is every reason to expect the details of the concept's prototype structure will vary gradually over time, as we gather new information about what is and what is not typical of the objects to which we apply the phrase. From a theoretical perspective it would seem to be deranged to suggest that such changes must be changes in the meaning of the phrase: The prototype structure is not replaced, but modified in a way best theorized in terms of the prototype diachronically persisting. Gradual variation in the prototype in the face of new information is best understood and best theorized as a matter of learning, not of meaning change. But of course such gradual changes in prototypicality over time may bring about changes in what one is and is not willing to call—and eventually what is and is not—a bluecar.

The same thing can be said of the meaning of 'bluecar'. At the moment of stipulation it is a harmless bit of idealization to say that the phrase means the same as 'blue car', for at that moment the history of the use of 'blue car' has been appropriated to be what we are to consciously consult in figuring out how to use the novel term. The stipulation launches a word with the beginnings of a meaning into the world, but that meaning can and probably will diverge from the meaning of 'blue car'. Idealizing, we say 'bluecar' starts out sharing a meaning with 'blue car'. But that meaning is embodied in two different ways in the cognitive world of the stipulator. The two instances of the meaning can evolve independently, so that the way the instance attached to 'bluecar' evolves is quite different from the way that attached to the phrase evolves.

Summing things up: Stipulating that expression E is to mean what expression E' means—if it's something that really occurs, a performance by a normal speaker of a natural language with normal psychology of the sort that humans normally have—can be expected to have as a consequence that a number of properties and relations contribute to constituting the meaning of E. Those properties and relations will come in degrees and magnitudes, degrees and magnitudes that vary independently of one another and whose interactions determine the semantic properties of E. Stipulation—real stipulation, not an abstract philosophical fantasy—fixes meaning, but it need not create synonymy. And once we think about meaning in an appropriate way, we see that there is a sense in which two expressions—a phrase p and a term t introduced by stipulating that it is to mean what p does—can, at the time t is introduced, share a meaning that evolves, as annexed to t and to p, in different ways. So the stipulation that 't' refers to 'p' or that 't' is to mean what 'p' means can give t and p the same meaning in a way that need not secure co-reference between them. So there is precious little reason to think it could create analyticity.

Return now to the regimentation we gave of the argument, that stipulation creates analyticity and a priori knowledge:

1. We can add phrases to our language and assign them meanings.
2. If we can assign phrases meanings, we can assign a novel phrase the same meaning as one already in use.

3. If we do this, sentences which differ only by uses of the two phrases will have the same meaning.

4. If sentences have the same meaning, bi-conditionals in which they sit to the left and to the right are analytic.

5. So, it is possible for there to be (many, many pretty interesting) analytic sentences in our language.

6. If a sentence of our language is analytic, the proposition it expresses is a priori for us.

7. So, it is possible for there to be (many, many) claims that are a priori for us.

I haven't objected to the first premise. I'm willing to allow that qualified, the second premise is true—but only if it is allowed that whether the phrases have the same meaning at the time of stipulation is not really under our control. The third premise in some sense involves a false presupposition: It assumes that a meaning is a static, unchanging sort of thing like a Fregean sense. But if assigning phrases the same meaning is nothing more than transiently making the history of one of the phrases the arbiter of conscious cogitation about how to use the other, there is no reason to think that assigning phrases the same meaning guarantees that as they carry their meanings into the future, each instance of the meaning evolving independently of the other, substitution of one phrase for the other preserves meaning.

Putting all this to the side, I've questioned whether in interesting cases we would know that instances of premises 2 and 3 were correct, at least without extensive empirical investigation. And I've suggested that even on a deeply internalist picture of meaning—one on which what I mean is determined by my mental state—meaning, and thus synonymy, will be opaque to a thinker. If this is correct, premise 4 is just wrong, wrong, wrong. Frankly, I think the argument from 1 through 4 to 5 suffers from something like massive presupposition failure—only someone with an empirically uninteresting notion of meaning would be tempted by it.

6. A Digression on Logical Truth

How, if at all, does this bear on the purported analyticity of logic? One might suggest it doesn't show that logical truths could not be analytic. The argument is this. Logic is tied to inference; while some inference is unconscious, much is under conscious control. It is perfectly possible to resolve that conscious inference turning on the logical particles is to be evaluated relative to a particular standard, one codified, say, via a system of natural deduction. Once we so resolve, we have a norm that determines logical truth. By making such a resolution, we adopt the norm. Once it is adopted, it governs our inferential practice. If we are conscious of making the resolution, we know thereby that it governs our practice, and we can tell whether an inference accords with the norm. Thus, our resolution gives sentences derivable using just the rules of our system an epistemologically significant status, one that entitles us to accept and assert them, come what may. This isn't to say that we couldn't come to reject our codification.

But that would be moving to a different framework; and while doing that may 'dis-entitle' us from asserting certain things, that such movement is possible doesn't imply that logical truths are not logical truths, nor does it show that we don't have a special epistemological relation to them.

Why exactly is the situation here supposed to be different from the case of stipulating the meaning of 'bluecar'? Well, launching a word into the cognitive Umwelt via stipulation is a birthing process over which we have imperfect control at best—it is not completely under our control what the word launched via stipulation means. But here we resolve to hew to rules and norms when engaging in a particular, consciously supervised activity—reasoning supervised by the central processor. Our resolution, insofar as it's meant to govern only our consciously directed inference, is to be understood as insulated from whatever else might be going on in the morass of the subconscious. A person who has pledged allegiance to classical natural deduction may be persistently moved by forces subconscious to affirm the consequent; this does not mean that he has given up his normative allegiance.

The argument here is not an argument that what passes for logical truth in the speech of those who have not explicitly resolved to follow certain rules is analytic or a priori. Rather, the argument is that of course one could make such a resolution; were one to do so, one would, for the reasons just rehearsed, create analyticity.

There are two problems with this line of argument. First, it is hard to see why subconscious inferential tendencies are irrelevant to the meaning and reference of logical particles when someone has resolved to use those particles in a particular way. Suppose I resolve that a standard natural deduction system is to govern my inferential practices, so that the argument schema

1. If A, then B
So, 2.   If A, then if C, then B

is according to my logical resolutions valid. I may still resist instances of this schema. For example, I may think that

(A)   If there is not massive voter fraud, then either Trump or Clinton will win.
       So, if there is not massive voter fraud, then if neither Trump nor Clinton wins, either Trump or Clinton will win

is patently invalid. My resolutions concerning 'if', 'or', and 'not' do not make my tendency to resist (A) irrelevant to the question of whether it is valid. This tendency is presumably coeval with my resolution about logical particles; what those particles mean is determined (assuming, as I am for argument's sake, an internalism about meaning determination) by the sum of facts about my usage broadly conceived, not just by my resolutions and stipulations. To think otherwise, I would say, is to invest resolution and stipulation with magic powers.

The second problem is this. We can agree that the resolution in question imposes a norm on the use of sentences in which the logical words occur. But argument is needed to make out that the norm has to do with truth as opposed to something else. We can of course say, for example, that

(CI)   If B may be inferred from the premises in S along with the premise A, then *if A, then B* may be inferred from the premises in S alone.

This warrants us inferring (2) from (1). But why should we go on to say that this warrant and the truth of (1) guarantees the truth of (2), as opposed to saying that this warrant and the assertibility of (1) gives us some amount of warrant to assert (2)?

7. Grice, Strawson, and Varieties of Synonymy

The author of 'Two Dogmas' has often been criticized as follows: Quine doesn't just think that there are no analytic sentences; he thinks there is no distinction to be drawn between analytic and synthetic sentences. His view seems to be, as Grice and Strawson put it,

not merely that the distinction is useless or inadequately clarified, but also that it is altogether illusory, that the belief in its existence is a philosophical mistake.

(Grice and Strawson 1956, 142)

Grice and Strawson wonder how he can possibly hold this: Quine allows that one could define a notion of analyticity in terms of 'cognitive synonymy', a notion that

seems to correspond, at any rate roughly, to what we should ordinarily express by [speaking of two expressions as having] the same meaning...If Quine is to be consistent...then it appears that he must maintain that...the distinction we suppose ourselves to be marking by the use of the expressions 'means the same as', 'does not mean the same as' does not exist either...But...we frequently talk of the presence or absence of relations of synonymy between...expressions...where there does not appear to be any obvious substitute for the ordinary notion of synonymy...Is all such talk meaningless?   (Grice and Strawson 1956, 144–5)

I respond on Quine's behalf: No, everyday talk of sameness of meaning is perfectly significant. At least it can be understood in a way that renders it significant. But understood so that it is significant, the notion of synonymy is of limited philosophical interest; it certainly can't be used to do the sort of explanatory work which those who wanted to explain a priori knowledge in terms of analyticity wanted to accomplish. I realize that some will take this response as not Quinean in spirit, much less in letter. But I think the story I'm about to tell is in fact Quinean. Let me tell it, and then explain why.

Think of a word's meaning, as I have been asking you to, as something historical, more of a process than a thing. To fix ideas for a moment,[7] think of the meaning of a phrase in an idiolect as the unfolding history of what is, was, and will be relevant to

---

[7] I am *only* offering this example to make the discussion concrete. More realistic proposals might include a variety of things not involved in securing reference.

determining its extension, and suppose that what is so relevant and how it is relevant can shift over time. Thinking of words in this way, we can associate with a phrase p a function, p(t), that maps a time interval t to the things that are relevant to determining its reference at t; I'll call this function the phrase's semantic history. Once you think of meanings in this way, it is clear that there are various sorts of relations that phrases might bear to one another within an idiolect that could be called synonymy.

Here are three. We say that phrases p and p' are transiently synonymous in an idiolect when there is some interval for which the values of their semantic histories are (non-empty and) identical.[8] (I'll sometimes speak of phrases being synonymous at t when their semantic histories overlap in this way at t.) We say that phrases p and p' are synonymous tout court if their semantic histories are identical. And we say that phrases are essentially synonymous if there is an interval when both are used and an event which occurs during that interval which is such that, of necessity, if that event occurs in the history of the use of those two words, then at every subsequent time at which the words are both used, they are synonymous at that time. The idea behind essential synonymy, if it's not clear, is that someone might do something—perhaps say, 'By "bluecar", I mean exactly what I mean by "blue car"'—that would somehow make it essential to a word that it mean just what some other phrase means; this is not guaranteed by mere synonymy tout court.

I read the Quine of 'Two Dogmas' as sensing (correctly) that many people who speak of analyticity are presupposing that words have (many or even all) aspects of their meanings essentially—they thought that if we are individuating words in such a way that words are things with meanings, then shifts in what constitutes a word's meaning must be shifts in the identity of the word. Meanings do not stand to words as shirts do persons. Quine thought (correctly) that this was nonsense and the root of much nonsense. He thought that everyday (non-philosophical) talk of sameness of meaning was clear enough for everyday (non-philosophical) purposes; certainly we can make decent sense much of the time of what is being said or judged when it is said or judged that the meaning with which x uses phrase p is constant within the interval i. But when we speak this way, we must be understood as using 'same' not to indicate identity but one or another sort of similarity.

While essential synonymy is a silly idea, transient synonymy is not. Sure, words can be transiently synonymous, but so what? If we introduce a word ('force') by saying that it is to be understood in terms of some formula that already has a meaning ('mass times acceleration'), we are launching a word into the world. There is nothing that can guarantee that the semantic history of the word will stay in lockstep with that of the phrase. It is not even clear that when we introduce the word via the phrase, the relevant identity ('force is mass times acceleration') is thereby made true: If we think of the introduction of the term as simply the beginning of the process of fixing its semantic properties, and

---

[8] 'Transient synonymy' is being used somewhat differently here than the way it was used in Section 4, when discussing Quine's willingness to grant that stipulation could create a sort of transient synonymy.

allow that what happens in the future is relevant to what the term picks out, then it seems clear that in realistic cases—cases in which a term is introduced in order to do real work in a real theory—the 'introductory definition', taken as an assertion, may turn out false.[9]

The response to Grice and Strawson I am making on Quine's behalf, then, goes so: We can clean up everyday talk about sameness and difference of meaning in one or another way so that it makes sense. Transient synonymy is one way of doing this; using similarity relations that approach transient synonymy in the limit is another. For non-philosophical purposes much talk of sameness of meaning can be understood in such ways. We may, in fact, be able to theorize about meaning in a profitable way once we think of it as a matter of the dynamics of certain mental states within populations of speakers. But those who wanted synonymy to do epistemological work—in particular, to contribute to defining a notion of analyticity that could be used to explain the possibility of philosophically significant a priori knowledge—are going to need something much stronger than transient synonymy. And there is no reason to think that anything strong enough is available.

8. Conditional Credence and Connotation

Or is there? In some interesting recent work, David Chalmers (2011, 2012) suggests a way of defining conceptual continuity which he thinks shows the arguments in 'Two Dogmas' to be without merit. Chalmers' proposal is particularly interesting insofar as it is (in effect) an attempt to both identify meaning with something ahistorical—something that can be 'totally determined' by one's intrinsic properties at a particular time—and to accommodate the facts that 'Two Dogmas' so forcefully brings to the fore—for example, that such things as inferential dispositions can vary (dramatically) over time without anything that would intuitively count as a change in meaning occurring. We can learn a good deal from Chalmers' proposal.

That proposal is a 'refined' version of Carnap's response to Quine in 'Meaning and Synonymy in Natural Language' (Carnap 1956b). Carnap suggested that the meaning-cum-intension of a predicate in an individual's idiolect is determined by her (potential) judgments about cases. Suppose we describe a 'possible scenario' to a speaker and ask if an object therein is a unicorn. So long as the speaker doesn't make mistakes in reasoning, her answer tells us whether the intension she associates with 'unicorn' is true of the individual in the scenario. Analogously, the meaning-cum-intension of a sentence in an individual's idiolect is determined by the idealized judgments she would make about the sentence's truth, given complete descriptions of all possible scenarios.

This much is more or less familiar stuff. Chalmers adds an interesting twist. He suggests that what a speaker means by a sentence S is what is encapsulated by her

---

[9] Gil Harman may be making pretty much this point toward the end of Harman (1996).

conditional judgments about S. It is not just X's judgments that S would be true or false were this or that (complete!) description of the world correct that are relevant to what X means by S, but X's judgments that it is likely to such and such a degree that S, given this or that evidence. Thinking of meaning in this way, we can operationalize the notion of conceptual continuity by adopting a Bayesian framework and explaining conceptual continuity in terms of a speaker's holding her assignments of conditional credence constant. Chalmers takes the Bayesian to assume the truth of a principle like

(CS) Let t1 be later than t2; let cr1 and cr2 assign a subject's credences (both absolute and conditional) to her sentences at t1 and t2 respectively. If the subject is fully rational and E specifies the total evidence she acquires between t1 and t2, then if the content of S does not change between t1 and t2, $cr2(S) = cr1(S/E)$.

Given (CS), we can define conceptual continuity in terms of (relative) stability of conditional credence. Chalmers' practice is to say that there's a shift in sentence S's meaning for x if (and only if), for some evidence E, there is the sort of shift in conditional credence that occurs when x's conditional credence for S given E moves from low to high or vice versa. If we call such shifts in conditional credence seismic shifts, the idea is that there is conceptual continuity for x's understanding of S between t and t' if and only if, for some piece of potential evidence as encapsulated by a sentence E (whether this be potential 'total evidence' or some more partial piece of evidence), there is a seismic shift in x's credence in S given E between t and t'.[10]

Here is one of Chalmers' examples. Let 'E specify evidence confirming that the furry, apparently feline creatures that inhabit our houses are actually remote-controlled robots from Mars, while the other creatures we see are organic' (2011, 402). Suppose Sarah accepts

C: Cats are animals

at t1, then accepts E, and consequently rejects C at t2. Let cr1 be Sarah's t1 credence function. If $cr1(C/E)$ is low and Sarah is rational, this, Chalmers tells us, suggests conceptual constancy on Sarah's part. And we can thus conclude that C wasn't analytic for Sarah.[11] On the other hand, if $cr1(C/E)$ is high, then either Sarah changed her conditional credence for C given E—and so, says Chalmers, the meaning of C—between t1 and t2, or she is being irrational in rejecting C. Either way, Sarah's judgment does not show that one can rationally reject C without assigning it a meaning different from the one she assigns it at t1.

---

[10] Chalmers is, of course, concerned with intrapersonal continuity of meaning. It is no part of his project to explain what we might have in mind when we assert or deny that different people mean the same thing by a sentence, or that a sentence in one public language means what a sentence of some other public language does. Indeed, it isn't clear that there is a sensible way to generalize his proposal from the intra- to interpersonal case.

[11] We must, harmlessly, assume that Sarah considered E possible at t1.

Among the virtues of this proposal is that it does not predict that there are any analyticities.[12] Analyticity of sentence S in x's idiolect in this framework is a matter of x's credence for S being very high relative to all potential bits of evidence. So if, for example, it is already determined by our credence functions that we would, if confronted with E, reject C—and probably many of us would—and that (counter)fact(ual) is reflected in our current conditional credences, then C isn't analytic for us. The proposal also appears consistent with the spirit of the gradualist argument. After all, conditional credences might change incrementally over time. My credence that cats are animals given any claim whatsoever might start out high; as weeks go by, my credence that cats are animals given certain claims might remain high, but not as high as it once was...until one day, my credence that cats are animals given claim X is clearly quite low. (Whether this is a problem for the story Chalmers is telling I will take up below.)

9. How Credence Relates to Meaning

The proposal is ingenious. But I think it is wrong-headed—it gets the relation between whatever facts there might be about meaning and our judgments of probability backwards. I will give an example, and then pontificate a bit.

In the words of the poet:

All along the watchtower, princes kept the view
While all the women came and went, barefoot servants, too.
Outside in the distance a wildcat did growl
Two riders were approaching, the wind began to howl.

If you are like me, you didn't find this a bit odd when you first heard it. If you are like me, you have been able to recite it for years, and it has never struck you as in the least odd. But some do find it odd. Dave van Ronk, for example, grumbles, 'A watchtower is not a road or a wall; you can't go along it'.[13] If my (and your) linguistic module had already made it determinate that one can't move along something oriented perpendicularly to the earth's surface, we should find the words of the poet infelicitous. Or we should at least have a 'Lucy in the Sky with Diamonds', 'Oh he's trying to be psychedelic' attitude toward this verse. I don't, and I suspect that you don't either.

A reasonable guess at the explanation of the absence of such a reaction is this. We have all acquired 'along' by hearing it applied to movement across surfaces more or less horizontal with the earth's, thereby acquiring a category—that is, a disposition to label some movements as movements along a surface, and other movements as not such. A first guess about the nature of this category is that it is a representation that involves something iconic—let's call it an icon—that helps categorize perception of movement

---

[12] Nor does it predict that there aren't any.

[13] This is part of a complaint that the poet wrote carelessly when he realized his audience would allow him to. Van Ronk is cited at http://en.wikipedia.org/wiki/All_Along_the_Watchtower (accessed February 4, 2019).

on a surface as movement along it. The icon also contributes something to determining when movement is not movement along a surface. For example, movement that deviates from the surface in the way a loop-the-loop would is not movement along the surface. But the fact that only certain sorts of resemblance to the icon prompt categorization does not imply that sorts of movement that would not trigger along-categorization would be miscategorized if they were categorized as movement along a surface. The category is simply silent about certain sorts of movement. In particular, it does not classify vertical surface movement as along or as not along. It has been left open whether such movement is movement along a surface.

Suppose this is the right story to tell about the category *movement along a surface*. It does not follow that we would have no dispositions that determine an assignment of a probability to *elevators travel along buildings* or *the princes were keeping watch all along the watchtower* relative to one or another piece of evidence. After all, if we hear someone using these sentences, we will have one or another reaction to the use, given the situation we find ourselves in. But what the story just told about the category *along* suggests is that what dispositions we have are not ones that are determined simply by the concept *along* or by the meaning of the word 'along'. One expects that how we react to novel uses of 'along' is highly contingent on matters that have nothing to do with the meaning we assign to the word. If our first encounter with the phrase 'along the watch-tower' is the poet's confident use, we will probably conform our use to his; if our first encounter is with Van Ronk's, we will find the poet's use deviant. In either case, our reaction will not be (merely) reflecting pre-existing facts about what the phrase meant in our vocabulary.

Categorization often involves a natural but underdetermined extension of an existing category. The fact that a category will naturally be applied (or withheld) in a certain way in a particular situation does not show that the category would have been misused or 'had its meaning changed' if it had been withheld (or applied). When a case is novel—when the question, Does this category apply in this sort of case?, has never been posed—there may be a very natural answer to the question. The fact that an answer to the question is natural, or even more natural than any other answer, though, does not by itself imply anything about whether the category 'demands' that answer, or whether deciding the case in another way would involve a change in meaning or replacing one category with another.[14]

This point carries over to our actual and hypothetical judgments about conditional probability. It may be extremely natural for me at time t in situation s to judge that it is very probable that y is more or less horizontal relative to the earth's surface, given that there are Fs all along x. It does not follow that if I assign a different conditional probability at a later time in a different sort of situation, I have 'changed the meaning' of 'along'. What determines the credence I assign to S given E is a fluid confluence of factors, some linguistic, some happenstanceal. Variation in one factor can shift

---

[14] Some of what I say here echoes claims Mark Wilson has argued for. See, for instance, Wilson (1982).

conditional credence. Since not all of the determinants can be thought of as aspects of meaning, shifts in credence cannot be identified with shifts in meaning.

I said above that Chalmers' proposal about the relation between credence and meaning gets the relation between them backwards; at this point, I hope it's clear why. Conditional and absolute credence, insofar as they are determinate to begin with, do not determine or constitute what our sentences mean. Rather, such facts as there are about meaning along with non-linguistic facts about our psychology determine our dispositions to do such things as accept one sentence on the supposition that another is true; these facts, in turn, determine under idealization such facts as there are about conditional credence.

10. The Rational Fixation of Belief

Part of the point in the last section—that our conditional credence functions will be (extremely) partial, even when limited to (the propositions expressed by) relatively short sentences we understand—strikes me as quite general. Return to the case of Sarah, who is confronted with Putnamian evidence E that cats are robots. If she is a typical non-philosopher, there is no reason to think that $cr1(C/E)$ is defined—no reason, that is, to think that Sarah has an opinion of how likely it is that cats are animals, given the robotic scenario. We may fairly assume that she has never considered a fanciful scenario like Putnam's and is, when she first hears it, at a complete loss about what to say about it. She will, of course, eventually come to have an opinion—life goes on, after all. But it is hard to see why such a decision must reflect a prior, more or less determinate (constrained range of) value(s) for C conditional on E to which Sarah was already committed. Presumably there is nothing about the meaning of C (as Sarah uses it) that would, along with a normal suite of beliefs, dictate that $cr1(C/E)$ must be high, low, or around 0.5.

But if the relevant conditional probability is undefined at t1, why think that rationality must make any demands whatsoever on Sarah as to what attitude she takes toward C given E? Sarah can quite rationally hold the meaning of 'cats are animals', insofar as it has a determinate meaning, constant and think whatever she likes about feline animality after she accepts E.[15]

The general point is that our linguistic training and extra-linguistic opinions or knowledge often don't determine what we would—much less should—say about many possible (and even actual) cases. No one laid down rules about what to say should we discover that the things we hail with 'kitty' are and always have been remotely controlled robots; who knows what we would say about such a case? We might have a response to a detailed description of a scenario of the sort Putnam describes; but why

---

[15] This needs to be qualified. If, for example, Sarah has no conditional credence as to whether prairie dogs are animals, given that they are robotic Martian spies, rationality might demand that her conditional credence on this be in line with her newfound conditional credence about feline animality.

think that prior to hearing the description there was a particular reaction we needed to have, if we were to maintain what we meant by C? This, of course, is essentially the point Putnam makes in discussing his example:

Once we find out that cats were created from the beginning by Martians... it is clear that we have a problem of how to speak. What is not clear is which of the available decisions should be described as the decision to keep the meaning of either word ('cat' or 'animal') unchanged, and which decision should be described as the decision to change the meaning. I agree with Donnellan that this question has no clear sense.   (Putnam 1962, 660–1)

Extending use in the face of unanticipated contingencies is poorly described as 'change in meaning' when what was determinate in meaning is preserved in the extension. The approach to meaning constancy Chalmers proposes has it that when one's conditional credence for S given some evidence has a large shift, that is a change in S's meaning. A shift from undefined to much higher than 0.3 is surely a large shift. So on the present approach, whatever Sarah decides about her kitten, we are witnessing fairly profound meaning change. But as just said, this doesn't seem an apt way to theorize. Generalizing, since pretty much any sentence one likes could be 'Putnamized' by coming up with a possible scenario E that would leave us at a loss as to what to say about the sentence, this suggests that Chalmers' approach gets the facts wrong about pretty much every sentence.

One might object that it follows from the fact that someone has a credence in C&E and a credence in E that they have conditional credence (C/E), equal to the first credence divided by the second; but surely it's not too much to assume that people have unconditional credence in sentences they understand.[16] Sarah, for example, presumably thinks at t1 that C is very likely, E very unlikely.

Even if conditional probability is definable via the ratio rule[17]

One's conditional probability of C given E is equal to one's absolute credence in C&E divided by one's absolute credence in E

it is no more plausible to think that the relevant unconditional probabilities exist than it is to think that the conditional ones do. Grant for the sake of argument that if either side of the equation

(R)   cr1(cats are animals/the robotic cat story is true) =
cr1(cats are animals & the robotic cat story is true) / cr1(the robotic cat story is true)

is defined, it's true. Since Sarah (and Putnam and you and I) has no idea what to say about whether cats are animals if the robotic cat story is true, we presumably don't have much of an idea about what probability to assign to 'cats are animals and the robotic story is true'. If it has a probability, it's somewhere between zero and the probability of

---

[16] Some things Chalmers said in correspondence suggest that he is at least tempted by such a response—though don't hold him to this.

[17] Which has been—reasonably, I think—questioned; see Hajek (2003).

'the robotic cat story is true'—which is just another way of saying (given (R)) that the conditional probability of cats being animals given the robotic story is something between 0 and 1, which is a way of saying that we have no idea what the conditional probability might be. There is no good reason to think that either side of (R) is defined.[18]

One way to respond to the sort of argument I've been giving has it that if a speaker understands the words in S and E at time t, then she does in fact assign a probability to S conditional on E, befuddlement when first encountering the question 'if E, then is it likely that S?' notwithstanding. Chalmers says some things that suggest this kind of response. He remarks that

For most S and most E, the subject will have some relevant dispositions involving S and E, for example, involving her willingness to accept various bets involving S and E. In many cases, these dispositions will line up in a clear enough way that [it will be determinate that the probability of S given E is determinately high or determinately low]. In other cases, the dispositions will be enough of a mix that it is hard to say. (2011, 413)

He then observes that the Quinean might well say that in this last case cr(S/E) is indeterminate, so that (even if the subject's prior probability for S was extremely high) rejecting S does not show that one is violating (CS) or being irrational. And then, so long as we can Putnamize a sentence, it will be rationally revisable without a change of meaning.

Chalmers in essence says that such cases are not possible. We can assume that the subject, on being confronted with the robotic cat story and accepting it, will eventually come up with a probability for 'cats are animals'. But

If the subject if fully rational, then the subject's dispositions to accept S on supposing E and on learning E should be the same, assuming no conceptual change. That is, if a fully rational subject rejects S on learning E and thinking things through, then if the subject were to have been initially presented with the supposition that E and had thought things through, the subject should have rejected S conditional on that supposition. (2011, 413)

Chalmers here assumes that, if one can rationally reach a conclusion about a sentence's probability, then (holding the sentence's meaning fixed) that conclusion is unique in the sense that no other conclusion could have been rationally reached by that subject. For if this isn't so, the subject might quite rationally reach one verdict when she makes a supposition relevant to the sentence, and with equal rationality come to another verdict about the sentence when she learns what in the previous case she supposed.

---

[18] Perhaps it will be said that I am rejecting the entire Bayesian framework for understanding rational change of belief, since it can't be applied to someone unless she has a well-defined conditional credence function. But there is no need to think that the Bayesian framework is inapplicable to a person who fails to assign conditional credence to every pair of claims. Suppose a subject's conditional and unconditional probabilities are (with some idealization) defined for humdrum (and not so humdrum) claims. That doesn't imply that they will be defined for the sorts of cases that might lead to our at least considering revision of what pass for analyticities. Why should this make the Bayesian framework inapplicable to the subject? Since these later sorts of cases never come up, confining a credence function to the cases that actually *might* come up isn't going to hamstring us.

In thinking about Chalmers' view, it is worth considering how Quine himself might have responded to it. Recall Quine's Duhemian reflection in 'Two Dogmas': 'A recalcitrant experience... can be accommodated by any of various alternative reevaluations in various alternative quarters of the total system [of our beliefs]' (1951, 44). One way to state what Quine has in mind here is in terms of what ways of revising one's beliefs— thought of as assignments of conditional and unconditional credences—are rational. Quine's idea was quite simply that there will not be a single rational way for an individual to react to an experience, recalcitrant or otherwise. At any time a rational person has open to her a number of ways of changing her assignments of probabilities to claims. Her dispositions to react to and evaluate evidence and then change belief determine these strategies, but the determination is one–many.

How do we choose among them, if we are rational? Well, essentially in terms of pragmatic factors: for example, 'our natural tendency to disturb the total system as little as possible' (Quine 1951, 44) often leads us to choose ways of updating our beliefs that ceteris paribus leave the absolute probabilities of certain claims (that there are brick houses in North Carolina, that cats are animals, that $1 + 3 = 4$) more or less as they were. Of course, other factors—our desire for simplicity, feelings that one explanation is 'more satisfying' (for example, it 'unifies the sciences' better) than another, convenience in computation, efficiency as a predictive device, and so on—may lead us to non-conservative updates.

A rational person will often, perhaps usually, be disposed to change her credences in the light of new evidence in a particular way. How she will be inclined to do this is a function of many things, including the ways in which she balances and is moved by the sorts of pragmatic considerations just mentioned. It is a very odd suggestion indeed that there is but a single way for a rational person to go about doing this; it is just as odd to suggest that, of the various different ways in which one might revise belief in the face of recalcitrant evidence, only one way of doing so is both rational and preserves the meanings of one's terms (if you prefer: does not involve conceptual revision). It is particularly odd to suggest that there is a single rational, meaning-preserving way to react to surprising, much less bizarre, turns of events. What seems a reasonable thing to say—something very much in the spirit of Quine—is that for each t at which a person X is forming beliefs there will be a set of R_t of strategies, thought of as conditional credence functions, that are available to X for (rationally) learning from experience. This set will be determined by X's dispositions to react to and evaluate evidence. It will be constrained by the pragmatic factors mentioned at the end of the last paragraph.

Being determined by X's dispositions toward possible evidence, the members of R_t can be expected to more or less agree about the conditional probabilities of sentences relative to pieces of potential evidence that don't go beyond the bounds of what X (currently) takes to be more or less likely. Thus, the members of R_t can be expected to tend to yield more or less the same credence functions when one conditionalizes them on E's that summarize total evidence accumulation over short periods of time. These facts form the basis of a justification for the claim that Bayesianism provides a decent first approximation to the truth about confirmation and rational belief revision. For they suggest that in the short term and in the case of 'normal science', the Bayesian paradigm may give a decent description of rational belief revision and evidentiary relations.[19]

As I am reading Quine, he thought it was absurd to think that a particular member or even a small set of members of a person's R_t (the set of strategies at t she might rationally adopt for belief updating) were the only strategies the use of which would preserve the meanings of one's sentences. If one insists on tying meaning to rational belief revision, one should say that the facts about what one's sentences mean are given by the ways in which one might rationally revise one's beliefs in the face of recalcitrant evidence.

It is obvious that on this picture there might be a very wide divergence indeed among the ways in which one might rationally revise one's credence in, say, 'cats are animals', given that one comes to think that the furry pets that go 'meow' are robotic.

It is not as if this means that we have to completely abandon the Bayesian framework for thinking about evidence and learning. We have to modify it in various ways; but that, I think, has been obvious for quite some time now.

It seems to me that the picture I have ascribed to Quine has considerable intuitive appeal. In particular, it sits well with (what I take to be) the obvious point that what it is rational for us to think as we make our way through the world is a joint function of the variety of ways we can see to make sense of the evidence we acquire and more or less practical constraints on how we might theorize, given our interests and abilities. Indeed, I think the broadly Quinean picture just sketched sits far better with this point than does the rigid Bayesianism that is required to get Chalmers' enterprise off the ground. For this reason alone, a Quinean view of meaning is much more likely than Chalmers' to be close to correct.

---

[19] A complicating factor is that almost no serious Bayesian thinks (it is even a reasonable idealization to say) that people assign crisp conditional or unconditional probabilities to many or any sentences beyond logical truths and untruths. The standard view amongst Bayesians is that we can assign a *range* of credence functions to an individual at a time; the facts about her credences are those claims about her credences that are true relative to any function in the range that represents her. This sort of multiplication of the individual's credence functions is of a quite different sort than the one I am suggesting Quine would insist on. Taking it into account would complicate exposition considerably, so I am ignoring it.

3

What Are Meanings, That We Might Share Them?

I say that meanings are like species. You should say: What do you mean by 'meaning'? I could mean something like the determinant of reference and truth conditions—something like what David Kaplan calls character. Or I could mean something that can be asserted, believed, and so on, that's associated with a sentence's use by convention and context, or more idiosyncratically by a speaker. Or I could mean meaning in the sense of that with which one must be in cognitive contact in order to qualify as a competent speaker in a population.

What I mean is the last; my primary goal in this chapter is to sketch the beginning of an account of meaning in this sense. On this account, meanings supervene on mutual presuppositions about how people (presuppose people are inclined to) understand one another.[1] The meaning of the word 'cousin' as used by, say, the English-speaking residents of Provincetown MA is to a first approximation a collection of humdrum assumptions—that 'cousin' is a word one uses to talk about cousins, that cousins are relatives, that your cousins are the children of your folks' sisters and brothers, that people have cousins but dogs and bumblebees do not, etc., etc. What makes these assumptions part of the word's meaning is, again to a first approximation, that it is mutual knowledge in the group that when someone uses the word, they can expect others to have these assumptions at the ready for making sense of the sentence in which the word is used.

Why think that if this is what meanings are like, meanings are like species? Well, a species is constituted by a population lineage, a collection of individuals related by descent. But that's just what constitutes the meaning of 'cousin' when meaning is thought of in the way just suggested. Each resident of Provincetown makes assumptions that they take to be mutually shared by all the other Provincetownies about what

---

[1] Eyebrows may rise at this. The last chapters argued that that we could accommodate Quinean qualms about meaning by thinking of it as species-like. And it is indeed my intention that we arrive at a picture of meaning that a Quinean could endorse. But you say, eyebrows in ascension: Quine endorsing a picture that explains semantic phenomena in intentional terms—in terms of presuppositions? *Obscurum per obscurius.*

Well. A high-church Quinean can admit presuppositions cashed out in terms of such things as dispositions to accept sentences, or to behave as if certain sentences are true. And even if high-church Quineans don't like talk that involves the intentional idioms, we evangelical low-church Quineans are perfectly happy to speak of beliefs, assumptions, and the like.

speakers expect audiences to have at the ready for interpreting the use of 'cousin'; these sets of assumptions 'reproduce' themselves as the word 'cousin' is handed off by parents and teachers to children and others learning the ambient language. And just as a species evolves when the environment favors one phenotype over a variant, so the assumptions that constitute the meaning of 'cousin' can change as the linguistic environment shifts.[2]

I said that my primary goal in this chapter was to begin sketching this way of thinking of what anchors linguistic competence, and this is the task of Sections 3 through 10. I've bookended those sections with a discussion of philosophical analysis. I do this because I think that, beyond its cohering with much that Quine has to say, a motivation for thinking about meaning in the way I'm proposing is that it helps make a case for the importance of something much like philosophical analysis as it is traditionally conceived. Let me explain.

A dozen or so years ago, most analytic philosophers would have found the following picture self-evident: Much, though by no means all, philosophy involves the generation of ingenious cases about which philosophers have relatively strong and consistent intuitions; such intuitions are a significant source of evidence for philosophical analysis, which is the task of articulating the structure of our concepts. Of late this picture has come under attack. Some say 'intuition' is nothing more than a pompous word for 'belief', and that our beliefs are not—simply because they are our beliefs—a source of philosophical evidence. Some observe that intuitions are supposed to have various hallmarks—they are supposed to have a particular phenomenology or issue simply from insight into conceptual structure; they complain that they are unaware of any such phenomenology and dubious about conceptual structure. Some say that since intuitions vary with the culture of their possessors, their usefulness as evidential fodder is compromised or worse.[3]

A subsidiary goal of this chapter is to develop and defend a version of the picture most of us used to find self-evident. Philosophical analysis, on this picture, is the attempt to uncover, articulate, and regiment the sort of meaning I've suggested anchors our competence as speakers; as such, philosophical analysis is first and foremost a kind of 'conceptual analysis', an attempt to spell out the nature of the concepts our words express—or, if you prefer to put it in linguistic mode, to spell out the meanings of the words that express our common concepts. This sort of analysis is, I'll argue, important if for no other reason than that often enough what we are talking about with philosophically

---

[2] It's a delicate question as to exactly what individuals constitute a word's meaning. I've written as if those individuals are (something like) enduring idiolects, with an idiolect thought of as something that is embedded in a particular person and social situation. On this way of thinking of things, aspects of such idiolects—in particular, the idiolect's lexical entries, thought of as incorporating assumptions about how audiences understand words—reproduce themselves via the linguistic intercourse of their hosts—via, that is, the behavior of parents and teachers in producing new token idiolects.

Other ways to answer the delicate question are taken up in Chapter 6.

[3] For a summary of some worries about intuitions as having philosophical significance and a response thereto, see Sosa (2007). Cappelen (2012) gives an extended negative discussion of the role of intuitions in philosophy.

fraught phrases like 'free will', 'equality', or 'knows' is not determinate—use may narrow down what we are talking about when we speak of knowledge, equality, or responsibility without yielding a best candidate. In such cases there is not anything more for philosophy to do, beyond articulating and then evaluating the various ways our thought and talk can be understood.

My bookending looks like this. In the first two sections of the chapter, I explain what I take intuitions to be, and say something about the idea that philosophical analysis involves but is not exhausted by conceptual analysis. I think there is something to this idea that even a Quinean could endorse. I then lay out the picture of meaning introduced above. The chapter ends with a discussion of the relations between intuitions and philosophical analysis. Intuitions can be and often are evidence for philosophical analysis. But their initial role in philosophical theorizing is as data, not evidence. Intuitions are something we have; a good philosophical theory should (among other things) strive to explain why we have the intuitions we do. When a theory does that well, intuitions become more than data—they become evidence. I compare the view I sketch with that of Cappelen (2012), Cappelen being no friend of the idea that philosophy needs intuitions. There is, I think, not all that much distance between the view I outline here (and the views of many others who think that intuitions are philosophical evidence) and Cappelen's view. There may, however, be at least one substantive difference between Cappelen and me, one that has to do with what we can reasonably expect philosophical analysis to deliver.

1. Intuitions

I won't try to define 'philosophical analysis'. But it is the sort of thing that philosophers are doing when they offer or criticize what are meant to be illuminating accounts of the conditions under which objects have a property or relation. It's the sort of thing you find when the philosopher, after twenty or so pages of Chisholming away at various definitions, triumphantly displays something of the form

(K)   S knows that p iff...

and declares the Gettier problem solved.

A case, as I shall use the term, is a description of a(n apparently) possible situation. Intuitions are things that are made manifest by strong, relatively stable inclinations to apply something predicative—a phrase or a concept—to something as described in a case.[4] This doesn't yet tell us what intuitions are, but it does have implications about what they are not. There is no need for an intuition to involve distinctive phenomenology, for example, since the strong and stable inclinations that manifest them generally do not. Intuitions presumably don't correspond to spontaneous or 'snap' judgments, at least not to ones that are immediately accessible to consciousness. Confronted with a

---

[4] I assume that the norm is that such inclinations are manifestations of intuitions.

putative counter-example to an analysis of (say) *x acts freely in F'ing*, I may at first not know what to say about it, in part because I 'go back and forth' between an inclination to think the case is a case of free action and an inclination to say it is not. Indeed, we have all found on occasion that our intuitions are at war with one another: I may after reflection have a strong inclination to say that something is a case of free action (perhaps in part because it so clearly patterns with paradigms of free action) as well as a strong inclination to say that the case is not such (perhaps because it has elements that I am committed to saying are incompatible with free agency).

So what, exactly, are intuitions? There are, I think, two primary possibilities: they are psychological states—judgments or inclinations to judge—focused on propositional contents, or they are the contents of some such states. The dominant use of 'intuitions', I think, identifies them with judgments about possible cases, so that (for example) my intuition about Alvin Goldman's barn case is either my making a particular judgment about it, or is the content of that judgment.[5] Because conflicting intuitions need not issue in judgments, I don't think this is the best way to use the term. Better, it seems to me, to identify intuitions with either strong and stable inclinations to make a judgment about a case, or with the content of the judgment one is thus inclined to make. I will be non-committal about the content of the relevant judgments, though I am inclined (following Malmgren 2011) to endorse the idea that, for example, the content of the intuition that Alvin Goldman is focused on, when he presents the case of Henry driving about fake barn country, is something like

p1: It is ('metaphysically') possible that someone be as Henry is in [here insert Goldman's description of the case] but not know that he is looking at a barn.

But nothing I will say turns on niceties about the content of an intuition.

Goldman's intuition is thus either his strong and stable inclination to judge p1, or it's the content of that potential judgment. Which one is it?

2. Conceptual Analysis

Philosophers who toil at finding biconditionals like (K) often call what they are up to conceptual analysis. I take it that those who use this moniker think that a successful philosophical analysis would, among other things, tell us something not just about a property or relation but about our concept of it. The idea is that a philosopher who offered

(K')   Knowledge is reliably generated true belief

(along with an account of 'reliable generation') as an analysis or philosophical account typically means to be doing two things: (1) she's telling us that the concepts of being reliably generated, being true, and being a belief are 'part of', or 'help constitute', our

---

[5] The case is in Goldman (1976); it's discussed in Section 12.

concept of knowledge; (2) she's telling us that the relation of knowledge is instantiated just if the properties and relations mentioned in (K')'s predicate are instantiated in the right way.[6] This implies that when philosophical analysis is successful, it tells us something about 'conceptual structure'.

This idea needs elaboration. It is not always clear what philosophers have in mind when they speak of concepts, and it is certainly not clear what conceptual structure is supposed to be. And it is not totally clear why an analysis of, say, the concept of knowledge—which one would think is something that is in some sense psychological—would be helpful to someone who was looking for illumination about the relation to knowledge.

How shall we understand the philosopher's talk of concepts? On any way of understanding it, concepts have a semantics: they (or their applications) can sensibly be said to be true or false of objects. Philosophical pictures of concepts diverge along two dimensions: over whether concepts are individuated in terms of the psychological structures that realize them, and over whether their semantic properties are to be assigned 'internally' or 'externally'.

Some see concepts as closely related to categories, enduring psychological structures that are involved in classification, are in some way involved in occurrent beliefs and memories, and are in language users connected with the meanings of the words we use to form their canonical names.[7] Categories are naturally thought of as idiosyncratic to their possessor, as they are structures naturally individuated in terms of knowledge and perceptual abilities that vary across individuals. Others views of concepts take them to be more or less semantic entities. Extreme versions of such views individuate them in terms of just their extensions (or possible worlds intensions, or the property or relation they determine); a somewhat less extreme version of such a view might individuate a concept in terms of its (ex- or intension and) semantic relations to other concepts. Views that take concepts to be partially semantic, partially psychological are of course possible.

For the moment I'm somewhat less concerned with these sorts of differences than with differences over how the semantic properties of concepts are determined. Some think the semantic properties of a concept are determined more or less narrowly—an extreme version of such a view is one that holds that they are determined in such a way that the semantics of the concepts of physiological duplicates can't differ. Others think of concepts as shared by different individuals, so that, for example, normal adult humans have the same concepts of physical object and agent, and normal English speakers express the same concepts with the word 'accident'. Given the variation across people in categorical realizations of the concept *accident*, this way of thinking of concepts seems committed to the idea that a concept's semantics is in good part determined

---

[6] Eventually I'll suggest that the relation between philosophical analysis and 'properties out there in the world' is somewhat subtler than this suggests.

[7] By this last I mean, for instance, that there is an intimate relation between the meaning of my word 'cat' and my concept *cat*.

by social and environmental relations among users. If you think of word meanings as one kind of concept and think that members of a single-language community typically mean the same thing when they use everyday vocabulary items, you will probably be partial to this view.[8]

If the idea that philosophical analysis involves uncovering conceptual structure is part of a proposal about how to best understand philosophical practice, we should take the concepts philosophers analyze to be shared ones. For whatever the target of such analysis may be, it is something that is public in the banal sense that when different philosophers try to give an account of knowledge, or reasons for action, or reference, or whatever, they presuppose that they are all trying to give an account of the same thing. I infer this last bit from the way in which (what is usually identified as) philosophical analysis proceeds. If you look at arguments over cases and over what our intuitions about them tell us, it is striking that we do not argue from intuitions—that is, from judgments about cases—that we do not take to be widely shared; the weight we are willing to assign to an intuition seems to be a function not of how strong our own inclinations are, but of how widely the intuition is shared. And one just doesn't see philosophers retreating when their intuitions are disputed, by saying that they are only trying to give an account of their own concepts. We all agree that if A's analysis of knowledge is correct and B's intuitions conflict with it, B's intuitions are messed up, even if they accurately reflect his idiosyncratic category of knowledge.

Suppose this much is accepted. What, exactly, is the conceptual structure that analysis illuminates? What is it for p's being true to be 'part of the concept' of my knowing p?

Well, we are thinking of a concept as something, like word meanings, that we first and foremost share with others. Many, perhaps most, of our concepts and meanings are acquired in dialog with others: We learn the rudiments of concept and word application from others; we work with them to decide how to apply word and concept in difficult cases; when differences over application are manifest, we argue and negotiate.[9] Even when a concept or meaning (apparently) has an innate basis—as, presumably, the concepts *object* and *actor* do—their contours are elaborated through social interaction. Having a concept and understanding meaning is in part a matter of being connected to a social network, a group of people who make use of the concept in particular ways, who recognize one another as using a word with the same meaning, and who typically share presuppositions about how the two are to be applied, even in novel cases. The sort of sharing I have in mind here is roughly the sort which is present when a claim is 'common ground' among a group G: the members of G all presuppose

---

[8] The two dimensions of variance are perhaps to some extent correlated—those who see concepts as primarily psychological tend to be sympathetic to internalist accounts of semantics; those attracted to externalist semantics for concepts often speak as if differences in the categories that realize a concept are not terribly relevant to its individuation.

[9] Part of having a concept is having a sense of the range of ways in which it can be applied, and thus having a sense of how far someone's use of a concept can diverge from one's own and still be a use of *that* concept.

the claim; they all presuppose that they all presuppose p; they all presuppose *that*; and so on.[10] These presuppositions and the behavior that manifests them make significant contributions to what our concepts are true of, though they do not by themselves determine reference: at the very least, we need to combine them with our relations to our environment and historical and broadly social facts about linguistic practice before we have something that even might determine reference.

Some of these presuppositions are more or less readily available to consciousness. Some may even qualify as consciously accessible mutual knowledge: not only do we pretty much all see immediately on reflection that we presuppose that brothers are siblings, we all pretty much immediately see that we know this, know that all know this, that all expect that we all know this, and so on. But many such presuppositions are not articulated: they have not been voiced, nor have they been thought explicitly, nor are they recorded subpersonally in some algorithmic form, nor does passing reflection give easy access to formulae which spell them out. And among such presuppositions, many can't be said to be known or even objects of belief. Take Austin's shopworn but nice examples from 'A Plea for Excuses' that illustrate the difference between doing something by mistake and doing it accidentally.[11] Do all or even most competent speakers know, before they read Austin's footnote, that someone who knows what it is to do something by accident expects anyone (who knows what accidental action is) to know that in the case in which the donkey Austin aims at moves and he thus shoots the neighbor's donkey, it was done by accident, not by mistake?

I would say no, and not just because most people are unfamiliar with the Austin example. Most people who have the concepts of acting by mistake and acting accidentally have not thought very hard about them. They have picked up the concepts by seeing them applied in various cases, acquiring dispositions that more or less match those of everyone else, at least in a broad range of everyday cases. They have stable inclinations to apply the terms, ones that overlap with those of others, but they have not articulated those inclinations to themselves or to others. When the competent speaker reads the footnote and judges this one's by mistake, that one's by accident, she

---

[10] At this point, I'm not giving a definition but a preliminary elucidation of an idea. Aficionados are of course aware that the notion of common ground I am alluding to has been trenchantly explored by Bob Stalnaker—see, in particular, Stalnaker (2014)—and that the nature of the attitude involved in presupposition is a delicate matter. There are also delicate issues here about members of a community who possess a concept but are in some way deviant—people, for example, who (to borrow an example from Tyler Burge) have the concept *sofa* but think that sofas are not furniture but religious paraphernalia. For now I ignore such issues but will return to them below.

[11] Austin writes:

> You have a donkey, so have I, and they graze in the same field. The day comes when I conceive a dislike for mine. I go to shoot it, draw a bead on it, fire: the brute falls in its tracks. I inspect the victim, and find to my horror that it is your donkey. I appear on your doorstep with the remains and say—what? 'I say, old sport, I'm awfully sorry, etc., I've shot your donkey by accident'? Or 'by mistake'? Then again, I go to shoot my donkey as before, draw a bead on it, fire—but as I do so, the beasts move, and to my horror yours falls. Again the scene on the doorstep—what do I say? 'By mistake'? Or 'by accident'?   (Austin 1979, 185)

is not applying an explicit rule from which the judgment is an easy consequence. She is not doing something that she had an articulate expectation that she (or anyone else) would do; neither did she have prior articulate knowledge from which such an expectation is an easy consequence. This is not to say that she didn't know what it is to do something by mistake or by accident; it is rather to say that the latter knowledge does not require very much in the way of conceptual articulation.

What is surprising is that while most people cannot articulate the difference between mistake and accident,[12] almost everyone immediately 'gets' the example and makes the judgments about them Austin expects. There is presumably something about our practice of labeling things as mistakes or accidents, something in the presuppositions about accidents and mistakes that are shared by those who have the concepts *accident* and *mistake*, that leads to convergence here—there is some set of properties and relations, or some degree of some magnitude, or something else made manifest in the examples, to which our classifications are sensitive, and which explains our convergence. When this sort of thing is true of a concept, say that the concept has implicit content.

Implicit content is implicit, and it needs to be articulated.[13] Though pretty much everyone agrees in their judgments about Austin's cases, it is actually pretty difficult to project from the cases to an account of the difference. Such an articulation would involve claims along the lines of ones like

(A)   We take such and such properties to suffice for something to fall under the concept *accident*,
We take such and such properties to be are necessary for something to fall under the concept *mistake*,

where the properties in question are ones sensitivity to which explains our converging judgments. Since implicit content is what sparks application, and our common patterns of application can be erroneous, articulations of such content need to be made in this form, though of course it will often turn out that something stronger can be said, something along the lines of

(A')   Such and such properties suffice for something to be an accident,
Such and such properties are necessary for something to be a mistake.

As I see it, those who think that philosophical analysis involves uncovering conceptual structure think such analysis aims at uncovering implicit content in the sense I've been trying to elucidate. Their hope is to come up with truths that look like the claims in (A); they suspect that often enough those truths will lead to truths like those in (A').

---

[12] As Austin observes, many people will *say* that they are the same thing.
[13] *Some* of what I have characterized as implicit content is already articulated in the minds of most speakers—that something falls under the concept *brother* only if it is male is an example. Not much of the articulated content of a concept will be of philosophical interest.

3. Linguistic Competence and Concepts

The suggestion in the last section is pretty darn vague. You might reasonably say that you haven't any feeling for the conditions under which one of the many presuppositions we all share is a part of a concept or meaning. It is common ground that it usually snows in Boston in winter. So it is common ground that cousins are such that it usually snows in Boston in winter. But it would be a disappointing account of the nature of concepts indeed that delivered the conclusion that part of the concept cousin or the meaning of 'cousin' is that (cousins are such that) it usually snows in Boston in winter. This and the next few sections try to say something useful about this.

A good place to start is with a proposal by Jim Higginbotham about linguistic competence.[14] Higginbotham himself starts with the question of what might be salvaged from the Davidsonian proposal—that knowing a truth theory for a language would suffice for being in a position to understand it—in the face of objections like John Foster's.[15] His suggestion is that what someone has to know in order to be a competent speaker of a language is not simply facts about reference, satisfaction, and truth conditions. Rather

What they must know…consists of: facts about the reference of expressions, about what other people know and are expected to know about the reference of expressions, about what they know about what one knows and is expected to know about the reference of expressions, and so on up.

From this point of view, meaning does not reduce to reference, but knowledge of meaning reduces to the norms of knowledge of reference…To a first approximation, the meaning of an expression is what you are expected, simply as a speaker, to know about its reference. As a speaker of English, you are expected, for example, to know that 'snow is white' is true iff snow is white; to know that 'snow' refers to snow, and that 'is white' is true of just the white things.

(Higginbotham 1992, 257)

The proposal is that linguistic competence is (in the first instance) a matter of knowing certain disquotational claims about reference and truth and knowing that those claims are common ground among speakers. To know the meaning of 'snow' is, roughly, to know: (a) that it applies to snow; (b) that English speakers know (a) and presuppose that others do; (c) that English speakers know (b) and presuppose that others do; and so on.

---

[14] In Higginbotham (1992), which develops material in Higginbotham (1989). References are to the reprinting in Richard (2003).

[15] See the essays in Davidson (1984) for Davidson's proposal. Foster (1976) observes that a truth theory for L in L′ might correctly characterize truth conditions with theorems (in the language L′) of the form '*S' is a true sentence of L iff S*', though it is never the case that the L sentence S and the L′ sentence S′ are in any sense synonymous. This will happen, for example, if a truth theory for French in English employs axioms like *x satisfies-in-French 'chien' iff (x is a dog which is such that the interior angles of a triangle sum to 180 degrees*, since something is of necessity a dog iff it is a dog such that the interior angles of a triangle sum to 180 degrees). Since the only apparent way knowledge of a truth theory for L in L′ might allow one to understand L is to (speak L′ and) use the right-hand side of T-theorems to interpret sentences mentioned on the left, an L′-speaker using such a theory would misunderstand L.

One wants to know what it takes to have the relevant disquotational knowledge—to know, for example, that 'snow' applies to snow. Does this sort of knowledge actually suffice for linguistic competence? Does knowing the fact about snow and 'snow' suffice for understanding the word 'snow' or for 'having the concept snow'?

Consider the child learning a language. The child hears mom say that dad's tie is gamboge. The child (subpersonally) infers that 'gamboge' is an adjective; he knows how adjectives work. Since the child is raised in a high-church Davidsonian household, he now assents to *'gamboge' is true of gamboge things*. If this assent expresses knowledge—not simply knowledge that the sentence ' "gamboge" applies to gamboge things' is true, but knowledge that 'gamboge' applies to gamboge things—then it seems unlikely that the sort of knowledge Higginbotham is appealing to can ground understanding. For surely the child does not understand 'gamboge' simply because he knows it's an adjective—he might not even realize that gamboge is a color. And adding knowledge that it's common ground that 'gamboge' applies to gamboge things (whatever the heck they are) is not going to magically induce understanding.

Higginbotham in fact holds that the child in such an example does know that 'gamboge' applies to gamboge things; he holds that one can know this while only partially understanding the word 'gamboge'. And the child, Higginbotham says, does partially understand it—he knows, for instance, that it is an adjective, and that whatever it means, it means something that one can sensibly ascribe to a tie.

Why, you may ask, should we say that the child is in a position to think, much less know, truths expressed with the word 'gamboge'? The crux of the argument is that

Our words do refer to certain things, at least are held to refer to them, even when our knowledge of reference is incomplete. Moreover, it appears that incomplete understanding does not even prevent attribution of the same concept to the ignorant as to the learned...we should [view the language of the learner]...as having an interpretation that is only partially grasped.

(Higginbotham 1989, 155)

The argument seems to move roughly so: Even if the child has an imperfect understanding of his idiom, still the child uses and speaks a language in which S says that p; so, when the child seriously utters S, the child says that p; so the child can be credited with the concepts expressed by the words (and/or thinking that p).

One problem with the argument, if I have it aright, is that there is a gap between saying in the sense in which the child can be said to (be able to) say that the tie is gamboge and the child's understanding (having the right concepts for thinking) that the tie is gamboge. It is perfectly clear that there are senses of 'say' on which x may say that p (e.g., a sign may say that a house is protected by the Acme Alarm Company), though x does not know or even grasp what it says when it says that p. It is of course true that we will credit the child with saying that the tie is gamboge: the child is in the course of acquiring the ambient public language; it would thus be beyond perverse not to assign the words he produces their ambient interpretation; thus the child is saying that the tie is gamboge in a sense not altogether unrelated to the sense in which signs say things.[16] But it does not follow from this, nor from this and the fact that the child simply knows that 'gamboge' is an adjective (or even from this and the fact that he knows that it picks out a color), that the child understands the word 'gamboge' or knows what it is for something to be gamboge.[17]

My point is not (so much) that Higginbotham's proposal is wrong, but that it is annexed to a dubious account of what it is to have a concept or grasp a phrase's meaning. But there is something right about Higginbotham's suggestion. This is the idea that talk about a word's meaning—meaning in the sense in which a word's meaning is what one has to 'grasp' in order to be a competent speaker—is to be elucidated in terms of what is common ground among those who use the word. In particular, our talk about meaning should be understood as talk about mutual expectations about how we will be understood.[18]

Return to the child who doesn't yet understand 'gamboge'. What would it take for him to understand it? Well, what do we expect of someone when we use 'gamboge' in a sentence? Certainly that they know that gamboge is a color. And not just any color—someone who identifies ripe apples, as opposed to French's mustard, as gamboge has not cottoned on to what it is to be gamboge. Is more required? Well, if they know that gamboge is a color, they had better know that colors are perceptible; that among the colors are red, yellow, blue...

Is yet more required? I say that this is an empirical question. There is clearly information that adult users of 'gamboge' have at the ready, that is in some interesting sense 'ready to be invoked' in the task of making sense of what someone is trying to get across with a use of 'gamboge'. Much though not all of this information is information that the user expects others to have at the ready in the task of making sense of uses of the word,

---

[16] Perhaps the child says that the tie is gamboge in a sense that the sign does not. The child is *acquiring* the ambient language, after all.

[17] Complicating the dialectical situation here is the fact that Higginbotham's proposal is a proposal about what suffices for one to be a competent speaker of a language. The relevant notion of competence, of course, can be spelled out in a number of ways, some that preserve ties with everyday criteria for understanding, some of which sever these ties. If we think of competence as something that is in good part divorced from understanding—it is what one has when the parameters for (Chomsky-style) universal grammar have been set, the syntactic, phonetic, and morphological features of everyday vocabulary items are entered into the lexicon, and there is relatively fluid production and parsing of sentences—the proposal Higginbotham makes is not unreasonable—though remarks below, I think, show that it still isn't correct. With regard to this notion of competence, the point in the text can be recast so: Since competence in this sense is in large part a non-semantic notion, we should not be surprised that competence does not imply comprehension.

[18] 'Meaning', of course, is used in different ways. Some talk of meaning is talk of what one must 'grasp' or mentally associate with a word in order to be a competent user of it. Some talk of meaning is talk of what determines (relative to a context of use) the input to compositional processes that determine reference and truth conditions. Other talk about meaning is talk about what determines (relative to a context of use) what a use of a sentence says (or what question or command it expresses). I am currently discussing meaning in the first sense. I will take up the question of how meaning in this sense is related to meaning in the other senses later in this chapter and in Chapter 4.

information that the user expects the other to expect to…well, you know the drill here. On a first pass, this information is what constitutes the meaning of 'gamboge'; it constitutes our common concept *gamboge*.

I spoke just now of information, but I mean information in the sense in which some information is misinformation. It is not the job—well, it is not the exclusive job—of our concepts and meanings to determine in any interesting sense of 'determine' what we are talking about. Perhaps meaning determines reference in the boring sense that (setting issues about context sensitivity and polysemy to the side) words that express the same concept must have the same reference. But to say this is simply to comment on strictures on when two people can be said to share a concept; it does not mean that one can explain why a word refers to what it does in terms of the information that (helps to) constitute its meaning. Neither does it imply that an interesting superveni-ence thesis holds between the information that contributes to constituting a concept and the concept's reference: since things like social and environmental relations typic-ally make large contributions to determining reference, shifting a concept to a new environment while holding constant the common ground that facilitates understand-ing may not preserve reference.

An upshot is that the idea that meanings or concepts are constituted by presupposi-tions about knowledge of reference is not right. A linguistic community may manage to refer to, say, light with 'light', though they mutually presuppose that 'light' applies to something iff it is the movement of minute corpuscles though an ether. But this is not what light is.

The presuppositions I invoked above—that gamboge is a color, a variety of yellow—we expect to be articulate within a population. But presuppositions may be present—they may be common ground—without being articulate. A society of materialists may presuppose that light is made up atoms—not because they have heard the idea articulated, but simply because they are disposed to tenaciously affirm that all there is are atoms and the void. This may dispose them—though they might initially be a bit surprised to realize that they thought this—to tenaciously affirm, should it come up, that light is made up of atoms. They may not only accept this, but be disposed to behave in ways that imply that they expect everyone else accepts this claim, and expect…Concepts may, and often do, have both more or less explicit and deeply implicit bits.

What constitutes understanding a word or having a concept on the view I am outlin-ing is not so much having a particular body of information at one's disposal as it is a matter of participating in a common practice, one that is held together in good part via shared expectations. Obviously such shared expectations can change over time. Today it is mutually expected that (people expect that) fire engines are red. There is good rea-son to think that this will not be mutually expected in fifty or so years, since white fire engines turn out to be visible under a wider range of conditions; if fire engines become more or less universally white, that will become common knowledge. Presuppositions change with changes in the world. So concepts can be expected—in line with the prem-ises of the gradualist argument set out in Chapter 1—to evolve over time.

Quine complained in 'Two Dogmas' that there was no sharp line to be drawn between change in meaning and change in belief; so much the worse, he concluded, for the idea that we can identify a certain store of information as constituting the meaning of our terms. But exactly what follows from the claim that there is no sharp line between change of meaning and change of belief?

Suppose we understand the 'no sharp line' claim to be in part something like this:

Let S=ϕ(F) be any relatively simple sentence of a person X's language in which the term F is used. X's revising her opinion about S—either moving from accepting to rejecting S or the reverse—is not intrinsically a change of what F means in X's vocabulary, as for there are (many quite) possible cases in which X can revise her opinion about S (in either direction) that can be perfectly well described as changes in belief, not changes in meaning.

Then it would certainly seem to follow (given some weak extra assumptions) that no piece of information p (expressed by a sentence ϕ(F)) is essential to the meaning of F in the sense that one can't continue to mean what one does by F unless one accepts p.

But it doesn't follow that there is not a (fairly) crisp, robust distinction at particular times between the information that 'makes up' or constitutes a particular word meaning or concept: one must simply broaden one's gaze and look not just at the beliefs (and expectations) of a single individual (including her beliefs about what others expect others to believe or know), but at what expectations are shared within a community of users. It can be perfectly correct to say that it is 'part of the meaning' of 'cousin', as we use it at present, that cousins are children of one's parents' siblings, even if it is also correct to observe that this is not essential to the word's having the meaning it has.

Of course, one can't know this sort of thing—what constitutes the meaning of a word at a particular time—a priori. Quine's conclusion, that a priori knowledge is not to be grounded in knowledge of meaning, is surely correct. The goal of philosophical analysis—knowledge of the 'contents of our concepts'—is possible. What is impossible is getting this sort of knowledge a priori: I have to have a good deal of knowledge of how we all conceptualize the world if I am to know how I conceptualize it.

Perhaps it will be said that meanings and concepts as I am suggesting we understand them are vague, messy affairs, unfit for serious study: if our business is 'limning the true and ultimate structure of reality', we do best to ignore concepts thought of in this way altogether. For there is no saying where the boundaries of the population that constitutes a concept begins or ends; no saying, for example, whether we should say there is a single concept fire engine shared by all those Americans who speak English or a profusion of concepts, one particular to residents of New York City, another to the denizens of Helena, Montana, a third confined to the members of a particular family. After all, shared presuppositions are going to vary as we vary a population. Best to follow Quine and leave talk of concepts by the wayside.

I find this reaction puzzling. Structurally, the same sort of thing is true of biological populations. There are any number of ways one can divvy up a population with more or less similar genomes to make up sub-species: one can do it so that all of the beetles in all of the fields in a particular county count as one species, or one can do it so that species vary as do the fields. Each way of proceeding may be apt given the right interests and purposes, and each way of proceeding is based on 'true and ultimate' structural features of the relevant populations. If the way we cut up species—or concepts—turns in part on the population whose properties we are at the moment studying, that does not imply that the subject of our study is phony, or scientifically or philosophically uninteresting.

Someone might insist that I am ignoring serious problems. Suppose the population we are focused on in our study of meanings or concepts consists of adult Bostonians of 2015 with a high school education. All these people presumably understand (pretty much) all of the words that are used in, say, the Sunday *Boston Globe*'s magazine section. But why on earth should we think it common knowledge among all these people that, for example, cousins are children of one's parents' siblings? Some people have weird beliefs, some people just get things wrong, some people have doubts about what they see as hard cases (are the children of my wife's brother's ex-wife's new husband's brother cousins of my children?), some will have Matesean worries that others haven't mastered elementary facts, etc. When one reflects on this, one begins to wonder whether any information goes to constitute any of the concepts of the target population, since it begins to look as if there might be no information which everyone in the population presupposes, expects others to presuppose, presupposes that others expect all to presuppose, etc., etc., etc.

I do not see that there is a serious problem here. There is a question, quite apart from the current proposal, about how we ought to understand claims that p is common ground within a group G—that is, how to understand the claims made when we say such things as

Gs presuppose p
Gs presuppose that Gs presuppose p
Gs presuppose that Gs presuppose that Gs presuppose p

and so on up. I rather doubt that people who speak of what is common ground in large groups would on reflection want these sorts of claims to be cashed out as simple, unrestricted universal quantifications; I don't think they mean for us to understand (for example) the second as ascribing a presupposition in a simple, unrestricted universal quantification. I certainly don't want to be so understood here. A much more useful notion of common ground will understand the claims in the list above as generics, so that, for instance and on a first pass, 'Gs presuppose p' has truth conditions along the lines of *all normal Gs presuppose p*, while the second says something to the effect that all normal Gs presuppose the first generic claim.

Explaining normality is not something I propose to try to do here, but here is a crumb of elucidation. I assume that for normal As to be Bs is not a matter of statistics, but of there being some explanatory connection between being an A, the situations

As (normally) find themselves in, and tending to be a B.[19] Put crudely, to make the generic claim is to claim that there is a collection of mechanisms M (that are in some sense normal for As and their situation) such that in propitious circumstances M tends to lead to As being Bs. If we think of generics and of common ground in this way, then to say that the claim

p: cousins are parents' siblings' progeny

is common ground amongst adult Bostonians does not imply that every Bostonian presupposes p (or that every Bostonian presupposes that every Bostonian presupposes p). What it does imply is that there is some sort of mechanism that in the normal course of things would bring Bostonians to presuppose p, to presuppose that Bostonians presuppose p, and so on. And of course there is such a mechanism—the Boston public school system.

Presumably one of the most important 'mechanisms' that keeps speakers of a language more or less in synch about what everyone presupposes about how a word will be interpreted (and what word a particular pronunciation or orthography makes manifest) is speakers' ongoing use of the language to express their thoughts, along with auditors' ongoing attempts to interpret such expression. Both thought expression and interpretation involve hypotheses—about what the other (you) presupposes the other other (me) thinks will be mutually presupposed about how a word is to be understood. Such hypotheses tend to become firmer—thought of as behavioral strategies, they tend to be reinforced—when they are successful. When the hypotheses lead to misunderstanding, they tend to be modified in a direction that, over time, leads to their being more or less in line with what others expect. The facts—that speakers are for the most part able to coordinate when they talk so that (relevant) expectations are matched, and that when speakers do not so coordinate there is a tendency for them to change their expectations about mutual expectations to ones that (in the long run usually) lead to all (more or less) sharing expectations—are the glue that holds a linguistic community together and make it a unity. The facts—that there is variation across the members of a community in the relevant presuppositions, and that for one reason or another, changes in presuppositions are partially driven by something that looks like speakers optimizing something associated with those presuppositions—are what make meanings historical entities, liable to something that looks in many ways like evolution.

I claimed above that, understood in a certain way, Quine's dictum that there is no sharp line between change in meaning and change in belief is obviously correct. There are stronger claims Quine seemed inclined to make that I do not want to endorse. One might read Quine as holding that there is no determinacy whatsoever—'no fact of the matter'—as to whether any change in the pool of information that (as I would put it) constitutes the meaning of a word is a change in what the word means, as opposed to a

---

[19] I here help myself to the rudiments of the view of my colleague Bernhard Nickel (2016).

change in the beliefs or presuppositions of users. The strongest plausible version of this claim, I think, goes something like this:

(B)   Pick two times t and t' at which a population P of speakers use a word w. Let G and G' be the pools of information that constitute the meaning of w as used in P at t and t'. If G and G' are distinct, then it is not the case it's determinate that w means the same thing at t and t'.

To hold a view like this is, I think, to hold that our talk about meaning has no theoretical utility whatsoever.

(B) is deeply counter-intuitive. It is (pretty much exactly) as counter-intuitive as analogous claims about species—for example, where there is any change in the phenotypical profile of a population lineage, or any change in what alleles are fixed in the genotypical profile of a lineage, there is no saying whether or not speciation has occurred. To say that it is counter-intuitive is not, of course, to show that it is wrong. Part of my project in this essay is to make a case that (B) is far too extreme to be a tenable position. But at this point I think it is worth making a weaker point about claims like (B).

It is plausible that much of our pre-theoretic talk about meaning tracks something very much like the sort of common ground I'm proposing is a kind of meaning. Certainly the sorts of things one finds therein are the sorts of things that are naturally adduced as answers to the question, what does such and such a word mean? Our judgments about whether a word has changed its meaning over time are sensitive to changes in this common ground—the more pronounced the change therein (and the faster it occurs), the more likely we are to judge that change in meaning has occurred. Even if there is a fair amount of indeterminacy as to when a form as used at t is synonymous with that form as used at t', that does not mean that our talk about meaning isn't tracking something real. Interpretive common ground is a real phenomenon, something it seems that we can in principle theorize about.

Our talk about meaning, like our talk about species, tracks something that is event-like, more process than product. Our talk about meaning, like our talk about species, tends to be cast in terms that are more appropriate to something that is not event-like: thus the attraction of the views that species have some sort of essence, and that a word's meaning can be identified once and for all with a definition or a Fregean sense or something of the sort. Because of the apparent lack of fit between what our talk about meanings and species tracks and the conceptual box that talk creates, we might at the end of the day decide that rather radical conceptual engineering is called for: we might even recommend dropping talk about species or meanings in favor of talk about populations related by descent or lineages of lexicons linked by various relations of communication. To do so in the biological case is not to suggest that species talk does not track a real phenomenon, or that the claims and generalizations biologists make in speaking about species are empty or unverifiable or false. Ditto, for the linguistic case.

4. Interpretive Common Ground

The meaning of a simple expression in a population is a certain set of presuppositions that are common ground in the population; I'll call them the expression's interpretive common ground, ICG for short. My goal in the next few sections is to say more precisely what ICG is, how it is related to linguistic competence, and how it is related to such things as the notion of 'what is said'.[20]

Talk of common ground is liable to make linguists and philosophers think of Robert Stalnaker's use of the notion of common ground in semantics and pragmatics. For Stalnaker, common ground is something that accompanies a conversation—it is the set of claims that for conversational purposes conversants treat as true (the claims that they accept, in Stalnakerian parlance), and that they accept that all accept, accept that all accept that all accept, and so on (Stalnaker 2014). For Stalnaker, claims are sets of possible worlds. This allows for a certain elegance in theory: a conversation's common ground can be represented as the intersection of those p's that conversants accept (and accept are accepted, etc.); assertion, when unchallenged, changes the common ground, again through intersection.[21]

There are differences and commonalities between Stalnakerian common ground and the ICG I propose to identify as meaning. One difference involves the way we think of claims, aka propositions. I take propositions to be much more finely individuated than Stalnaker. The proposition expressed by a sentence's use is a structured entity: its parts correspond to the phrases in the sentence that pick out objects and properties; its structure encodes relations in which these must stand in order for the proposition to be true. There is a certain loss of elegance in thinking of propositions in this way. But the loss is more than compensated for by ridding us of the burden of identifying necessarily equivalent claims, of allowing us to deny that (there is any sense whatsoever in which) someone who thinks that red is a color thereby thinks that every integer has a unique decomposition into powers of primes.

Something I want to carry over from Stalnaker's framework is the idea that to presuppose p is not necessarily to believe it, but to be disposed for certain purposes to act as if one believed it. Conversational presuppositions are, for example, claims that those involved in a conversation are disposed for the purposes of the conversation to treat as being true. For you to have such a disposition, in turn, is for you to be disposed, when your behavior is meant to help achieve conversational goals, to behave in ways that would be brought about by the belief that p in a person who had that belief and was otherwise like you (in terms of mentality and situation). A person may make

---

[20] This section and its surround owes a lot to comments from many people, in particular Liz Camp, Louise Hanson, Sally Haslanger, Jeff King, Eliot Mendleson, Kevin Scharp, and Barry Smith.

[21] Why can common ground be so represented? On this view, the claim that X is the set of worlds in which it is true that X. So the set of worlds in which P and Q is true is just the set of worlds in which both P and Q are true—i.e., the intersection of the claim that P and the claim that Q. Thus, adding a claim to common ground—which is like conjoining it to those already in common ground—changes common ground by intersection.

presuppositions he doesn't believe are true, as when, conversing with someone I think is an idiot, I force myself to behave as if I think his opinions are worth taking seriously, or when I decide not to challenge a friend's political opinions and allow her to think that I agree with them.

My use of *X presupposes p* is thus elliptical for *For purposes Q, X presupposes p* which, in turn, is elliptical for something along the lines of *In situations in which X has purposes Q, X is disposed to behave as if X believed p*. Somewhat more precisely, it is elliptical for *In situations in which X has purposes Q, X is disposed to behave as would a person who was like X (insofar as she had a similar mental state to X, was in a similar situation, and had purposes Q), who believed p, and whose Q relevant behavior was in part determined by that belief.*[22] That is just too much of a mouthful, though. So mostly I just speak of speakers presupposing P.

Interpretive common ground is a collection of presuppositions. Which, exactly? Roughly put, the ICG of 'cousin' in the group of English speakers includes such things as

C: Cousins—that is, what English speakers are talking about with 'cousin'—are parents' siblings' progeny

as well as

A.   English speakers who use 'cousin' presuppose that they—that is, the things the word applies to—are parents' siblings' progeny.

B.   English speakers who use 'cousin' expect their audience to recognize that in using the word they presuppose C, and they expect their audience to (be ready to) use that fact in interpreting their use of the word.

These last two might sound like fairly sophisticated assumptions, ones beyond the ken of, for example, the competent five-year-old. But that's not so.

A five-year-old who has acquired 'cousin' and grasped how the word is used knows that cousins are parents' siblings' progeny. He also knows that the people around him think this and that they call cousins 'cousins'. He may not use fancy semantic terminology like 'call' to express this; he has not mastered the intricacies of mention and quotation. But with what he knows, he can answer the question, 'What do people mean by 'cousin'? He will tell you 'they mean people like uncle Gus's daughter Sue and Aunt Sadie's son Fred'. As he knows that Gus is his dad's brother and Sadie his mom's sister, his answer displays that he assumes that when people use 'cousin', they assume that they are talking about parents' siblings' progeny. That is, he presupposes A.

Furthermore, the child's attempts to make sense of others' use of 'cousin' are driven, in part, by this knowledge. In being so driven, he is behaving in interpretation as would someone whose interpretation was in part controlled by the belief that when

---

[22] This way of characterizing presuppositions is not Stalnaker's, though it is certainly in the spirit of Stalnaker's characterizations.

someone uses 'cousin', they expect people to take them to think C and to use this fact in understanding them. And this suffices for our five-year-old to presuppose B.

Fix a group G. Consider the collection of those claims q such that

1. Members of G who use 'cousin' presuppose q.
2. Members of G who use 'cousin' expect their audience to recognize that in using it they presuppose q and expect the audience to use that fact in interpreting their use of the word.
3. (1) and (2) are common ground among Gs.

This is the ICG of 'cousin' in G; the general definition of which this is an instance I trust is obvious. Clearly, the ICG of 'cousin' among English speakers includes C. It should be clear from the discussion of the average five-year-old a few paragraphs back that I take it that (given that q is a 'non-intentional' claim, one not about the expectations or assumptions of others) if

1. Members of G who use 'cousin' presuppose q;
2. Members of G who use 'cousin' expect their audience to recognize that in using it they presuppose q and expect the audience to use that fact in interpreting their use of the word

are true and are common ground, then

1. Members of G who use 'cousin' presuppose that members of G who use 'cousin' presuppose q;
2. Members of G who use 'cousin' presuppose that members of G who use 'cousin' expect their audience to recognize that in using it they presuppose q and expect the audience to (be ready to) use that fact in interpreting their use of the word

are also true and are common ground. Given that this is so, the fact that C is part of the ICG of 'cousin' in group G means that A and B are as well.

I've written as if I thought that the notion of something's being 'common ground' or 'mutually presupposed' was to be cashed out in terms of indefinitely iterated attitudes—p's being mutually presupposed is a matter of our presupposing p, presupposing we presuppose p, presupposing that, etc., etc. If this is our understanding of such notions as common ground, the implication in the last paragraph would seem to be assured. But I am not sure that the best way to understand notions like the notion of common ground is in terms of endless iteration of attitudes. (I'm not sure it's not, either.) So officially I'm taking the notion as a primitive. Continue, if you don't want to take it as a primitive, to assume that the notion will at the end of the day be cashed out in terms of some sort of hierarchy of iterated attitudes.[23] In any case, when I speak of a word's ICG,

---

[23] Thanks here to Liz Camp.

I assume that when it includes things like 1 and 2 and q is non-intentional, it includes things like 1' and 2' as well.

A word's ICG in a group G is a set of presuppositions made by members of G about how Gs use the word. If someone makes an assumption about Gs, something makes it the case that they are making a presupposition about Gs. One might wonder how this comes to be. How, for example, does our five-year-old manage to identify a particular class of speakers? For that matter, even if we adults explicitly think that English speakers who use 'cousin' think that they are parents' siblings' progeny, how does it come to be the case that we are making presuppositions about a particular class of speakers?

The presuppositions in question are in the first instance certain behavioral dispositions associated with language use and interpretation. Exceptional circumstances to the side, when someone speaks (or interprets), they obviously (behave as if they) believe that they and their audience (they and the speaker) speak the same language. A speaker and her interpreters obviously do presuppose, for example, that 'speakers of the language we are speaking who use "cousin" presuppose that they are parents' siblings' progeny'. To a first approximation, the group that 'speakers of the language we are speaking' picks out is the class of speakers with whom, in the terminology of the next chapter, the speakers and the auditor are 'linguistically coordinated'. For the moment: to say that X and Y's are so coordinated is to say that X and Y reliably and projectively interpret each other so that if Y is disposed to use entry E of his lexicon to interpret X's use of entry E' of X's lexicon, X is disposed to use E' to interpret Y's use of E, and vice versa.

The speaker (and auditor) presuppositions that constitute a word's meaning are (for the most part) not one-off assumptions, ones that materialize for the purposes of a conversation only to be abandoned at its end. Or so I would say. After all, independently of any particular conversation, there are an awful lot of people out there who my dispositions equip me to interpret, and people whose dispositions equip them to interpret me, with our dispositions doing this in a way that achieves, modulo such things as loud music and fatigue, the sort of equilibrium I just called linguistic coordination. These people's dispositions typically equip them to interpret one another in a way that achieves linguistic coordination. So there is a (vague around the edges) group so related to my (and your) linguistic practice that is linguistically linked in this way. My and your presuppositions about people with whom we can communicate—people who 'speak our language'—are presuppositions about this group.

There is a good deal more to be said here; I say some of it in the next chapter.

5. Ways of Being a Competent Speaker

The idea we are investigating is that the meaning-cum-anchor-of-linguistic-competence of a word in a population at a particular time is its ICG. If so, then to understand a word is to have 'the right sort' of cognitive contact with its ICG. But what, exactly, is it to have the right sort of contact with the ICG of 'cousin'?

ICG being a collection of presuppositions that speakers make and expect others to make, a natural answer to this question is that understanding a word is a matter of participating in its ICG by making the presuppositions contained in it in the relevant conversational situations. Doing this does seem sufficient for understanding.[24] But there are at least two reasons for thinking that it's not necessary.

Suppose that Ruben is fanatical about cousins: not only does he think only males are cousins, he is on a tear about it, challenging anyone who has the temerity to say something that implies that there are female cousins.[25] Then he is not presupposing for conversational purposes that cousins are (all and any) parents' siblings' progeny. This is certainly grounds to avoid Ruben at family gatherings (and otherwise, probably), but it's not grounds to say that he doesn't understand the word 'cousin'. So long as he recognizes that everyone else assumes that cousins are (all and any) parents' siblings' progeny (and recognizes, for each p in the basis of 'cousin', that users of 'cousin' presuppose p and expect others to recognize that presupposition), Ruben understands 'cousin'.

To understand a word, it suffices to know how it's 'supposed' to be used; knowing that doesn't require that one use the word in that way. Putting the point in terms of the notion of interpretive common ground: ICG contains not only first-order claims like

C.   Cousins—what users of 'cousins' are talking about—are parents' siblings' progeny

but also 'higher-order' claims such as

D.   Speakers who use 'cousin' expect their audience to recognize that in using the word they presuppose C.

D and C are in the ICG of 'cousin' because it is common ground that both are accepted by speakers. In talking about a word w's ICG, it's useful to have a term for the 'first-order' claims like C that occur in w's ICG, as opposed to 'higher-order claims' like D that populate it and that are in some loose sense in w's ICG because first-order claims like C are there. Let us call the first-order claims that play such a 'generative role' for a word's ICG its *basis*. Ruben doesn't presuppose (all of) the basis of 'cousin', but he is nonetheless competent because he presupposes the higher-order claims in the ICG of 'cousins', the claims that are common ground about how 'cousin' is used.

Here is a second reason for thinking that understanding a word doesn't require complete participation in its ICG. It has been claimed that autists 'lack a theory of mind'—they are unable to ascribe beliefs and intentions to others, or at least unable to ascribe such things as beliefs that others believe p and expectations that others will believe that p. If so, this means that high-functioning autists are unable to fully participate in ICG: an autist may make all the assumptions in the basis of 'cousin', but not, say, believe that people presuppose that people presuppose that users of 'cousin' expect

---

[24] Given that one has mastered such things as syntax, phonology, and morphology.
[25] 'Fanatical' here alludes to Burge's (1986) discussion of 'sofa fanatics'.

people to recognize that they assume that cousins are parents' siblings' progeny. But an autist may be a competent speaker for all that.[26]

There is clearly a sense of 'competent speaker' in which autists can be competent speakers, even if they 'lack a theory of mind'. But what this shows at most is that there is more than one relation to (the common ground that constitutes) a word's meaning that fosters understanding. Ceteris paribus, someone who simply presupposes the basis of a word's meaning is thereby a competent speaker. Even if high-functioning autists—and for that matter, three-year-olds in the process of acquiring a language—do not make higher-order presuppositions about the expectations of others about presuppositions, they do clearly master the basis of the ICG of the ambient vocabulary; this is what makes them competent speakers. The way to respond to this objection is simply to observe that there are three relations to a word's ICG that can, all else being equal, foster competence: one can presuppose all of it; one can presuppose only the higher-order bit; one can presuppose only the basis.

While this seems a perfectly apt response, I think it might concede too much to the objection. Consider an autist or a child who would qualify as a competent speaker. Part of what constitutes their competence are beliefs and knowledge (better, belief-like and knowledge-like) states that are in some sense realized linguistically. The autist or child does not simply assume that cousins are parents' siblings' progeny; he does this by doing something like tokening or being disposed to token in a belief-making way the sentence 'cousins are parents' siblings' progeny'. It is because this presupposition is encoded by or associated with the word 'cousin' 'in the right way' that the child is able to mobilize it in speech and interpretation. But having higher-order presuppositions like B and D is simply a matter of having certain sorts of dispositions for the purposes of conversational interaction. For the sorts of reasons given in discussing the average five-year-old speaker, there's good reason to think that autists and three-year-olds often, perhaps typically, have the relevant dispositions and thus make the higher-order presuppositions.

6. Illocution and Meaning

You might object as follows: I grant that there is such a thing as what we mean by our words. What we mean by our words is the lowest common denominator of what everyone means by those words. But this lowest common denominator—what everyone thinks and thinks everyone thinks, etc.—is surely exhausted by a word's reference. What everyone knows about 'Obama' is that it names Obama; one doesn't need to know or even believe that he was once the president. What everyone knows about the German pronoun 'du' is that it refers to the person addressed with it; there is nothing more to know. The view just sketched is acceptable, but surely it reduces in the case of names and demonstratives to what used to be called a 'direct reference' or 'Millian' view of

---

[26] Objections to Gricean accounts of meaning along these lines can be found in Gluer and Pagin (2003). Thanks to Eliot Michaelson for pressing this sort of point.

meaning; and surely it will also reduce to such a view in the case of common nouns, verbs, adjectives, and adverbs.[27]

It is simply not true that, for example, one understands (one 'grasps the meaning' of) the German 'du' as it is used by Germans simply by knowing that 'du' refers to the person who is addressed with it. If this were so, then there would be no difference between the meaning of 'du' and polite 'sie'. But there is a world of difference between them, as 'du' is familiar and 'sie' is formal—they are like 'tu' and 'vous' in French—and to not know this is to be an incompetent speaker. It is simply not true that one was able to understand the way 'Obama' was used in the United States in 2015 if one did not know that 'Obama' named the president: when people said things like, 'If you want to know what will happen in Afghanistan, you should listen to Obama tonight', they not only meant in part that (given the antecedent) you should listen to the president; they expected that you would understand them to mean this. You were not equipped to make sense of the way 'Obama' was used if you did not know this. There is such a thing as the way a word is used in a population—there are generic facts about a word is used—and understanding is a matter of having mastered such facts.

Davidson (1967) asked, What could we know that would enable us to understand linguistic behavior? The proposal of Higginbotham (1992) exposited a few sections back was an attempt to provide a partial answer to that question, as it was an attempt to describe what people 'must know if they are to be competent speakers'. The proposal I have been developing in the past few sections is also meant to provide a partial answer to the question. Speaking very roughly indeed, Davidson's answer was that it suffices to know first-order facts about reference and truth. Higginbotham's was that one must know those facts about knowledge and reference that one is expected to know. The answer I have sketched thus far is that one must be in cognitive touch with those presuppositions that are commonly involved in interpretation.

Here is a worry about all three proposals. To interpret a language requires knowing what its speakers are doing with their words. But knowing a truth theory for a speaker's language, knowing that certain facts about reference are common knowledge, or recognizing the sort of ICG I have been discussing is not sufficient for knowing what someone is doing when she assertively utters 'snow is white'. One needs to know something along the lines of the following: in uttering 'snow', the speaker is referring to snow; in uttering 'is white', the speaker is ascribing the property of whiteness to what she referred to with 'snow'; to do this sort of thing—refer to x and go on to ascribe y to it—is to assert that x is y.

The point is correct, but perhaps it does not constitute a big worry. What one needs to insert into Davidson's, or Higgy's, or my story is what we might call 'pragmatic information'. One does indeed, if one is going to be a competent speaker of English as it is

---

[27] The idea that meaning is something like a 'lowest common denominator' is floated in Soames (2002), though he would not endorse the idea that this implies that there is nothing to the meaning of a singular term beyond its reference. Herman Cappelen has wondered in conversation about an objection like the one in the text.

spoken in these parts, need to be cognizant of such generic facts as: speakers use 'snow' to refer to snow; speakers use 'is white' to speak of whiteness; speakers use sentences of the form *Name plus Verbal Phrase* to ascribe to what they refer to with Name what they speak of with Verbal Phrase. One needs to know facts like the fact that when a sentence S is used to assert p and sentence T is used to assert q, the sentence S and T is used to assert the conjunction of p and q.

Knowing such things gives one knowledge that provides a place to begin in interpretation. It provides, for example, a first hypothesis about Sara's utterance of 'snow is white and grass is green': that it was an assertion that snow is white and grass is green. Of course, there aren't guarantees here. Davidson (1986) and others remind us that speakers can veer in their usage from the generic facts: malaprops, neologisms, 'creative' use—these occur all the time. That this is so means that there is nothing we can know that would guarantee that we are always able to make sense of what another is doing with her words. But to think that linguistic competence requires knowledge that guarantees that one will know what a speaker says is to set the bar for linguistic competence way too high. It's enough to be able to reliably come up with hypotheses about what speakers are doing that are naturally generated by the facts about what speakers normally do with the words uttered in the sort of situation in which they were uttered. This, one thinks, is not only a way to be a competent speaker but probably the way most of us are competent speakers.

Applying all this to our running example of the word 'cousin' requires a small reworking of the notion of ICG. Speaking schematically, we identified the ICG of a word w with those claims q such that

1. Users of w presuppose q;
2. Those users expect the audience to recognize (1);
3. (1) and (2) are common ground.

We need to add pragmatic facts. The right way to do this seems to be to identify w's ICG with this collection along with any generic claims to the effect that

4. Users of w use it to ϕ;
5. Those users expect the audience to recognize (4)

that are common knowledge. In the case of our running example, we add the claim that users of 'cousin' use it to predicate being a cousin and expect their audience to recognize this and to use that fact in interpreting their use of the word. Henceforth I will understand 'basis of word w' in such a way that it includes those claims of the form of (4) that are common knowledge.[28]

---

[28] This is simplified. Consider the phrase, 'I promise to be at Man Ray by 10pm'. What is common ground about this phrase is in part something like: When it is used as a free-standing sentence, it is used to promise to be at Man Ray by 10pm; when it is embedded in a conditional antecedent (e.g., 'if I promise to

'Cousin' is a word that is used to describe people. There are, of course, words that are used for purposes other than descriptive ones, and words that have a mixed use. David Kaplan famously reminds us that to understand words like 'hello' and 'oops' is not to have information about the non-linguistic world, but to know how they are used. You understand 'oops' when you know that people use it to express empathy about a minor mishap of which they are (usually) visually aware; to understand 'hello' is to know it is used to greet (Kaplan ms). There is, so far as I can see, nothing in the basis of 'oops' or 'ouch' or 'hello' beyond facts about how they are used.

Most interesting among words that have a non-descriptive use, perhaps, are those whose meaning combines descriptive and non-descriptive aspects. Consider as an example racial, ethnic, religious, and gender slurs. Such terms are (often) emblematic of prejudice and disrespect. Their central linguistic use—at least, we all believe their central linguistic use—is one that makes prejudice and disrespect manifest. Not only do we presuppose this, we expect that others presuppose it and that they bring the presupposition to the fore if called upon to interpret a slur's use. Slurs are typically— not invariably, but typically—used to express contempt or derogation of their targets. This generic claim—that slurs are used to express contempt or denigrate—is something that we all presuppose, something that we all expect that auditors of these terms will presuppose. All this—the generic claims about what users of slurs presuppose and about how they use them, that we presuppose these claims and that users expect us to invoke them in interpretation—is common knowledge among competent speakers. It is thus part of the words' meanings.

In the case of many slurs, there will also be descriptive presuppositions in ICG. At least at some points in the history of the word, users of 'Kike' quite generally assumed that Jews are a group one ought to think negatively of; they assumed that it is quite all right to display disrespect for them, and that an especially good way to express contempt for Jews is by calling them Kikes. Everybody knew that users of the term so thought, that they expected their audience to recognize this, and so on. At least when this was the case such presuppositions were part of the term's ICG, partially constitutive of its meaning. Something similar may sometimes be true of some of the 'information' involved in stereotypical ways of thinking of the groups targeted by a slur. It's not implausible that at the time the term 'Kike' gained currency, users assumed that Jews were aggressive and greedy and expected the audiences of their uses to recognize this; it's also not implausible that as the use of the term spread, these presuppositions became common knowledge.

Assuming that all this is correct, we arrive at a picture of the meaning of 'Kike' on which its meaning is in part constituted by its illocutionary role—that the word is

---

be at Man Ray by 10pm, I will I be there'), it is used only to express the claim that I promise to be at Man Ray by 10pm. Similar remarks, of course, apply to the original remarks on ICG: even prescinding from polysemy and ambiguity, facts about what speakers presuppose when using a word are often conditional: in a sentence like this, a speaker presupposes blah, in one like this she presupposes blee…

used to express contempt and derision for Jews is constitutive of the word's meaning.[29] Its meaning is in part constituted by 'information' about the group that is the target of the term—it is (assuming that the sort of assumptions mentioned at the end of the last paragraph are part of ICG) 'part of the meaning' of the slur that its targets are greedy and aggressive. To say that the illocutionary fact (that the slur is used to evince contempt for Jews) helps constitute its meaning is, of course, not to say that it does not have application or satisfaction conditions; to say that the (mis)information that those to whom the term 'Kike' applies are greedy helps constitute the meaning of the term is not to say the term is true of or applies to someone only if they are greedy. Nor is it to say that anyone who understands the term assumes this about Jews—as we saw above, one way to understand a term is to know, of its ICG, that it is its ICG. Knowing that is not to thereby participate in it; it is not to make the assumptions that users of the term make.

I see all this as a virtue of the proposal that we think of word meaning, and thus in particular of the meaning of slurs, as I've been suggesting. Many philosophers— myself included—have thought that (non-assertive) illocutionary facts are central to the meaning of slurs, but have struggled to explain how this could be without ending up saying something that seems to imply literal uses of those terms invariably involve a display of contempt or the like.[30] The proposal on the table makes the relevant (generic) fact—that users of 'Kike' use it to display contempt, disrespect, or derogation for Jews— constitutive of the word's meaning without making any use of the term that is non-derogatory a misuse. Many philosophers have thought that slurs have descriptive meanings that encode (false) stereotypical information about their targets, but have struggled to find a way to reconcile this with the obvious fact that, for example, people use 'Kike' to talk about and refer to Jews, which would not be so if the term were narrowly synonymous with something like *Jew and thereby despicable*.[31] The proposal on the table makes the relevant (mis)information constitutive of the slur's meaning, but does it in a way that does not threaten the truism that 'Kike' is a nasty term for Jewish people.

7. 'What Is Said' and Literal Meaning

Philosophy of language and linguistics try to give an account of meaning. There are three sorts of facts—and thus, reifying, three sorts of meaning—that one might be trying to uncover and explain when doing this. There are facts about what one must know or cognize in order to be a competent speaker, c-facts. There are r-facts, ones about reference and truth conditions. And there are p-facts, those we cite in providing an illuminating, systematic answer to questions about what sentence uses say, about the 'content' of the attitude such a use expresses. I have suggested that we identify c-facts with facts about ICG; r-facts are—well, they are facts about reference and satisfaction

---

[29] That is to say: the generic claim, that the word is so used, is part of the basis of its ICG.

[30] See for example Dummett (1973) and Richard (2008).

[31] See, for example, Hom and May (2018).

of (uses of) simple expressions, facts about the compositional determination of reference and truth, and whatever facts explain why those facts are facts.

How are c-facts related to r-facts? One attitude you might have—it's not mine—is that once we have uncovered the c-facts, we've uncovered pretty much all there is to be said about reference and truth. You might, for example, say that while of course it is true that 'snow' refers to snow and 'is white' is true of what's white, it is a mistake to think that these truths are truths in virtue of a substantive relation of reference-and-satisfaction relating words and world. It is analytic, or as close to analytic as anything could get, that 'snow' refers (in my language) to snow, that 'is white' is true of what's white, and that 'snow is white' is true just in case 'is white' is true of whatever 'snow' refers to. It is a central fact about how we use 'refers' and 'true' that these and related claims are to be taken as truths; this is in fact what makes the claims true. There's nothing more to be said about reference of theoretical interest.

So, at least, might you say. As I said, this is not my view. For one thing, there are more facts about reference than disquotational ones. Words undergo substantive changes in what they refer to; for example, 'pasta' as used by speakers in England in the late nineteenth century (arguably) did not refer to such things as congealed agar flavored with bacon and extruded from a tube, though (arguably) now it does.[32] Such facts are theoretically significant facts about reference. Presumably they have explanations; certainly they are not explained by reciting the disquotational fact that 'pasta' refers to pasta. One thinks that such explanations will have to involve accounts how shifts of patterns of use (and environmental and social relations of speakers) bring about changes in reference; one hopes for an account of how changes in such things as ICG, deference, and environmental relations are related to referential change. If this hope is not misguided—I say it is not—that is reason to think that there is a substantive relation of reference.

In any case, there are reasons to think that the facts descriptive formal semantics studies are unlikely to be reducible to or even completely contained in c-facts. Here are two. (1) c-facts—at least if they are facts about ICG—are, so far as reference goes, a miscellaneous mixture of fact and fiction. It may be common ground among a group that users of 'Muslim' presuppose (and expect you to recognize the presupposition) that the word is true of just those people of the same faith as Barack Obama; that doesn't mean that 'Muslim' as those people use the term is true of Christians instead of Muslims. There is no recipe for defining r-facts in terms of c-facts. (2) It is (not im-) plausible that the process of speaking and interpreting speech is governed by cognitive structures that in some sense embody the sort of information about semantic structure that one would find in a good semantics textbook. But it does not seem plausible that—beyond the relatively superficial level of such things as 'snow' refers to snow—this sort of information is common ground among speakers. Not every cognitive structure that

---

[32] Such examples raise hard questions. One *feels* an inclination to say that: 'pasta' changed its reference in English between 1860 and 2016; the meaning of 'pasta' has (in some sense) remained the same; meaning determines reference. But we can't say all three, can we? (And I ask with Whitman: Listener up there, what have you to confide in me? Talk honestly, no one else hears you, and I stay only a minute longer.) Chapter 4 discusses such questions.

is shared by speakers and governs their linguistic and interpretive behavior is to be glossed in terms of presupposition or propositional attitudes.

Suppose, simply to make this point clear, that it is a fact that the semantic scope of a quantifier phrase as it occurs in a sentence is identical with its syntactic domain in the sentence's surface structure.[33] This can be a fact, one which determines the truth conditions of utterances and which governs the processes of speech and interpretation, without its being common ground among the speakers whose behavior it governs. After all, there are many processes that have semantic impact—that shape what mental states mean—that are not common ground. Suppose that David Marr's hypotheses about the way perceptual processes proceed is correct. Then those hypotheses are facts that shape what information vision conveys, and thus what vision represents. But such facts are not known (much less commonly known) by perceivers. There is every reason to think that baroque facts about morphology and phonetics are in the same boat.

The upshot is that ICG does not contain, much less explain, r-facts. To theorize about competence is not to theorize about reference or vice versa, even though theorizing about the one is theorizing about something relevant to the other. Meaning—if by meaning we mean what we know when we are competent speakers—is of course relevant to what we are talking about and to what our words refer to. But meaning in this sense does not determine reference.

What is the relation between c-facts and p-facts? First off, what exactly are p-facts? I said that they are those facts that provide an illuminating, systematic answer to questions about what uses of sentences say, and about the 'content' of the attitude such a use expresses. Alas, that is not enough of a job description to nail down what exactly p-facts are supposed to be. I discern three attitudes that one might have about the shape of p-facts, the facts about 'what proposition is expressed' by our (declarative) sentences.

(a) One might take one's cue from the way we talk about and apparently quantify over assertions, beliefs, and the like. One, for example, assumes that a sentence like

A. Laura said that bicyclists are good companions

says that Laura is related (by the saying relation) to something determined by the complement 'that bicyclists are good companions'; the phrase 'what Laura said' in

B. Mark doubts what Laura said

functions as a quantifier that ranges over a domain (of 'propositions') that includes what A's complement determines; and such facts explain the validity of the inference from A and B to

C. Mark doubts that bicyclists are good companions.

---

[33] This hypothesis was put forward in Reinhart (1979); the formulation here is borrowed from the (extremely useful) critical discussion in Szabolcsi (2010).

And one might further take the p-facts to be the facts that determine what complements in sentences like A and C determine—their 'semantic values'—and what domains phrases like 'what Laura said' range over.

(b) One might think that this is a rather narrow picture of 'the content of an attitude'. One might think, for example, that 'the content' of the thought Laura expresses with 'bicyclists are good companions' is surely richer than the semantic value of A's complement. After all, the semantic value of 'that bicyclists are good companions'—what it contributes to determining the truth or falsity of sentences in which it occurs—is surely the same as it occurs in A, C, and such things as

D.   It's true that bicyclists are good companions.

Why think that there is much more to this content than a collection of work-a-day semantic values—extensions, or possible worlds intensions, or objects, properties, and relations? But what Laura thinks about the goodness of cyclist companionship, after all, is in part determined by how Laura thinks of cycling and good companionship and is likely to be idiosyncratic to Laura; ditto for Mark. Someone who so reasons will take the p-facts to be a highly various collection, with the p-facts about Laura's thoughts and assertions being in good part distinct from those about Mark's.

(c) The contents of assertions and beliefs are likely to be pretty thin if one thinks of them as the semantic values of sentences. If one thinks of them as involving the rich but typically idiosyncratic cognitive structures associated by a speaker with her words, those contents are likely to be, well, idiosyncratic: contents perhaps in principle shareable but in practice unlikely to be shared. It is natural to think that there must be some middle ground. One thinks, for example, that the sentences 'Robert is a Jew' and 'Robert is a Kike' (i) at a thin level—at the level of truth and reference—say the same thing, as each classifies the same individual as a member of the same group, but (ii) since it is in some sense 'part of the meaning' of (only) the later sentence that Jews are fit objects of derogation, the sentences in an important sense express different thoughts or states of mind. And this is a fact about content or meaning in a public sense: it is a fact about the meaning of the sentences in the language that we speak. Of course much the same sort of thing might be said of a pair of sentences like 'Donatien Alphonse François was a mediocre writer' and 'the Marquis de Sade was a mediocre writer': these sentences differ in meaning, one might say, in part because in some sense it is 'part of the meaning' of the name 'the Marquis de Sade' (but not of Sade's given name) that the Marquis was an author.

The view I've been sketching suggests an account of content or what is said in the sense of (c). In thinking about how such an account might go, begin by thinking about what we do in understanding one another's assertive utterances. A reasonable first hypothesis is that in interpreting another, an auditor begins by using her knowledge of the ICG associated with the other's words, as well as rudimentary semantic knowledge. To understand an utterance of 'many cousins are French', one takes one's knowledge of the semantics of the frame *many As are Bs*—that its instances are true just if many of the As are Bs—and of the referential facts—in this case, that 'cousin' refers to cousins and 'French' applies to things French—and combines this with what one knows users of 'cousin' and 'French' presuppose and expect to be seen as presupposing. Doing this, the auditor arrives at an understanding of the utterance, understanding it as one in which the speaker, inviting the audience to think of cousins in this way [insert here the basis for 'cousin'] and of French things in this way [insert here the basis for 'French'], represents that many of the former are the latter. If we think of sentence content in this way, we think of it as a synthesis of semantic values—of the words used and of their syntactic modes of combination—with the ICG of the words used.[34]

One notion of 'what is said' is the notion of what is in some sense associated by convention with a sentence-as-used-in-a-particular-sort-of situation; what is said in this sense is what the competent interpreter brings to the table in trying to understand what another is doing in speaking. It is the default interpretation, the interpretation that the competent speaker will expect the auditor to begin with (if nothing signals that another interpretation should be sought) and that the competent auditor will begin by assigning (again, if nothing signals that another interpretation is to be sought). 'What is said' in this sense is what one gets if one assumes that a speaker is speaking as a member of a particular population and combines the ICG of the words used in that population with the relevant semantics in the way just outlined. It is a reification of what one entertains if asked, outside of particular contexts of use, to think about what a sentence says. If there is such a thing as literal meaning, this is it, and the notion of what is said limned one paragraph back strikes me as as good an account of this notion of content as we are likely to get.

Take this for what it is: a proposal about the content conventionally associated with a sentence as it is used in a population. It is not a proposal about the semantic value of (uses of) the complement *that T* as it occurs in such things as *Mariam thinks that T, Ernie said that T*, or *it's true that T*. Neither is it a proposal about 'what is strictly and literally said' by a use of a sentence. At least it is not such a proposal if such a proposal is supposed to tell us what someone, speaking literally, asserts when she assertively utters a sentence. It is clear enough that a sentence T may be used—may be used when speaking

---

[34] I'll not attempt here to address the fact that sentences like 'I'm cold' do not have a single proposition associated with them by convention, but rather have something like a function from uses to 'conventionally associated propositions'. I think it's relatively straightforward to extend this paragraph to do so.

You might protest that while I purport to be giving an account of the content of an utterance of a sentence S, I am making use of clausal complements: to grasp the content of an utterance of *many As are Bs*, I just suggested, is to take oneself to be invited to think of As and Bs in certain ways and, while doing so, to represent *that many of the former* [the As] *are the latter* [Bs]. But isn't the content of the utterance just whatever is picked out by the complement clause?

Some of Chapter 4 and much of Chapter 5 could be read as a response to this. For the moment, let me say this: As I suggested above, I take it that there is a notion of shared 'strict and literal content' that is richer than the notion we get if we identify such content with something like a Russellian proposition or a structured intension. What the text suggests is a way of 'adding to' referential content to get to the richer notion of 'what is literally said'.

strictly and literally—to assert various things that are related in various ways to what convention associates with a sentence. It is clear enough that we can and do use the complement *that T* to report such sayings. And it is clear that we can and do ascribe a variety of thoughts with the complement. The complement itself is presumably univocal in meaning through all this. I would identify the semantic value of a complement clause with something along the lines of the articulated propositions introduced in Richard (1990)—combinations of words and their everyday references. I would say that when we report what someone says or think with a sentence like (A) or (C), we offer the complement as a contextually good 'translation' or 'representation' of what the individual says or thinks, with the standards of goodness shifting with the context of our report. I have argued for this elsewhere (Richard 1990, 2013) and will discuss the matter in Chapter 5.

It will be asked: if the proposition conventionally associated with T is not what we are referring to when we say that Rene said that T, if it need not be what we are saying Rene asserted when we utter 'Rene said that T', of what theoretical importance is it? The response, I hope, is obvious: it's what convention and our linguistic abilities associate with the sentence. It is the starting point for understanding an utterance of the sentence T; it is what the auditor is more or less forced to process in trying to interpret the utterance and what the speaker knows full well the auditor is more or less forced to think in the process of interpretation. It is what we, on first pass, understand the speaker to have said, though we can and usually do add and subtract to what linguistic convention associates with a sentence in the course of trying to make sense of an utterance.

8. Epithets and Assertion

The use of a slur, even a non-slurring use, typically causes a distinctive sort of offense, one that the user can be held responsible for even if his intentions in use are benign. It's a virtue of the account of content just sketched that it offers a straightforward explanation of why this is so.

Imagine that Robert offers Rachel the paella he made, full of chicken and chorizo, saffron and clams. Rachel says, 'Robert, you expect me to eat this trayf? You know we Kikes don't do pork and shrimp!' Rachel does not intend to display contempt for herself and other Jews, and anyone who hears her will know that. Still, someone—Robin, say—who hears Rachel may well be offended, even if she recognizes that Rachel isn't being contemptuous of herself or anyone else. Why?

What happens when Robin interprets Rachel's—or any other—utterance? Well, she takes the speaker to be a member of a certain group: she takes her to be an adult English speaker, or a member of her family, or a resident of Birmingham, Alabama, whatever. She has some sense of how the relevant group uses the words in the sentence uttered. This sense of how the word is used informs her attempt at interpretation. Making use of what she takes to be ICG for the utterer relative to the group, she recovers what she takes to be literally said by the utterance. She may go on to embellish or alter this interpretation if it seems that some interpretation other than the default interpretation provided by ICG is called for. Robin thus begins by awarding Rachel's utterance its literal interpretation relative to the population in which she takes Rachel to speak. Recognizing that Rachel is being friendly toward Robert, she then amends her understanding, replacing it with another. Robin won't be aware of running through a variety of interpretations of Rachel's utterance, interpretation being for the most part fast and outside of the purview of consciousness; all one is usually aware of is the final result. But the default interpretation, on the picture I sketched above, is the starting place for interpretation.

What happens when Robin generates this default interpretation? Well, this depends on the common ground—that is, the meaning—that Robin uses in constructing it. If someone utters something of the form *As are Bs* and the ICG of A includes the presupposition that As are Cs, then Robin understands the speaker as having said, inviting her to think of As as Cs, that As are Bs. If the common ground—that is, the meaning—of the words used involves facts about illocution, Robin takes the speaker to be performing the relevant illocution. If, for example, the speaker utters 'hello', Robin will take the speaker to be greeting the addressee. This is so, even if subsequently— several milliseconds later—Robin revises the interpretation, as she will when she realizes that the speaker's 'hello' wasn't a greeting but an attempt to get a daydreaming addressee to pay attention.

So what happens when Robin hears Rachel's remark to Robert? The hypothesis I've been developing is that Robin begins by situating Rachel as a speaker from a particular population that uses its words in a particular way, and then recovers the default interpretation of the utterance, using the ICG surrounding the words used (and rudimentary semantic knowledge and facts about the utterance context). If there are illocutionary or expressive facts in the meaning of some of the words used, Robin uses those facts to construct a first understanding of what it was that Rachel was doing. And this explains why Robin may be offended, even deeply offended, by Rachel's remark. For suppose that Robin takes Rachel to be speaking—as she is—the language spoken in the United States.[35] Robin takes there to be a standard use among the speakers in the US of words like 'Kike', 'pork', 'shrimp', and so on. If she is like most of us, she will take the standard use of 'Kike' to be one on which its use displays contempt for or denigrates Jews. And so Robin, at least initially, interprets Rachel's utterance as an act of displaying contempt for and denigration of Jews. She milliseconds later corrects the interpretation, taking Rachel to be speaking jocularly or to be honoring Robert by using 'Kike' in an in-group way.

---

[35] A speaker is always part of many populations: Rachel, after all, is a speaker of US English, an American Jew, a resident of California, Robert's sister-in-law, etc. So it is something of an idealization to say that Robin places Rachel in one particular population. Better, perhaps, to say several interpretive strategies may be activated, some more strongly than others. This doesn't affect the point I'm pushing.

But the initial interpretation was made. And to make the initial interpretation, given that the relevant ICG of 'Kike' includes the generic claim that people use the word to display contempt, is to understand Rachel as displaying contempt. And so to make the initial interpretation is to be in a situation that is phenomenologically just like the situation one is in when one witnesses someone using 'Kike' to display contempt for and disparage Jews: to so interpret Rachel just is inter alia to see her as slurring Jews. Such an act is offensive; witnessing such an act produces offense. Even though the interpreter revises the interpretation, the offense is caused, and the physiological and psychological effects of witnessing the act occur: the limbic system is activated, hormones causing stress are released, associations the word triggers are made.

On the story I'm offering, offense is sometimes a function of where the interpreter situates the speaker in the socio-semantic landscape. And so an interpreter may not feel offense at Rachel's remark. Robert may take himself to be a certain sort of friend of Rachel, and so understand himself as being honored by being addressed in a particular register. If so, the meaning he initially assigns the utterance may not involve illocutionary facts about other uses of the words uttered. Other interpreters—think of those who have repeatedly witnessed second-person slurring—may be unable to interpret any use of the term in any way other than as a slur, even if they know that some use the term non-slurringly. For them, the offense felt may be particularly intense.

The non-slurring use of a slur typically causes a distinctive sort of offense, one the user is often held responsible for even when his intentions in use are benign. Why the responsibility, when the user means no harm? Return to Rachel's utterance, and assume that Rachel meant to be speaking in a particular register, a somewhat intimate one due to her long friendship with Robert. Still Rachel spoke, as we all pretty much always do, in public. It is not really in our control in what register, as a part of what group, we are taken to speak. Rachel is many things: an American, someone from California, a Jew, Robert's sister-in-law. She can be interpreted as speaking the idiom—as assuming the ICG—of the various groups she is a member of. She has a responsibility to anticipate how she can be, or at least is likely to be, interpreted. If her audience is likely to think of her in interpretation as simply another American, or as a resident of Alabama, or as speaking as part of some other group whose members, should they use 'Kike', use it slurringly, then she has a reason to avoid the term. To fail to do so is a kind of linguistic negligence.

To utter a sentence is to more or less force the audience to process what the sentence means. If the sentence uttered is one in which a slur is used, what the sentence means—in many populations, in many registers—is in part a record of illocution displaying prejudice and contempt. In some populations, in some registers, the meaning of the sentence is literally made up of such things as the fact that those who use the words that occur in it hold Jews in contempt and think it acceptable to display such contempt. Understanding a use of a sentence containing a slur as being in such a register—even if it is not, even if one corrects one's understanding in microseconds—is understanding it as—at a certain level it is no different from witnessing—a slurring act. Witnessing such acts causes a special kind of offense; hearing a slur used, even when not to slur, is thus liable to cause the same sort of offense.[36]

9. Compositionality

I have suggested that understanding a lexical item is a matter of participating in one way or another in the item's interpretive common ground.[37] ICG is a kind of meaning, and one expects that, like other kinds of meaning, it is possessed not just by lexical items but also by complex phrases. Meaning is generally held to be compositional—roughly, the meaning of a complex phrase is determined by its syntax and the meanings of the phrase's parts. Is this sort of meaning—let's call it c-meaning—compositional?

It will be said that it has to be. Competence encompasses an ability that suffices, prescinding from the limits mortality puts on processing, to understand an infinitude of sentences. Assuming that grasping the c-meaning of an expression is required for understanding it, competence requires being able to grasp the c-meaning of arbitrary sentences. How else could we possibly have the ability to do that for infinitely many sentences, save by using some algorithm that allows us to determine the c-meaning of the whole from the c-meanings of the parts and the way they are strung together? But the existence of such an algorithm insures that c-meaning is compositional.

For reasons that I will come to, I don't think this is a very interesting argument. But let us go slowly.

One could argue that one sort of compositionality is more or less guaranteed for c-meaning. The c-meaning of a lexical item is its ICG. The ICG of an expression includes assumptions about that very expression, assumptions that presumably won't be in the ICG of other expressions.[38] The ICG of 'cousin', for example, includes the assumption that 'cousin' is used to talk about relatives; this assumption is presumably absent from the ICG of any other lexical item. But then no two lexical items will have the same ICG. Assuming more generally that the c-meaning of any phrase involves assumptions about the phrase that do not figure in the c-meaning of other expressions, we are pretty much guaranteed a weak sort of compositionality, since no two phrases will have the same c-meaning. So phrases that have the same c-meaning must be such that they are c-meaning isomorphic all the way down.[39]

---

[36] Thanks to Daniel Harris for discussion of the topic of this section.

[37] Thanks to a reader for Oxford for persuading me to address the issues addressed in this section.

[38] More precisely: the ICG of an expression e contains presuppositions about e that will not be in the ICG of any expression that has a syntactic complexity equal to or less than that of e. The ICG of a complex expression—'swanky disco', say—might include presuppositions about its sub-expressions—e.g., that 'disco' is a name for places where people dance.

[39] Again, this needs to be stated more carefully. Assume that we can order phrases in terms of complexity, measured by the number of lexical items and constructions used to form them. Modest assumptions will then assure us that at each level of complexity n, the c-meaning of any expression e of complexity n is (because it contains presuppositions about e) distinct from the c-meaning of any expression other than e which is of complexity less than or equal to n. (One of the modest assumptions is that the c-meaning of an expression of complexity e does not involve presuppositions about expressions of complexity greater than e.)

The argument here turns on the fact that, since the meaning-cum-ICG of an expression is in some sense partially constituted by that expression, different expressions will have different c-meanings. You might think that this is a bug, not a bonus. Do we really want to say that intralinguistic synonymy is impossible?[40] But if you think about it, you'll see that the answer is: well, yes. If the meaning of an expression is constituted by the facts about that expression one has to know in order to understand how it functions in its language, then it looks like intralinguistic synonymy is impossible, as the things one has to know about a word are facts about that expression, not other (simpler) expressions.

This isn't to say that we can't define a kind of c-meaning that allows different expressions (even expressions of different languages) to be synonymous. We have been thinking of the ICG of 'cousin' as a collection of presuppositions; let's pretend that the ICG of this word consists of just the claims made by the sentences

'cousin' is used to speak of cousins
cousins are parents' siblings' progeny.

To presuppose these is to 'ascribe (to 'cousin') in presupposition' the property one gets if one conjoins these claims and abstracts on the vocabulary item 'cousin':

being an expression e such that e is used to speak about cousins and cousins are parents' siblings' progeny.

Call the property so obtained from an expression's ICG the expression's abstracted common ground; its ACG. If we take c-meaning to be ACG, there's no bar to introducing a word, 'cuzine', that has the same c-meaning as 'cousin' and so is (transiently, at least) synonymous with 'cousin'. Since the viability of such a notion of synonymy is (pretty much) orthogonal to questions as to whether c-meaning is compositional, most of the rest of this section will ignore this way of thinking of c-meaning.[41]

Nothing that's been said so far commits us to a particular view of how one gets from the c-meanings of the parts of complex phrase to the c-meaning of the whole. The

---

It follows that we never find expressions, with the same syntax and parts with the same c-meaning, that differ in c-meaning, which is a weak kind of compositionality.

[40] Obviously interlinguistic synonymy of syntactically distinct expressions is ruled out as well.

[41] A good deal of detail has been left out. For example, one needs to make a decision about what to say about the c-meanings of complex phrases when their ICG involves presuppositions about their constituents. Suppose we introduce 'cuzine' as imagined in the text. The two terms will have the same ACG. Suppose that the ICG of 'first cousin' involves assumptions about the word 'cousin', as well as about the phrase 'first cousin'. Once 'cuzine' is introduced, people may treat it like a variant of 'cousin', and so speak of 'first cuzines'. Presumably the ICG of 'first cuzine' will be just like that of 'first cousin', save that in it, 'cousin' has been replaced by 'cuzine'. Should 'first cousin' and 'first cuzine' be said to be synonymous? The proposal in the text isn't gussied up enough for us to give a positive answer to this. At least given certain idealizing assumptions, we could complicate it to achieve this. I don't propose to try doing that here.

I've ignored for present purposes the complications brought in by the idea that meaning is species-like. Think of the issue under discussion as whether what Chapter 2 called transient synonymy of different expressions is possible, and, if it is, whether when we consider only a very small temporal slice of a language, ICG is compositional.

simplest story one might tell has it that the c-meaning of a complex expression involves the ICGs of its lexical items and the semantic values of both its lexical and its complex phrases. A version of this story was behind the suggestion in Section 7 about what is 'strictly and literally said' by a sentence. Fleshing out that suggestion: Suppose that relative to a context, the referential semantic values of phrases are the sorts of things Russell would have said they were: objects, properties, (sometimes functional) relations, and complexes thereof. Suppose that $S = S(e1, e2, \ldots, ek)$ is a sentence whose lexical items are exactly e1 through ek. Let c be a context of use and G a group of speakers relative to which we can assign the lexical items ICGs. Relative to c and G, S may be said to strictly and literally express a thought that one thinks if one thinks the Russellian thought expressed by S in c while thinking of the semantic values of the lexical items in S in the ways in which one does when, in thinking of them, one presupposes the ICG of e1 through ek. On this way of thinking of c-meaning, sentences are assigned c-meanings that are fusions of the referential meanings of their parts with the c-meanings of their lexical items; so long as referential meaning is compositional, this sort of meaning will be as well. It is straightforward to extend this idea so that complex subsentential phrases are assigned c-meanings that are fusions of referential meanings and lexical c-meanings.

One could recast it so that the c-meaning of a simple expression is its ICG, the c-meaning of a complex something representable as a tuple of the c-meanings of its immediate parts, and what is 'strictly said' by a sentence a fusion of c- and referential meaning. Pretty obviously, on either way of proceeding, c-meaning is compositional in a fairly strong sense—not only is the meaning of the whole a function of the parts, it is a straightforwardly computable function thereof.

But shouldn't there, one might ask, be more to c-meaning than this? Take a phrase like 'swanky disco' as used by, say, upper-class Manhattanites of the 1980s. Surely there were presuppositions (that it was common knowledge among these people) that users made when they used 'swanky disco' which they expected their audience to pick up on and use if needed in interpretation. One thinks that these presuppositions did not have to be a function of the presuppositions attached to 'swanky' and 'disco'. Speakers might have presupposed that all would recognize Studio 54 as the paradigm of swanky discos; but that doesn't mean that users of 'disco' needed to assume that the audience would think of Studio 54 when they used 'disco' alone, or that they would think of it when they used 'swanky' in a sentence like 'Pretty swanky pinky ring there, Morris'. The emergence of Studio 54 in the ICG of the phrase 'swanky disco' is unpredictable from the ICGs of its parts. But then surely it's not a function of the ICGs of the parts.[42] But then how could c-meaning be compositional?

A cognate worry can be raised if we return to the idea that lexical meaning is abstracted interpretive ground. The fact that 'disco' is simply a truncated version of 'discotheque' suggests that, abstracting from the fact that each term's ICG involves

---

[42] There is of course a parallel here to the relation between the prototype associated with a complex phrase and the prototypes associated with its parts.

presuppositions about itself, those ICGs are identical; so if we identify c-meanings with ACG, the terms have the same c-meanings. But this doesn't suggest, much less entail, that the c-meanings of 'swanky discotheque' and 'swanky disco' are the same. If you are like me, you expect your audience to find 'swanky disco' ironic bordering on sarcastic; if you are my wife, you recognize this and know that I know that you recognize it. But none of this is true of 'swanky discotheque'. A nation of ironists like me and my wife thus associate different interpretive expectations with the complex expressions. But my wife and I make and expect the same generic interpretive assumptions about 'disco' and 'discotheque' when speaking to each other. This is a failure of compositionality for c-meaning.

There is a fairly obvious, but I think misguided, response to this argument: if my wife and I have different mutual interpretive presuppositions about 'swanky disco' and 'swanky discotheque', surely that implies that we don't have exactly the same mutual interpretive presuppositions about the two nouns. If part of the common ground of 'swanky disco' for us is

S: When we use 'swanky disco', we are being ironic

then surely part of the common ground of 'disco' for us is

T: When we use 'disco' in 'swanky disco', we are being ironic.

But there won't be a corresponding claim in the ICG of 'discotheque'. So the ICGs of 'disco' and 'discotheque' are different. Compositionality vindicated.

I don't subscribe to his response. For a claim p to be in expression e's ICG, the generic

U: People who use e expect their audience to recognize that in using it they presuppose p and expect their audience to use that fact in interpreting the use of e

must be true. But I doubt that in the sort of example we are discussing the generic

V: People who use 'disco' expect their audience to recognize that in using 'disco' in 'swanky disco' they are being ironic and expect their audience to use that fact in interpreting the use of 'disco'.

The subject of V is 'people who use "disco"'. So V is a generic about—well, people who use 'disco'. It's true only if the norm among such people is to expect their audience to use the fact that people who use 'disco' in 'swanky disco' are being ironic in order to interpret their use of 'disco'. But surely this isn't the norm. When I say to my wife, 'I want to see Liz Phair at the Sinclair, so let's not go to the disco this week', I am neither being ironic nor intending her to anticipate what I would be doing when I spoke ironically of the venue Machine as a 'swanky disco'. A presupposition like V is not normally mobilized or otherwise contributing to the control of linguistic behavior when 'disco' is used, even assuming that T is always mobilized when 'swanky disco' is used. Neither do users of 'disco' when the use is not embedded in 'swanky disco' expect their audience to have anything along the lines of T held at the ready for interpretation.

Suppose I am right about this response. Should we conclude that c-meaning isn't compositional, or that it can't play the role of the anchor of linguistic competence? Not at all. What the example we are discussing shows is that one cannot in general predict the ICG of a complex in a population given just the knowledge of the ICGs of its parts. That means that sometimes when a complex expression is generically used in a particular way or ways—so that it has a non-trivial ICG—competence requires one to learn the ICG of the complex, as opposed to constructing it from the ICGs of the complex's parts. This would be a counter-example to compositionality only if there were an unbounded number of complex phrases that have ICGs that are not simple 'sums' of the ICGs of their parts. But the ICG of a phrase is a collection of presuppositions that it is common knowledge its users make. There isn't an unbounded collection of phrases, complex or otherwise, that the users of an idiom use. Only finitely many phrases have been and will be uttered. So there are only finitely many exceptions to the rule of thumb,

The things it is common knowledge that users of phrase p presuppose and expect you to recognize they presuppose when they use p are the sum of those things users of the simple parts of p presuppose and expect you to recognize they presuppose when they use each of those parts.

What competence demands is that in tracking the way the ambient idiom is evolving, one use something like this rule as a default and make adjustments when called for.

The fact that 'swanky disco' has an ICG that is not straightforwardly determined by the ICGs of its parts shows that it is an exception to the general case. But so long as there are only finitely many such exceptions—and since such exceptions are a result of the exception's use, there can be only finitely many—we have no threat to compositionality. The finitely many exceptions to the rule function somewhat as do idioms like 'paint the town red', which can in principle be understood either idiomatically or literally.[43] Exceptions or additions to such default rules exist only because of exceptional linguistic behavior; the store of such behavior being finite, the exceptions will be as well.

10. Competence and Abilities

I have written as if what constitutes a meaning or a concept is simply a collection of presupposed information. But a picture of concepts on which they are just pools of information is too shallow.[44]

Users of color terms like 'red' and 'looks red' generally apply them on the basis of appearance; they expect others to recognize that they do this and to invoke such an ability in understanding them; all of this is common knowledge. When a practice (in this case, the practice of applying a term in certain sorts of situations on the basis of appearance) and/or an ability (here the ability to coordinate with others in the

---

[43] Thought of in this way, 'swanky disco' would in some sense be 'c-ambiguous', having two c-meanings. This might be the case even if one of those meanings was (like the literal meaning of 'paint the town red') difficult for speakers to access.

[44] This section is a result of Sally Haslanger's yelling at me.

application of 'red' on the basis of sensory input) is associated with a term in the way these practices and abilities are associated with 'red' and 'looks red' among English speakers, the practice/ability is in some sense integral to what the word means; it is, I'll say, meaning-constitutive. Confining attention for the moment to abilities, an ability to φ is meaning-constitutive for expression e as used by a population G when:

(1)   Gs who use e make use of their ability to φ in applying e;
(2)   Members of G who use e expect their audience to recognize that in applying it they make use of such an ability, and they expect them to invoke that ability in interpreting the use of w;
(3)   (1) and (2) are common knowledge in G.

The ability (A, call it) to identify paradigmatically red things as such in 'good' or 'normal' perceptual situations is meaning-constitutive of 'red' in the language we speak. But what, exactly, is that supposed to come to? Does this mean that a person unable to perceptually identify red things as red, because she is color blind, or blind, or for some kindred reason, does not understand the word 'red'? Of course not. One way to understand 'cousin' is to presuppose its basis; another is to know of its basis that it is generally presupposed. One way to understand 'shitbag' is to use it in accordance with the rule: apply 'shitbag' to a person to display extreme anger with or contempt for him; another way to understand the term is to (refuse to use the term but) know that this is the rule that users expect you to recognize they are following. Analogously, one way to understand 'red' is to have ability A and use it in applying (and interpreting applications of) the term; another way to understand 'red' is (to be without that ability but) to know that the term is so associated with A in the sighted.

So it doesn't follow from the fact that an ability is meaning-constitutive for word w that those who understand w have the ability. Indeed, since the conditions in the definition above are generic, it doesn't follow that anyone who understands the term has the ability, since users might find themselves in a (very) non-normal situation. This doesn't strike me as a bad result, since one can think of odd situations—the valley of the blind after the one-eyed king is deposed, perhaps—in which color words might be understood but no one could identify things as red.[45]

11. Conceptual Analysis Again

I've tried to give some substance to the suggestion I made in Section 2, that philosophical analysis tries to elucidate implicit conceptual structure, by giving an account of concepts and meanings on which they are things constituted (at particular times) by certain

---

[45] The class of terms for which abilities and practices are meaning-constitutive is far wider than the class of 'observational terms' like color and shape terms. The ability to visually identify stereotypical birds is arguably related to understanding 'bird' in the same way that the ability to identify red things is to understanding 'red'. How far this sort of thing extends deserves more discussion than I can give it here.

sets of mutual presuppositions and expectations. I'll return to developing this idea in the chapters to follow. But enough has been said about concepts that we can return to the topic of philosophical analysis.

It seems to me obvious that many philosophers have understood what they were up to in conceptual analysis as the attempt, first, to articulate meaning-cum-ICG and, second, to reflect on what is thus articulated in an attempt to determine what property or relation that common ground is tracking. Certainly Austin and other ordinary language philosophers did. Austin counsels us that at least sometimes in philosophy

we are to proceed from 'ordinary language', that is, by examining what we should say when, and so why and what we should mean by it.

...ordinary language...embodies...something better than the metaphysics of the Stone Age, namely...the inherited experience and acumen of many generations of men...If a distinction works well for practical purposes in ordinary life (no mean feat, for even ordinary life is full of hard cases), then there is sure to be something in it, it will not mark nothing: yet this is likely enough to be not the best way of arranging things if our interests are more extensive or intellectual than the ordinary...[Everyday] experience has...not been fed from the resources of the microscope and its successors...superstition and error and fantasy of all kinds do become incorporated in ordinary language...(only, when they do, why should we not detect it?). Certainly, then, ordinary language is not the last word: in principle it can everywhere be supplemented and improved upon and superseded. Only remember, it is the first word.

(Austin 1957, 185)

Austin suggests here that philosophy at least begins by understanding the conceptual connections and distinctions that are explicit and implicit in the 'experience and acumen of many generations', which is quite close to what I've suggested we take to be the structure of a shared concept. I would have thought it was obvious that a good many philosophers—Plato and Moore strike me as apt examples—would recognize themselves as engaged in cognate investigations.

I imagine that some will say that this is a misleading picture of philosophical analysis. When, for example, Alvin Goldman reasons about the case of Henry in fake barn country, he reasons quite explicitly to an account of knowledge, not to an account of our concept of knowledge. No matter what Austin might say, he is after an account of the difference between a mistake and an accident, not an account of the difference between our concepts of these. Save when they are doing some part of philosophy of mind concerned with concepts or representations, philosophers are concerned with analyzing properties, not concepts of properties.

To this, I respond that the suggestion was not that philosophical analysis was concerned solely with concepts and their structure. Of course we are as much interested in the properties and relations our concepts are concepts of as we are in the concepts themselves.

One might counter that dragging concepts into an account of philosophical practice only obfuscates it. A philosophical account of, say, knowledge or free action aspires to (something like) a true, illuminating, and (possibly) necessary account of what is necessary and sufficient for someone to know p or to act freely in doing such and such. 'Applying the concept of knowledge to cases' is nothing more or less than thinking about what's necessary or sufficient for knowledge. The idea that we are thinking about our concepts when we are thinking about knowledge is about as plausible, it might be said, as the idea that we are looking at a mental image when we are looking at a barn.

One reason to think that this response is too hasty is that it ignores the possibility that philosophical analysis may be a worthwhile enterprise in cases in which there is no property for the analysis to be an analysis of; all there is for us to analyze in many cases of philosophical interest is our concepts.

Take free action as an example. Some philosophers tell us that to act freely would be to perform an act, the performance of which was not determined by conditions over which one has no control. Others tell us that to act freely is, roughly put, to perform an act such that one could have decided not to perform it (and would not have performed it, had one so decided). Yet other accounts are on offer. There is no consensus amongst philosophers—or amongst non-philosophers, for that matter—about which of these accounts of free action we should endorse. This is in good part because all of the accounts have—I hope I will be allowed to put it this way—considerable intuitive appeal. Each of them invokes elements that are more or less central to the way we think about free action, elements that we are loath to write out of our way of thinking of it.

Why should we think that when we use the phrase 'free action' in speech or token it in thought, it is determinate that we are picking out the property isolated by one as opposed to another of these candidate analyses of free action? I do not ask this rhetorically. I am open to being convinced that we do determinately mean something more or less co-intensive with one of these analyses, or with one that no one has been clever enough to hit upon yet. But it seems obvious that: (a) we are owed an argument for this, given that our intuitions about free action are divided and wobbly; (b) it is not at all implausible that 'free action' does not determinately denote; (c) if it does not, then all those interested in philosophical problems linked to the notion of freedom can do is to describe the varying strands in our concept of free action and make recommendations, based on the interests we do or might have, as to how we might eliminate the vagueness of the concept.[46]

I do not say that all or even most of the notions philosophy investigates suffer from the kind of indeterminacy I've suggested may infect the notion of free action. But I do say that it is very probable that some, and not improbable that many, do.[47]

[46] The point I am making does not depend on what account of vagueness we adopt. The epistemicist about vagueness, for example, will say that if 'acts freely' is vague in the way I have suggested it might be, then while there is a fact about what property the phrase picks out, it is unknowable what that property is. But if it *is* unknowable, there doesn't seem to be much of interest for philosophers concerned with free action to do, beyond conceptual delineation and normative recommendations.

[47] Nor do I say I am the first person to suggest that this is so. See, for example, Unger (1984).

There is a somewhat different sort of indeterminacy from which many notions of philosophical interest arguably suffer, one that gives another reason to interpret philosophical analysis as at least in part a kind of conceptual analysis.

Consider my dog, who is capable of rudimentary thought. She can, for example, think that I have thrown a ball. Many such thoughts are presumably realized by mental structures that deserve to be called concepts—structures that are used in categorization, are invoked in memory, are implicated in the rudimentary planning and reasoning the dog engages in, and so forth. Consider, now, the project of determining the extension (or possible worlds intension) of the canine ball concept that helps realize the dog's belief that I just threw a ball. The project is not obviously absurd, and might even be worth contemplating, if only because it raises interesting questions about interpretation and intentionality. What is absurd is the suggestion that it is even close to determinate, for every ballish x, whether the dog's concept is true of x. Surely my Sheltie's dispositions to behavior and her 'knowledge of the world' support neither the claim that the concept mobilized when she thinks I threw a ball is true of a football the size of a car, nor the claim that the concept is false of such.

An investigation into the semantics of Sheltie thought is an investigation in semantics, and thus an investigation into what properties dogs are thinking about, in some sense of 'property'. But the properties in question are partial. And to get a grip on the way in which they are partial, we have no choice but to look at the structure of the canine concept and its deployment. Why exactly should we think that it is any different when it comes to the analysis of human thought? It is a banal observation indeed that we have not anticipated all of the cases in which we might be puzzled as to whether a particular word or concept applies. It is a less banal, but no less correct, observation that our dispositions, world knowledge, and environmental relations do not come close to determining what our reactions to novel cases will or should be.[48] It is implausible, in my opinion, that an appeal to some metric of naturalness or to 'reference magnetism' will erase very much of the indeterminacy, particularly when we come to the analysis of the concepts we use to think about the social world.

Like the dog's, our thoughts are partial in the sense that it is very often a vague matter whether their predicative elements are true or false of the things we are thinking about—there is either no fact of the matter, or there might as well be no fact, since the facts are unknowable. As in the case of Sheltie semantics, to get a grip on what we are thinking we have no choice but to look at the structure of our concepts and their deployment. If we as philosophers are interested in what we are thinking, when we think about knowledge, freedom, or the good, we have no choice but to pay as much attention to our common conceptual structure as to the properties that structure might be reaching toward.

---

[48] For a budget of examples see Wilson (1982, 2006).

12. The Role of Intuitions in Philosophy

Intuitions are supposed to provide evidence for philosophical analysis. Insofar as one of the targets of such analysis is implicit or explicit conceptual structure, surely they do something like provide evidence. When there is a widespread intuition about a case, this is sometimes best explained by supposing that that intuition reflects conceptual structure. When we so explain the intuition, the intuition has the status of evidence for the explanation we give.

To say this is not to say that the mere fact that I have an intuition—that is, that I have a strong and stable inclination to make a certain kind of judgment about a case—is in and of itself evidence that the judgment is correct. Neither is it to say that the mere fact that most everybody has such an intuition is in and of itself evidence that the judgment is correct. Intuitions are, in the first instance, data for philosophy, not (immediately) evidence, much as observations that are prior to physical theory are data, but not immediately evidence for physical theory. When a physicist is given a collection of observations, her task is to turn the data those observations provide into evidence, by coming up with a theory that both explains the data (typically by implying it when coupled with other theory and reasonable background assumptions) and makes novel predictions (again, when coupled with other theory and assumptions) that, if correct, serve to confirm the theory. This, it seems to me, is exactly how we ought to think of the task of the philosopher who finds that she and others have intuitions in the relevant sense about the application conditions of some philosophically fraught term. She should try to figure out what sorts of mutual, albeit implicit, presuppositions could be responsible for her inclination to make a particular judgment. Once she has a story about this that seems to explain the intuitions, she can go on to explore a variety of cases to see whether the story, coupled with other philosophical stories and apt background assumptions, makes predictions that are borne out.

For a concrete example, consider Alvin Goldman's discussion of Henry, who has unknowingly driven into an area where there are many fake barns and who, looking at a real barn, thinks that it is a barn (Goldman 1976). Goldman observes that if we are only told that Henry is driving around Pennsylvania, sees a barn, and thinks 'that's a barn', we will be inclined to say he knows that he sees a barn; if we are also told about the fake barns, we are inclined to say that in such a case, Henry doesn't know that he is looking at a barn.

Goldman considers various accounts of knowledge that validate these intuitions and settles on one of them, on which knowing p requires that one's belief that p be reliable in a particular way—the knower must be able to discriminate the actual state of affairs p from various relevant possible alternatives. Goldman explicitly argues for this proposal by observing that our 'inclinations' to make judgments about various cases are correlated with whether the case is described in such a way as to presuppose that Henry is unable to discriminate the area's fake barns from its real barns:

A person knows that p...only if the actual state of affairs in which p is true is distinguishable or discriminable by him from a relevant possible state of affairs in which p is false...In the original description of the barn case [Case C, call it, where there is no mention of fake barns] there is no hint of any relevant possible state of affairs in which the object in question is not a barn but is indistinguishable (by Henry) from the actual state of affairs. Hence, we are initially inclined to say that Henry knows. Given that the district Henry has entered is full of barn facsimiles, there is a relevant alternative...state of affairs...[that] is indistinguishable by Henry from the actual state of affairs...So, once apprised of the facsimiles in the district [in Case C'], we are inclined to deny that Henry knows.   (Goldman 1976, 774)

Call the property of Henry's belief that we sense to be lacking in the full-blown case reliability. Part of the argument here pretty clearly involves premises like:

1. We have a stable and strong inclination to say that Henry's barn belief is knowledge when given case C, and a stable and strong inclination to say that Henry's barn belief isn't knowledge when given case C'.

2. In case C, 'there is no hint' that Henry's belief is not reliable; in case C', there is a suggestion that it is not.

If we assume, as surely Goldman is assuming, something along the lines of

3. Nothing else about the cases is relevant to explaining the difference in our inclinations toward C and C'

we are in a position to explain (1) with:

4. Our stable and strong inclinations about cases like Henry's and about whether a belief is knowledge are sensitive to whether or not it appears to us that the belief is reliable.

But of course this pattern of explanation is one in which we explain the existence of an intuition—that is, we explain (1)—with a hypothesis about conceptual structure. Insofar as this provides a good explanation of the intuition—and provides the basis of an explanation for a variety of other intuitions about different kinds of cases[49]—what Goldman has succeeded in doing is turning the data provided by the intuitions mentioned in (1) into evidence. If we add to (4) something else that Goldman is presumably assuming:

5. When our judgments about whether something is F are sensitive to whether it is G, that is a reason, all else being equal, to think that Fs are Gs

we are in a position to conclude that we have reason to think that knowledge requires reliability.

It seems to me that many passages in analytic philosophy of the last 100 or so years, in which philosophers make points by appeal to examples, should be understood in much the way I'm proposing that this passage should.

---

[49] Something that Goldman of course tried to show in a variety of papers developing a reliabilist view of knowledge.

I'll close this chapter by comparing my take on the role of intuition in philosophy with Herman Cappelen's (2012). Cappelen is no friend of the idea that intuitions have a role in philosophy, while I am. But the distance between our views is not so great, and it is, I think, illuminating to see exactly where we do differ.

Acknowledging that there are different accounts of the nature and role of intuition, Cappelen focuses on the view that

A. Intuitions are mental states:
  1. with propositional content, either sui generis states ('seemings') or beliefs with a particular etiology;
  2. which have a distinctive phenomenology;
  3. that are based solely on conceptual competence;
  4. and that have a special evidential status—they are in some sense 'rock bottom' and need no justification.
B. Analytic philosophers rely on intuitions so characterized for evidence (at least as a source of evidence).

Cappelen is inclined to dismiss the idea that there is a distinctive phenomenology that accompanies what philosophers are voicing when they express intuitions, observing that he is unaware of any such funny feelings when he reads the work of Gettier, Goldman, or Kripke. I, too, am an intuition zombie. Let us agree to strike A.2 from the characterization of intuition; call the resulting job description for intuitions I.

Cappelen for the most part attacks views on which intuitions are the contents of beliefs that we give voice to when confronted with philosophical cases. For example, in discussing Goldman's barn example, Cappelen identifies the putative intuitions that Goldman would describe himself as invoking as consisting in 'two claims':

C1: In the first scenario [when fakes are not mentioned], Henry does know.

C2: In the second scenario, Henry does not know. (Cappelen 2012, 171–2)

On this interpretation, intuitions are beliefs-cum-contents-of-judgments about cases. It is not hard to show that these don't fit the job description I: As Cappelen argues, C1 and C2 are not candidates for 'rock-bottom' evidential status, and Goldman is not well understood as thinking otherwise.

All this marks a difference between Cappelen and me, but at least some of the difference is merely verbal. I do not identify intuitions with judgments about cases or with the contents of such judgments. Intuitions are, rather, certain psychological facts that often result in our making judgments with the relevant contents. I gave a reason for thinking of intuitions in this way at the beginning of the chapter: a single person's intuitions are often in conflict; we don't want to say that just because someone has conflicting intuitions, they have inconsistent beliefs.

Do the psychological facts with which I say we should identify intuitions have 'rock-bottom' evidential status? Frankly, I'm not a fan of talking that way about any evidence, being something of a fan of Quine's 'Two Dogmas'. But surely such facts have, for the person whose psychology they are facts about, 'rock-bottom' status as data. There is no denying that one has the relevant intuitions. You could probably convince me—with a lot of work—that I don't have a stable and strong inclination to judge that Henry doesn't know in the second scenario, just as the doctor in an old example of Keith Lehrer's manages to convince a patient that a state she reports as a pain isn't really a pain but an itch. But this doesn't mean that my knowledge about my inclinations isn't basic for me in an important sense.

To say this is not, of course, to say that intuitions have an indubitable evidential status—that given that I have an intuition that a concept applies in a case, I thereby have good reason to think that the concept applies in the case. What the intuition gives me is data, something that calls for an explanation. The null hypothesis, I should think, is that the intuition reflects something in conceptual structure. So the intuition gives me reason to think that there is something about the relevant concept that makes me have the intuition. And all this makes it reasonable to entertain the hypothesis that there is some aspect of the cases about which I have the intuition that corresponds to something in the structure of the concept.

This is related to a difference between Cappelen and me about what is going on in passages like the one from Goldman. I see the passage as involving, among other things, an abductive inference; Cappelen does not. Cappelen's main complaint about interpreting it as I do is that

in an abductive inference with c as the explanandum and T as the explanans, the question of whether c is the case is typically not under discussion.   (Cappelen 2012, 172)

The point is well taken. But surely what we should conclude is not that the relevant passages are not best reconstructed as abductive arguments. Rather, we should conclude that the explanandum of the argument is the fact that the philosopher—and (the philosopher assumes) most other philosophers—is strongly and stably inclined to make the relevant judgment. That is not up for debate; I'm sure Cappelen would not disagree.

Are intuitions in my sense 'based solely on conceptual competence'? Well, again, as a fan of Quine I am no fan of this way of talking. And, in any case, as I have characterized intuitions, they may be the result of any number of things, including contingent, collateral knowledge about the property a case is supposed to focus us on. This is one reason why, in my reconstruction of Goldman's argument, the final premise—the one that gets us from facts about concepts to ones about properties—is hedged with a ceteris paribus clause. Intuitions are the result of our applying our concepts to descriptions, without 'doing empirical investigation'. As things stand, they are a way to get some data about what we are and are not sensitive to, in applying a concept. I suppose I agree with Cappelen that saying that intuitions are 'based solely on conceptual competence' is a bad way of describing them. It doesn't follow that they aren't a source of data that, given an explanatory theory, counts as evidence for what I called above conceptual structure.

Cappelen and I don't disagree that there are intuitions, characterized as I have been characterizing them. We do seem to disagree about their role in philosophical argumentation, as well as about what it is that philosophical analysis is and should be trying to do.

The disagreement is not, I think, really about the range of things that play an evidential role in philosophy. Cappelen thinks that just about anything might play an evidential role in philosophy; he believes, I think, that the idea that intuitions have a distinguished role in philosophical evidence badly—very badly—overestimates their importance. I agree that just about anything can play an evidential role in philosophy, and that a great deal of what is evidence in philosophy comes not from gazing at our inner omphalos, but from the sciences.

I think where Cappelen I differ most fundamentally is about what philosophers are doing when they try to give accounts of things like knowledge or free action. Cappelen's view, I think, is that they are simply trying to say something illuminating about properties and relations, and that our concepts of these properties and relations are of no particular philosophical interest. Myself, I think we have no choice in philosophically interesting cases but to proceed cautiously, open to the possibility that there are no properties or relations that our words and concepts are directed on—not because those concepts are as empty of content as the concept phlogiston, but because they are often massively partial or painfully indeterminate. Since this is generally an open possibility, and surely sometimes how things in fact are, philosophical analysis has to be conceptual analysis, for often there is nothing else for it to be.

4

Conceptual Evolution and Reference

One hundred and forty years ago pretty much no one in the English-speaking world thought it was possible for people of the same sex to marry. Forty years ago pretty much no one—surely pretty much no one in America—thought so. But at some point toward the end of the twentieth century, squeaky wheels started questioning whether this sort of thing was really impossible. One anticipates that in another forty years the idea that a man could not marry a man will seem as quaint as does the idea that there is something sinful about sex outside wedlock.

When Jane Q. Public slowly changes her mind between 1995 and 2015 as to whether same-sex marriage is impossible, is that a change of meaning or change in belief? If it is a change in meaning or concept, then what happens is that 'marriage' expresses one concept in 1995, another in 2015; insofar as our beliefs, assertions, and the like are constituted by our concepts, this suggests that what was said or thought with sentences like 'it's impossible for men to marry one another' in 1995 is not what such sentences express today. If it is a change in belief, then the sentences say the same thing, but our view about its truth has changed. Quine, to whom we owe the pithy question, 'Change in meaning or change in belief?', would have said that there was no saying and no point in trying to say—here we have the argument of 'Two Dogmas of Empiricism' acted out in public. Quine would have said this because he thought that there was no principled story to tell about whether a sentence was analytic or otherwise; but if there's no principled story to tell, how could we say in a principled way whether Jane Q. was changing the meaning of 'men can't marry each other' or changing her mind about marriage mano a mano?[1]

I think Quine's pessimism is more extreme than is warranted. Real distinctions are not always sharp distinctions. It is a fact that we are conspecific with our children, and that we are not with our simian ancestors, though there are links in the line of descent where it's indeterminate whether we and the link are conspecific. Likewise, it is sometimes

---

[1] The decisions of Canadian courts about same-sex marriage from the first decade of this century are relevant here. In *Halpern v. Canada* 2002, for example, the court spends considerable time reviewing arguments for and against (what is in effect) the claim that it is true by definition that marriage is a bond between a man and a woman; at the end of the review it does something that appears very much like throwing up its hands in exasperation as to whether there is a fact of the matter about this. (The complete text can be found at http://www.canlii.org/en/on/onsc/doc/2002/2002canlii49633/2002canlii49633.html.)

indeterminate whether a word means the same at different times. It does not follow that it is never determinate that a word persists in meaning one thing in any interval, or that it is never determinate that a word changes its meaning, any more than from the occasional indeterminacy of whether a remark is insightful, it follows that there is no difference between the work of a genius and the work of a hack.

Questions of the forms:

Does this word, as used by these people in this situation, mean the same as that word, as used by those people in that situation?

Does this sentence, as used by these people in this situation, say the same as that sentence, as used by those people in that situation?

are by and large no worse off, no less the bearers of sensible answers, than are questions of the form:

Are these individuals, in this particular historical and ecological niche, members of the same species as those individuals, in that particular historical and ecological niche?

This chapter discusses the semantic questions.

Some signposting is in order. I will not try to provide necessary or sufficient—much less necessary and sufficient conditions for—diachronic sameness of meaning. Sections 1 and 2 say a bit about the idea that there is an analogy between biological entities, like species and population lineages, and semantic things like meanings and concepts. In particular, I say something about what gives a group of contemporaneous speakers the sort of cohesion that makes it appropriate to theorize it as a group that means the same things with its words or shares a language. Sections 3 through 6 discuss the conditions under which it is appropriate to say or deny such things as that sentence S, as used by a population P of speakers at time t, says the same thing as does S, as used at a later time by a 'descendant population' of P. That is, these sections discuss such questions as: When Cardinal Law said in 1984 'same-sex marriage is impossible', did he deny what Justice Roberts affirmed in 2014 when he wrote 'same-sex marriage is obviously possible'? Sections 7 through 9 discuss a view that I call referentialism. Roughly put, this is the view that (limiting ourselves to the use of a term within a 'linguistic lineage'—a sequence of populations whose later members acquire their language from earlier ones) identity of meaning or concept expressed by a word is a matter of sameness of reference. I am inclined to think that this is a bad way to think about conceptual continuity, and these sections explain why. Finally, Section 10 discusses some relations between the way of thinking of meaning that this chapter develops and views that put notions of truth and reference at the heart of talk about meaning.

1. The Linguistic and the Biological

Species are populations spread across time. The population lineage that constitutes a species consists of populations related by descent—today's orange bullfinches are the descendants of yesterday's; tomorrow's will be descendants of today's. Descent is—well, nature provides examples of various kinky processes of propagation: parthenogenesis, sporulation, fission, Iowa's precinct caucuses. But the biological paradigm of reproduction is the case in which two individuals create a new individual in such a way that the parents' characteristics (some of them, anyway) have an influence on the characteristics of the progeny—the beak of the baby goldfinch is likely to resemble that of the parents in certain ways. In biological reproduction the product inherits characteristics from the producers.

Not just any old sequence of populations related by descent makes for a species. If we start with Abraham Lincoln, Lincoln's wife, and seven orange goldfinches contemporary with Lincoln, and then trace progeny down through the generations, that does not constitute a species. The organisms that constitute a species at any time cohere in a biologically important way. What way is a matter of controversy. Some say that the cohesion is a matter of reproductive relations, species being collections of organisms that are able to reproduce with each other but not with members of other species; orange goldfinches are such because they can get it on with other (differently sexed) orange goldfinches. Others say that it is matter of shared properties: what unites a species at a time is a relation members bear to genetic, morphological, behavioral, or ecological properties. Orange goldfinches are such because they have the genetic profile of, and thus look and act like, orange goldfinches. For the moment we don't need to worry about exactly what properties and relations are the synchronic glue of species.

Species are population lineages diachronically related by descent and synchronically related by... by some synchronic species-making relation. In saying that linguistic entities are like biological ones, I mean to say that they are important players in processes analogous to those that constitute species. How exactly do they come to be players? If a meaning is really like a species, then it must be constituted at any time by a set of individuals, related by some synchronic meaning-making relation. What are these individuals? Furthermore, the populations that constitute a meaning at various times must be related by the linguistic analog of descent; thus, there must be linguistic analogs to reproduction and inheritance. What are these analogs?

Perhaps the two most obvious candidates for linguistic analogs to biological individuals are idiolects and the lexicons on which they are based. An idiolect is what the linguist has in mind when she speaks of an individual's internalized grammar. It is a language whose syntax and phonology are determined by the cognitive structures that constitute the individual's ability to manifest thought linguistically and to parse and interpret such manifestations by others. Its sentences are structured combinations of items (phrases) that are constructed from simple parts (words). The words of such a language are those things that can be generated from a set of memorized structures, the language's lexicon.

In what ways are idiolects and their lexicons like individual goldfinches qua members of a species? Well, take a population that we would describe as sharing a language—the English-speaking high school graduates of New York state, for example. Of course, they don't have identical idiolects or lexicons. But they have ones that are not just similar but are presumably related in ways somewhat reminiscent of the ways in which the genomes and morphology of various orange goldfinches are related. There is a relatively small collection of variant genes—alleles—that control (along with other genes and the environment) how the goldfinch's beak will look, what its song will sound like, and so on; likewise, there is a relatively small collection of sorts of entries for 'goldfinch' in the lexicons of New Yorkers, that control (along with other aspects of grammar and one's education and social situation) how the word will be pronounced, its syntactic behavior, the meaning it is accorded. Because of this similarity (in both individual 'goldfinch' entries and in New Yorkers' overall idiolects), speakers who have these idiolects are able to engage in (linguistic) intercourse with one another.[2] So there is, on either way of identifying the individuals that make a 'linguistic species', a clear analog in the biological case. There are also pretty obviously analogs to reproduction and inheritance: most obviously, there is what happens when one or more people teach another person a word or significant part of the lexicon.[3]

The analogy does not stop there. Species evolve. Inheritable characteristics come in variants—some of us are blonds, some gingers—and the distribution of those characteristics in a species can change over time. On occasion one variant becomes fixed; others disappear; new characteristics arise through such things as mutation and incorporation of genetic material from other species. Enough of this and a novel species may arise. Both sorts of change, evolution and speciation, have linguistic analogs. Pronunciation and morphology, for example, shift over time: 'shore' has come to sound like 'sure';[4] English has lost much irregular verb morphology in the last 500 years. If we think of what the last chapter called interpretive common ground (ICG) as part of the information in the lexicon—and if it is meaning in the sense of what the competent speaker must cognize for competence, this seems fair—it is clear that this, like pronunciation and morphology, changes as a result of interactions with the world, and that this in turn affects the frequency with which various lexical properties are instantiated. And over time, such things as geographical and cultural isolation can lead to changes in a group's language profound enough that the language the group speaks is different from that of its ancestors.

I do not say that the analogy is perfect. For one thing, the evolution of species is in good part due to natural selection—changes in allele distribution due to a reproductive advantage that certain genes (or the characteristics for which they are responsible) confer. It is not immediately clear to what extent there are processes like natural selection in the linguistic case; we'll take this up in Chapter 6.

---

[2] And because of differences between these idiolects and the idiolects of, for example, Spanish speakers who live in the same geographic area as the English speakers, English speakers can't have linguistic intercourse with Spanish speakers; the ensemble of English idiolects is 'conversationally isolated' in a way, like the way in which species are normally reproductively isolated from other species.

[3] As we will see, there are other, Lamarckian relations that also are like reproduction.

[4] The example is from a lecture by J.C. Wells: https://www.phon.ucl.ac.uk/home/wells/cardiff.htm; accessed February 4, 2019.

Here is a genuine disanalogy. Biological individuals, thought of as embodied genomes, are quite stable. There may be a certain amount of mutation in germ cell reproduction, but it is hardly massive. For the most part environmental factors do not rewire the genome so that what could be passed on differs from what was inherited.[5] Do we want to say the same thing about particular human vocabularies?

No and yes. Matt and Diane meet, marry, and bear Noah, who learns to speak by interacting with Matt and Diane. Noah's parents teach him nouns and verbs and how to put them together. There is a certain amount of variation in the way these words are realized in each of their lexicons, variations in pronunciation (Matt says *caw-fee*), morphology (Noah says *eated*), and assumptions about meaning (unlike the rest of the family, Diane doesn't suppose that adoptive parents are literally mothers). Some of these differences are transient (Noah will grow out of *eated*), some aren't (Matt was born and bred in New Yawk), and some persist only under certain environmental conditions (if people argue with Diane about mothers, she may change her tune).

It is natural to describe the members of our little family as literally sharing a vocabulary. Saying that, we can't identify the words of the shared vocabulary with feature sets—collections of morphological, phonological, syntactic, and semantic properties manifested in the user's speech. For if that's what words are, our family members do not have common words for 'coffee', 'eat', and 'mother'. If we are going to describe the family in the natural way, we need to think of words in some other way. What seems apt is to think of them in something like the way that we are taught in high school to think of genes. Genes come in different 'versions'—alleles—and different members of a species will vary as to which alleles of a particular gene they have. Likewise, words come in different versions, and Matt, Noah, and Diane have different versions of the same words.

If this is how we think of things, then linguistic individuals—embodied lexicons—are not stable in the way that embodied genomes are, for such things as morphology, phonology, and syntactic and semantic roles in a lexicon change over time. If Matt moves to Massachusetts and loses his New Yawk accent, this is the equivalent of trading in New York genes for Bawstonian ones. And if he does do this, what he will bequeath to those whose lexicons are shaped by interacting with him will be Boston-baked genes.

The observation so far is that lexicons and languages are species-like. And so are meanings themselves. At least they are when thought of in a certain way, as ensembles of mental structures. Take the meaning of 'cousin' to be constituted by those aspects of linguistic competence that realize the ICG surrounding 'cousin'—that is, by the ensemble of those sets of presuppositions that various speakers associate with the phrase by assuming that the phrase's users expect to be understood as making them. Then that meaning is an ensemble, each member of which actually or potentially interacts with

---

[5] A certain amount of cut-and-paste rewiring occurs in the generation of gametes, of course.

other members of the ensemble; those parts of the meaning that constitute it at one time give rise to those that exist at later times; they do this in a way that is like biological reproduction, as the traits that the 'parent meanings' have tend to reproduce themselves in the spawn. And of course the constitution of a meaning, thought of as ICG, changes over time, in some cases so dramatically that semantic speciation occurs.

2. Lexical Coordination

In the biological case, saying what makes two organisms—even two organisms that exist at the same time—members of a species is fraught. (Even given that the parents of each were conspecific, they needn't be conspecific; otherwise species would never go out of existence so long as their members have joint offspring.) The problem is so fraught it has a name: the species problem. Saying what binds together the vocabularies that make up the linguistic analog of the species is just as fraught. After all, saying this is tantamount to saying what it is for people to share a vocabulary. And since to share a vocabulary is to be a good way down the road to sharing a language, saying what binds individual vocabularies into the analog of a species is going a good bit down the road to saying what it is to share a public language. And this last is fraught. There is considerable skepticism that the notion of a public language is coherent; there is considerable skepticism that public languages, even if such things exist, are of any theoretical interest to linguistics or to philosophy.

The species problem might be divided into two parts. There is a synchronic part: What gives a synchronic population the cohesion that makes it a species? And there is a diachronic issue: What properties and relations determine whether populations that exist at different times are conspecific? In the biological case, what gives a synchronic population the cohesion that makes it a moment in the existence of a species is presumably its instantiating (many of) the relations and mechanisms that are invoked in various specific species definitions: the potential for its members to breed with each other, systems that identify others as potential mates, a common ecological niche, and so on.[6] A first step toward clarifying, if not resolving, the linguistic version of the

---

[6] This is in the spirit of a proposal by Kevin de Queiroz as to how various species notions are related. De Queiroz suggests that most contemporary accounts of species are partial, incomplete specifications of a *general lineage species concept*, according to which 'species are segments of population level lineages' (de Queiroz 1998, 60), a lineage being 'a single line of direct ancestry and descent' of populations. The various definitions of species that one finds debated in the biological literature—species are reproductively isolated interbreeding sequences of populations, or such sequences that have a system for recognizing mates, or all of the descendants of a particular node on a phylogenic tree, or all the organisms with a particular range of phenotypes, or interbreeding occupants of a particular ecological niche, or ... (most of) these should not be take to be 'definitions' of 'species' but as criteria that are useful for isolating one species from others. Speciation (and a species itself) is a process; species criteria are more or less useful ways *at particular points in the history of a species* for isolating what are and are not members. For example, reproductive isolation is not an absolute but something that comes in degrees, and is (more) characteristic of a species at a relatively advanced stage of speciation than earlier on. As I understand De Queiroz, he thinks that none of the species

species problem is to find relations that stand to individual vocabularies as relations like *being able to produce fertile offspring or instantiating mechanisms that identify one another as potential sexual partners* stand to conspecifics. This section tries to take a small step toward isolating one such relation.

In a successful conversation a speaker speaks, an audience hears and understands—the speaker, let us say, utters, 'I was there', meaning that she was at Woodstock; the audience takes the speaker to have said, 'I was there', thereby meaning that she, the speaker, was at Woodstock. What happens in this transaction?

Suppose for the moment that we buy into a picture associated with Chomsky (1980, 2000): the speaker and the audience do not really share a language; each speaks her own idiolect, which may be more or less similar in phonology, morphology, syntax, and semantics to the other's. Working from this picture, we will say that the speaker produces a sentence and the audience understands the speaker to have produced a sentence. The speaker, of course, produces a sentence of her language; the audience, working as he is in his language, interprets the speaker therein.[7] The speaker's performance involves selecting a set of words of her language (call this the utterance's basis), and applying constructions to these and to phrases that emerge along the way, winding up with the sentence which is uttered.[8] (Call this last the utterance's output.) The audience interprets this output as the result of applying certain constructions of the audience's language to some of the audience's words (the interpretation's basis),

notions (and no Boolean combination of them) that say something concrete about what distinguishes one species from another provides anything even close to necessary and sufficient conditions for marking the contours of a species from beginning to end. (Again, as I interpret De Queiroz) a species in some sense *is* the historical process of a lineage's becoming and remaining distinct from other lineages; since the mechanisms that distinguish an ongoing species may change during its history, none of the specific species notions defines what it is to be a species.

I'll return to De Queiroz's view in Section 9.

[7] The audience, after all, reacts to the auditory or visual onslaught of the speaker how? By applying *the audience's* linguistic abilities to parse said onslaught.

I am not suggesting that the audience experiences or thinks of the sentence it hears or reads—that is, the sentence it is aware of—as something like a representation of the sentence the other produces. When you talk to me, my experience is captured by reports like, 'I heard you say "I was there"'. Typically, I experience you as—a Chomskyan would say 'as if'—uttering words of my language: the sentence mentioned by quotation in the direct speech report is, after all, a sentence the reporter produces, which is a sentence of his language. (This is not always so, of course; I may experience you as producing a mishmash of bits of my language with something else if you say, 'he runned away'. And of course sometimes I am left at a loss for what it is that you did.)

If we begin with Chomsky's picture of each speaker speaking her own internalized language, the picture sketched in the text may seem inescapable. One goal of this section is to argue that this picture is perfectly consistent with the claim that there are such things as public vocabularies—and thus that Chomsky's picture is not incompatible with the claim that there are (things very much like) public languages. Insofar as these things can be modeled and investigated with the sorts of techniques employed in the study of population dynamics—something we will discuss in Chapter 6—it is hard to see why we should agree with Chomsky that public languages, even if they exist, are of no interest to the 'science of linguistics'.

[8] 'Basis' as it is used in the next couple of pages is being used in a quite different way than it was used in Chapter 3, when I spoke of the basis of the ICG of a phrase.

which is the sentence the audience understands the speaker as having produced (the interpretation's output).

This description does not suppose that there is anything like qualitative identity between the grammars of speaker and hearer. The feature sets that characterize the speaker's words may differ from those that characterize the audience's: phonological properties may vary ('you say *tomayto*, and I say *tomahtow*'), as may morphological properties ('you say *runned*, and I say *ran*'), as may semantic properties (what you take as a paradigm of redness may differ from what I do). Neither need there be isomorphism between the ways in which phrases are constructed, or in the structures of whole sentences.

Let us concentrate on the words the speaker and hearer use—on the bases of utterance and interpretation. Suppose that the speaker and hearer are regularly in communication, with the speaker sometimes speaking, sometimes listening, the hearer sometimes listening, sometimes speaking. What should the speaker and hearer hope for? A natural hope involves two elements: First, that when either of them uses a word—that is, whenever either them tokens an entry from his lexicon—the user can rely on the other recognizing what word is used (that is, what lexical entry is tokened), so that the user can anticipate being consistently interpreted; second, that when this expectation is satisfied, the auditor (all else being equal) understands the speaker.

One way—in some sense, the natural way—for the first of these to obtain is as follows:

(i) For each word x of X's language there is a word y of Y's language such that: were X to use x, X could reasonably expect that Y would interpret x with y; and were Y to use y, Y could reasonably expect X would interpret y with x, and;

(ii) The converse: for each word y of Y's language there is a word x of X's language such that: were Y to use y, Y could reasonably expect that X would interpret y with x; and were X to use x, X could reasonably expect Y would interpret x with y.

In this case, we say that X and Y's lexicons have an established coordination, a sort of interpretive bijection between the lexicons. Issues of homonymy and polysemy to the side for the moment, something approximating established coordination is what we arguably find in cases in which two people regularly communicate with each other 'in a single language'. There are, for example, words 'a', 'dog', and 'barked' of my language and words 'a', 'dog', and 'barked' of yours which are such that when I use one of my words, you consistently interpret me as having produced the corresponding one of yours, that word being the one which, when you use it, I consistently interpret you with the word I used. Which is just to say that when I or you say 'a dog barked', the other takes the speaker to have said 'a dog barked'.

I take it the generalization to a larger group is clear enough: The lexicons of the Gs have a (perfect) established coordination provided there is an equivalence relation R on the words of the G's individual lexicons such that for any w in some G's individual lexicon, $R_w = \{w'|wRw'\}$ has exactly one member from the lexicon of each member of

G, and a use by X of her contribution to R_w is such that X could reasonably expect of any Y in G that Y would interpret x with Y's contribution to R_w. It should go without saying (and will henceforth) that a community might be coordinated in this way only when we ignore various bits and pieces of individual lexicons that are specialized and hence not widely shared, and that a community might come close to established coordination without its being the case that it was perfectly coordinated on any vocabulary items.

Established coordination is often, perhaps almost normally, accompanied by mutual understanding. At least this will be so given that: when X and Y's lexicons are coordinated, that induces a ragged coordination of the sentences of X and Y's languages, as in the example of 'a dog barked'; X and Y participate in the same ICG for their coordinated words; they have internalized the same interpretive principles for syntax.[9] Indeed, when lexicons are coordinated and their users' presuppositions about what an audience can be expected to assume about the words more or less overlap, it seems like the right thing to say is that the lexicon's owners are using the same words: when lexicons are coordinated and ICG is shared, we can on a first pass identify common vocabulary with the equivalence classes R_w mentioned in the previous paragraph.[10] The R_w's are like genes, whose members are the gene's token alleles in the population.

Normally, the members of animal species are able to interbreed with one another to produce fertile offspring; the fact that a group is so able to interbreed contributes to, even if it does not constitute, the group's being a species. This does not mean that arbitrary (differently sexed) pairs of a species are perpetually hopping in and out of the sack—Ft. Lauderdale in the spring notwithstanding, the life of a species is not a nonstop orgy. Nor does it mean that every coupling between species members will lead to offspring, even if that's something like the norm when the couple are adult, normally developed species members.

Normally, those who share a vocabulary—and in virtue of that (at least part of) a conceptual scheme—are able to converse with one another in such a way that there is understanding. The fact that a group is so able to converse contributes to, even if it does not constitute, the fact that the group shares a vocabulary. This does not mean that arbitrary pairs of the group are perpetually talking to each other—the life of the normal adult American is not a non-stop orgy of posting his thoughts on Facebook where they are more or less immediately inflicted on all his Facebook 'Friends'. Neither does it mean that every conversational coupling between vocabulary sharers will lead to understanding, though that may be something like the norm when the conversants are adult, normally developed members of a vocabulary-sharing group.

---

[9] By this last, I mean that X and Y have dispositions like those of someone who accepts instances of schemata like, 'A use of *many Fs are Gs* is to be understood as saying, of Fs and Gs, that many of the former are among the latter'.

[10] 'Identify' is wrong if only because we want the public words to be things that endure through time. A bit better: If the G's lexicons are coordinated and ICG is shared at time t, we can on a first pass say that at t the common vocabulary the Gs share is constituted at t by the equivalence classes.

I suggested above that when people regularly converse with one another, there will be (something approximating) an established coordination between their lexicons. But I would want to say that I share a vocabulary with more people than those with whom I am in constant communication. For the most part, I share a good deal of vocabulary with—I use the same words as—not just Facebook Friends but with many of the Friends of the Friends of those Friends, even though I have not and will not interact with them. In this regard, regular conversation is more like attempts at actual interbreeding than it is like the ability to interbreed. The vocabulary theoretic analog of the ability to interbreed is the existence of mechanisms within a population that normally lead to established coordination between members of the population who attempt to speak to and interpret one another. I will say when there are such mechanisms in place within a population that the lexicons of that population are coordinated simpliciter.

What sort of mechanisms are these? Some of them are mechanisms whose existence is responsible for the more than merely modest success of modern morphology, phonology, syntax, and the sort of semantics pursued by those who study such things as argument structure, thematic relations, and the mechanisms employed in the lexi-con.[11] As children acquire their language, they acquire a language that is based upon and that typically closely resembles the language(s) of those around them. Part of their acquiring their language just is acquiring the ability to recognize when the words others use have (morphological and phonetic) form and (syntactic and semantic) function that is aligned with the form and function of their own words, and to base their interpretation—their identification of what sentence the other has just uttered—on the basis of this alignment. Learning a language just is, in part, learning how to coordinate one's lexicon with the lexicons of others.

To say this is not to say that everyone's language or lexicon is identical. Phonology, morphology, syntax, and semantics(-cum-what-one-presupposes in mutual knowledge held at the ready for interpretation) of course varies across (say) the English-speaking population of Newton, MA 02467. Why that should be thought to imply that there is not a theoretically interesting sense in which all the Newtonians are using the same words escapes me. The fact that there is considerable allelic variation across this popu-lation does not lead the biologist to say that there is no theoretically interesting sense in which the members of this population share genes. What's the difference?

I am of course making an (extremely vague) empirical claim about how individual linguistic abilities are related. This claim is somewhat—okay, it is way—ahead of the evidence: we don't have consensus about what a good model for the organization of the lexicon is. But doesn't the claim that lexical coordination isn't the norm strike you as a sort of unmerited skepticism, something like the claim that there is no theor-etically interesting sense in which some population lineages are biologically distin-guished in the way in which, say, *Anthonomus grandis* is?

---

[11] Examples of this last are Jackendoff (2002) and Pinker (1989).

3. Changes In and Changes of Meaning

We are accustomed to distinguishing between the things that constitute an object and the object itself. Theseus' ship, for example, is constituted by, but not identical with, the sum of its planks, nails, and such. Most of us think the ship can survive the loss of at least some of its constituting parts; most of us think that if we of a sudden replace all the ship's parts with novel ones, what we have is not the ship with which we began. If we think of meanings as ICG, we will want to make an analogous distinction between the things that constitute a meaning and the meaning itself. Most of us think that the claims that constitute the core of an expression e's meaning in a population—the basis of e's ICG—may change, at least a bit, without e's meaning changing; most of us think that if of a sudden the basis of e's ICG more or less completely changes, the word no longer means what it did in the population.

There are two ways in which word w's meaning in a population P can change between time t and a later t'.[12] First of all, the way w is used in P at t'—in particular, the presuppositions users associate with it—may be so different from the way that w is used in P at t that it is inappropriate to say that w's meaning in P is the same at t and t'. Secondly, the claims that constitute w's meaning in P—in particular, the basis of the ICG associated with w—may shift from t to t'; this may or may not be accompanied by a change of the first sort. It will be useful to have terminology for these sorts of change. Call the first s-change and reserve *change of w's* meaning for it. Call the second c-change and reserve *change in w's* meaning for it.

Changes of and changes in meaning are changes in what presuppositions are associated with a word. But there are several things that could be called changes in presuppositions, and thus it is less than clear (on an account that glosses meaning in terms of anything like ICG) what a change of or change in meaning is. Let me explain.

One expects that the presuppositions which constitute a word's meaning are realized in good part by standing cognitive states associated with dispositions to accept tokenings of sentences (in which the word is used) expressing the presupposition. When a presupposition is so realized, it is not too much of an idealization to think of it as being realized by something like a 'sentence stored in the head'. And even when what realizes a presupposition is not (a state associated with a disposition to accept) a sentence, a presupposition will often be realized by standing states with more or less natural, robust persistence conditions. So in general, when a presupposition is part of the basis of a word's meaning, there will be something—a state associated with accepting the sentence or some other persisting state—that we can identify as the vehicle of the presupposition. In the case in which a presupposition's vehicle in all or most of a

---

[12] Think for the moment of words and sentences as having identity conditions that are not semantic, but determined by such things as syntactic, phonological, and morphological (SPM) properties. Of course, the connections between word and sentence identity and these sorts of properties is messy, soritical, and just as puzzling as the connections between meaning and ICG. Still, an account that illuminated what sorts of changes (holding SPM properties constant) made for change of meaning would surely be useful.

population is (under idealization) the same, we can also speak of a vehicle for the presupposition at the level of the population as a whole.

The idea of little boxes in the head where I store the vehicles that determine what I presuppose about marriage, cats, and so forth will strike many as silly. But the idea that the states that determine presuppositions have fairly natural, fairly robust persistence conditions and tend ceteris paribus to persist—that idea strikes me as not silly at all. That's not to say that change in the vehicles of presupposition is never saltative— on Tuesday no one presupposes 'Der Horror-Clown ist der Fürher der Vereinigen Staaten'; on Wednesday everybody does. But change in the ensemble of the vehicles of a word's presuppositions is presumably something that's typically gradual. The ensemble of vehicles that realize the ICG of words like 'cousin', 'cat', and 'capellini' seems to persist with relatively small accretions and deletions in the short or medium term. Consider as an example the changes in the use of the verb 'marry' that occurred from 1975 to 2015 in America. For all the recent hue and cry about how these changes are leading to the end of the family, civilization, and country music, there really wasn't much of a change from 1975 to 2015 in what people accepted about marrying, thought people accepted about it, etc. In 1975, people accepted a litany of things about marriage that included:

(M)   Marriage is a contract between a man and a woman; one can't marry more than one person at a time; it is permissible for married people to have sex; it is widely thought to be wrong to have sex with a married person to whom one is not married; married people generally live together and share their property; married people mostly sleep in the same room; people very rarely marry before the age of sixteen; it is widely thought that people who have children should be married...

The first conjunct of (M) has, by 2015, fallen by the wayside. But all the rest is obviously accepted by all of us.

Now, 'accept' in the last paragraph is ambiguous. It is obvious that, save for the first, people of my advanced age accepted and would have assented to all the sentences in (M) in both 1975 and 2015. But one might well wonder whether those sentences (now) express claims that people (then) accepted. After all, we individuate claims partially in terms of their truth conditions: If I presuppose that S, you don't presuppose what I do unless you have a presupposition that's true iff S. And the truth conditions of the claim a sentence makes are determined (in part) by the reference of its parts: change the reference of 'marry' and you change the truth conditions of and thus the claim made by 'one can't marry more than one person at a time'.[13] But one might well say that as the word was used in 1975, 'marry' wasn't (and couldn't be) true of unions between members of the same sex, though as it's used today it is true of such unions.

---

[13] For those who think of truth conditions as sets of possible worlds as opposed to something like structured intentions, it's not *invariably* true that changing the reference of the part changes the truth conditions of the whole. But the issue here obviously arises in the possible worlds framework.

That is, one might propose that the reference(-cum-possible-worlds-intension or function from times to extensions or Kaplanian character) of 'marry' changed. Whether that's so is debatable, but it's certainly not obviously wrong. And so it's certainly not obvious that the claims made by members of (M) are constant across the decades.

But now take someone like me, who presupposed all of (what was expressed by) (M) in 1975 and today presupposes all of (what) it (now expresses), save for its first conjunct. How much of a shift in presuppositions about marriage did I undergo? If we focus on the underlying states that realize my presuppositions, it's not clear that there's much of a shift at all—I don't accept 'same-sex marriage is impossible' today; otherwise I accept pretty much what I used to. One way to understand talk about presupposition—and, more generally, attitude—retention is to understand it so that it suffices, for retaining a presupposition or other attitude, that the underlying psychological state persists.[14] On the other hand, we do appeal to reference and truth in identifying attitudes. And if we think about matters in this way, it looks as if we might have to say that—given that the reference of 'marry' has shifted—pretty much every presupposition I made about marriage in 1975 has been replaced by a new one.

How should we think about matters here? It's natural, of course, to follow ordinary usage. A non-philosopher wouldn't hesitate to say that in both 1975 and 2015 people assumed/knew/thought/believed that one can't marry more than one person at a time, that married people usually live together, etc., etc., etc. I suspect that many of your average non-philosophers wouldn't hesitate to say this even while also being ready to say that 'married' wasn't true of/couldn't be used to describe single-sex unions in 1975, though it can be now. Even a philosopher who recognizes the possibility that the reference of 'marry' has changed over time would say that people thought that one can't marry more than one person at a time and they still think so.[15] The upshot is that if we follow ordinary usage, we will say that even if the reference of 'marry' shifted from 1975 to 2015, the presuppositions that determined the meaning-cum-ICG of 'marry' didn't much change and so (all else being equal) there wasn't (in an interesting sense) a change in the word's meaning.

This is not an isolated case. Many of us are aware, or think we are aware, that 'water', as it was used by Boswell and Johnson, applied to things (e.g., urine) that it doesn't apply to today. But we will happily use sentences in which 'water' occurs to ascribe Boswell beliefs he would have expressed with those sentences; if we read, 'Johnson said that Scotland "consists of stone and water"', we happily say that Johnson said that Scotland consists of stone and water. Even apprised of the facts about usage, most of us would say that the word 'water' hasn't undergone (much of) a change in meaning.

We should try to take our practices of attitude ascription at face value. Someone who insists that we can't use the sentence 'one can't marry more than one person at a

---

[14] This needs to be stated with more finesse. Attempts to do so can be found in Perry (2000).
[15] If you doubt this, reread the first paragraph of this chapter and ask yourself if you disagreed with any of it on your first reading.

time' to report attitudes expressed by it in 1975 if the reference of 'marry' shifted from '75 to '15 is letting the tale of philosophers' theories wag the dog of use to which those theories are responsible.[16]

But how, exactly, are we to give the dog its due?

4. Referential Indeterminacy and Reported Speech

One way to try to answer this question is to engage in some paradox busting. Most of us would endorse each of the following—at least if it was presented to us apart from its comrades:

A. A use of a sentence says that Tim married Tina only if the use of the sentence says something that is (of necessity) true iff Tim married Tina.

B. If uses of 'marry' in 1975 picked out a relation different from the one current uses pick out, uses of 'Tim married Tina' in 1975 are not ones that say something that is (of necessity) true iff Tim married Tina.[17]

C. Uses of 'marry' in 1975 picked out a relation different from the one current uses pick out.

D. When Tom uttered, 'Tim married Tina' in 1975, he said that Tim married Tina.

But if you endorse all of these at once—well, laughing friends deride tears you cannot hide.

One thinks there must be truths in the neighborhood that we're attuned to, truths that we endorse and that are prompting our inclination to accept each of A through D in isolation. I think there are, and that the way to discover them is to reflect on how—and to what extent—the reference of our words is determined.

Suppose we begin with a Putnamian picture of how predicate reference is determined.[18] On this picture, at any time a predicate is associated with a set of paradigms ('good examples' of what the predicate does and does not apply to), principles for projecting from the paradigms to an ex- (and in-)tension, and a pattern of deference within the population of speakers, that helps determine how to apply the projective principles. Suppose (for now) that if we are confined to looking at the momentary facts about the three Ps—paradigms, principles of projection, and patterns of deference—for a predicate, there is a unique story to tell about what it refers to at that moment.[19] Does this make it plausible that there will be at each (or any) time a best story to tell about what the predicate refers to?

---

[16] There is a useful discussion of this issue in Dorr and Hawthorne (2014), who think the facts mentioned above are philosophically problematic. As will become clear, I am unconvinced that they are. Chapter 5 discusses Dorr and Hawthorne's article.

[17] For present purposes, think of relations as individuated in terms of their possible worlds intension.

[18] I mean something along the lines of the story told in Putnam (1975). I doubt that for present purposes it makes much difference which plausible account of reference determination we begin with.

[19] Or at least a very small number of more or less overlapping 'best stories' about reference to choose amongst. This disjunction should be understood as being carried over below.

Not at all. Use broadly construed, which includes the three Ps, shifts across time. What was and will be paradigmatic yesterday and tomorrow is relevant to the determination of what we're talking about today: we do not speak in a vacuum, without care to speak in continuity with those who came before and those to come. If a predicate's three Ps determine its reference at every time, it is because there is some non-arbitrary recipe that maps the progression of Ps associated with a predicate to the progression of references thereof. But why think there is such a recipe? Is the correct recipe ahistorical—let each instant decide its own reference? Or does it involve some sort of weighted averaging—the further away in time, the lower the weight—of instantaneous referents to find the referent at a time? Does the future weigh more heavily, since we acquire more knowledge of what we want to be talking about? Or does the magic recipe perhaps involve speakers' (counterfactual) judgments to determine a distinguished interval used to calculate reference? It is implausible that there is anything about patterns of use or the intentions and beliefs of users that makes one of these, or some other story, the acontextually correct story about reference.

Of course, the same sort of thing is true of instantaneous reference. Discussions of reference often seem to presuppose a picture on which a word's use is something like a collection of different forces, each pushing the word toward a particular part of the world, and thus a certain extension. To discover a word's extension on this picture, one sums the forces to get a single overall force; that total force gives the word a unique momentum through semantic space, thus determining a unique extension. Such discussions seem to assume that the various strands of a predicate's use must compose *somehow*, that there must be a recipe—a single recipe—for combining all the facts about the way we use a word so as to come up with a best candidate for the word's extension. But why on earth does that have to be the case? Consider, for example, the word 'dog'. Suppose that more or less the same 'mechanism' underlies all normal adult use of the word in perceptual situations. Given this, someone might suggest that to find the word's extension, we need to find the answer to the question, 'Which properties does this mechanism best register?' It would be silly to suggest that this question is irrelevant to the word's semantics. Someone else may observe that the word 'dog' is a member of a family of words that are associated with a kind of concept that has a long evolutionary history. She may claim that to find the word's extension we need to find the answer to the question, 'Which properties did this sort of concept evolve to register?' Again, it would be odd to suggest that the answer to this question is irrelevant to the word's semantics.

These questions point to different aspects of what is, broadly speaking, the 'use' of the word 'dog'. It is reasonable to think that both aspects—and many others besides—are relevant to the question, 'What are we talking about when we talk about dogs?' But why should we suppose that there is a best answer to the question, 'How do we balance the relevance of these two considerations, when they (as they probably will) pull in different directions?' Why are we to suppose that there is a single proper way to commensurate their differing effects in computing an extension?

My point is that if we confine attention to the sorts of facts that are usually taken to exhaust what our words are referring to, we will say that the reference of our terms is indeterminate. The indeterminacy is not the wild sort of indeterminacy that has it that it is as plausible that 'dog' is true of the members of some subset of the integers as it is that the word picks out things likely to be at the end of a leash. But it is an indeterminacy of more moment than that which arises because ... well, who can say which of the molecules detaching themselves from Rover's nose are actually part of Rover? The indeterminacy is not only synchronic (it's not completely clear whether 'dog' at the moment encompasses various canine/fox hybrids), but diachronic: it's often not determinate whether a word as used at one time has the same reference as it has as used at some other time.

If this is right,[20] then there is often no non-arbitrary answer to questions like

E.   Was 'dog' as used by Silke in 1820 true of the same things as 'dog' as used by Sara in 1950?

To say that there's no non-arbitrary answer to such questions is to say that there are incompatible answers to them that are equally good and no answers better than them. But to say this isn't to say there aren't any good answers to questions like E.

Talk about reference and truth conditions is partially beholden to the ways in which we interact with the world. We do not have to await consensus on the theory of reference to know that my domestic uses of 'Nancy' refer to someone who lives with me, and that my uses of 'woman' apply to people who resemble Nancy in various biological ways, while they don't apply to people who resemble me in other biological ways. Etcetera, etcetera. To say this is to acknowledge that something along the lines of Putnam's three Ps make up part of the story about reference, and to agree that there are what we might call causal constraints on an account of reference and truth conditions.

Talk about reference and truth conditions is partially beholden to the way we talk about modality, propositional attitudes, and truth itself. Such talk is talk about the properties of the claims our sentences make—we say that the claim, that Nalini's work on implicit bias was groundbreaking, is contingent, true, and believed by Susanna. Thus, the claims our sentences make are individuated in part in terms of reference and truth conditions. One does not have to endorse a Davidsonian principle of charity or humanity—on which it is something like a conceptual truth that most of what we say is true or at least justified—in order to think that humdrum claims about what others say and think ('he said that her work on implicit bias was groundbreaking') are routinely true and justified by what we think justifies them ('He uttered, "Nalini's work on implicit bias was groundbreaking"'). Surely routine claims about attitudes are by and large true and justified by what we take to justify them. To agree with this is to agree that there are what we might call interpretivist constraints on an account of reference and truth conditions.

[20] It is.

What makes an answer to a question like E a good answer is that it respects what our talk about reference and truth conditions is beholden to—it respects causal and interpretivist constraints—and does so at least as well as other answers to such questions.[21] Answers to such questions that have 'dog' talk being talk about a certain subset of the real line do not respect the constraints and so aren't good answers. But the causal and interpretivist constraints seem to leave considerable indeterminacy about the answer to a question like E, or for that matter,

E'. Was 'dog', as used by Silke in 2000, true of the same things as 'dog' as used by Sara in 2015?

But this should be something of a relief, given that we are trying to understand how it could be correct for Sara to report Silke's 'dog'-sayings homophonically—that is, if we are trying to understand why, when Silke utters, 'There's a large dog in my house' at t, it is routinely correct for Sara at t+n to use the report, 'Silke said that there was a large dog in her house', even though it might also be correct to assess Silke and Sara's uses of 'dog' as referring to different things.

Here's why. Assume, first of all, that when we ascribe an attitude with a sentence of the form *a Vs that S*, V a verb like 'says', we are ascribing a relation between a's referent and something determined by the complement *that S*. Assume further that what the latter is is something determined in part by the referential values and syntax of the sentence S—it is (at least in part) a structured proposition or structured intension, or a set of possible worlds, or a pairing of the sentence S with the meanings of its parts, or something of the sort. Since our worry at the moment is primarily about a lack of referential match between Silke's utterance and Sara's use of 'there was a large dog in her [Silke]'s house', these assumptions don't beg any questions. Assume as well that to say that it's indeterminate whether P is to say (something that implies) that abstracting from a particular context of utterance 'there's no fact of the matter' as to whether P, and that consequently (so abstracting) it's neither true nor false that P.

If Sara is a competent, tolerably well-informed speaker, her assessments of what Silke is talking about and what she is saying will be based on an interpretation *I* of Silke's vocabulary that respects the causal and interpretivist constraints mentioned two paragraphs back. This interpretation will match Silke's (uses of) words and phrases with Sara's (uses of) words and phrases; in using *I* to interpret her, Sara thereby assigns (Sara's) reference to Silke's utterances. It may well be that, abstracting from Sara's interests in making sense of Silke, it's indeterminate whether *I* is a correct interpretation of Silke. But if *I* does as well as any interpretation Sara can give of Silke and doesn't

---

[21] I'm open to the suggestion that I've missed a constraint on what makes an answer to E a good answer. For example, one might say that it is a constraint that it is done in a way that makes the behavior of the person being interpreted more or less rational.

I doubt that adding this constraint or other reasonable constraints floating around in the literature provides much hope of securing more determinacy for everyday talk's reference and truth conditions than is provided by the constraints just mentioned.

violate any reasonable constraint on interpretation, Sara can reasonably—indeed, correctly—take *I* to be a correct interpretation of Silke.

I don't expect much argument against the claim that if Sara's interpretation *I* violates no reasonable constraints and is as good a one as Sara could employ, then it's reasonable for Sara to employ it. But how, you might ask, can *I* be a correct interpretation when it is ex hypothesi indeterminate whether *I* is correct?

Well, it is only indeterminate whether *I* is correct in abstraction from a particular context and set of interests. But when the 'standing meaning' of an expression or construction manages to partially determine its reference—when the expression is vague or otherwise indeterminate—the interests and purposes of users in a particular context can and do sharpen reference. Those interests and purposes can and do make a particular mode of use—a mode which, outside of any context, is not determinately correct—correct. This sort of thing is quite generally true of terms with indeterminate or incomplete or not wholly fixed semantics. For example, we often sharpen meaning using the sorts of mechanisms David Lewis (1979) pointed out: we say things that would be true only if reference were sharpened in a certain way; if no one objects (ceteris paribus and within limits), reference is so sharpened.

In the case at hand, Sara brings a particular set of interests with her when she interprets Silke; in particular, she wants to make sense of Silke by interpreting Silke's linguistic behavior in Sara's own idiom. She proceeds to interpret Silke in a particular (more or less homophonic) way, in a way to which no one can object: given Sara's interests and what constraints there are on interpretation, there is no better way of interpreting Silke. This suffices to make Sara's way of interpreting Silke correct in context.

Of course someone with different interests, in a different context, might interpret Silke differently from the way in which Sara interprets her. And all else being equal—in particular, if the other interpretation satisfies whatever constraints there are on interpretation—that interpretation in that context will be correct. Likewise, for the case that sparked this discussion: Given the indeterminacy of what people are talking about when they use their words, a speaker can in one context correctly say something whose correctness requires that 'marry' in 1975 applies to what it applies to in 2015, while some other speaker in some other context can correctly say something whose correctness requires that the reference of 'marry' varies from 1975 to 2015.

5. Paradox Lost

We were wondering about the status of the apparently inconsistent quartet:

A. A use of a sentence says that Tim married Tina only if the use of the sentence says something that is (of necessity) true iff Tim married Tina.

B. If uses of 'marry' in 1975 picked out a relation different from the one current uses pick out, uses of 'Tim married Tina' in 1975 are not ones that say something that is (of necessity) true iff Tim married Tina.

C. Uses of 'marry' in 1975 picked out a relation different from the one current uses pick out.

D. When Tom uttered, 'Tim married Tina' in 1975, he said that Tim married Tina.

A and B express truths in any conversation. The truths of C and D vary from situation to situation, depending on what interests govern the projects of interpreting Tom and speech in 1975. Our practice of interpreting the speech of others is fluid, and whether we will interpret others using common words as referring to the things we refer to with those words is interest-dependent. Given that there is a certain amount of indeterminacy in whether another is speaking about exactly what we speak of with a word, it seems pretty obvious that our practice here is the best we could hope for.

Our interest in A through D was prompted by an interest in questions about propositional attitudes. We were wondering, first of all,

Q1.   How can we be entitled to think that our 'homophonic reports' of sayings and reports of others—especially reports of past thinkings and sayings—are correct, given that we have good reason to think that the reference of the words they and we use might have shifted, so that they referred to something different from what we do with the words?

Relatedly, we wanted to know the answer to

Q2.   Are we really entitled to think that we share many or even most of our presuppositions about marriage with our parents and grandparents?

So far as Q1 and Q2 go, I think the answer is clear. Our everyday practice is to pretty much invariably make ourselves the arbiters of the reference of those we interpret. If there's not been too much shift in the vehicles of the presuppositions that surround the words in a sentence like 'Tim married Tina' or 'Pasta is easy to make if you have a machine to roll out the dough', we generally interpret the other as talking about what we are talking about. If what I said about reference in the last section was correct, this is our right. Given that it is our right, we are entitled to be confident in thinking such things as that when someone writes, 'At the most fundamental level, a gay marriage is impossible because the same-sex couple can never consummate their marriage; they can never become one flesh (or unify)', they said that same-sex marriage is impossible.[22]

In the discussion in this and the last section I've presupposed that it's reasonable to say that 'marry' as I used it in 1975 picked out a different relation than the one it picks out when I use it now. But that's not the only reasonable interpretation of the word; it's not the interpretation we're using when we interpret utterances in the past homophonically—that is, for example, when we interpret a past utterance of 'Tim married Tina' as saying that Tim married Tina. Now, someone might insist that there has to be an 'ultimate', non-perspectival answer to a question like

---

[22] http://www.aboutcatholics.com/beliefs/why-gay-marriage-is-impossible. (Accessed February 4, 2019. Don't get me started.)

Q3. Did 'marriage' shift reference between 1975 and 2015?

Given what I said in responding to Q1 and Q2, I must say that there is no determinate answer to this question—that is, no answer that is, given any reasonable interpretive interests and purposes, the answer to Q3. But that's not to say we can't answer it. We can, for example, stipulate that the interests and purposes of speakers of 1975 are to be the primary determinants of what they were talking about with 'marry' and that our interests and purposes are the primary determinant of what we are talking about. That's a perfectly reasonable way to think about things, and it may well determine an answer. But it's not the only reasonable way to think about things; in fact, it's apparently not the way we usually think about such matters.

There are questions like Q3 that appear to have more determinate answers than it does. One can, for example, ask whether there has been a shift between 1975 and today in what would be a reasonable interpretation of someone's use of 'marry'. If reasonable synchronic interpretations are made reasonable in good part by what is common ground and by the typical or normal interests of interpreters, this sort of question may have a fairly sharp, more or less determinate answer.

If all this seems to make questions—in particular, diachronic questions—about reference nebulous: well, to a certain extent they are nebulous. But they are not that nebulous. There are, for example, no acceptable interpretations of 'married' on which it did not apply to Dick and Pat Nixon, Eric Clapton and Patti Boyd; there are none on which it does apply to JFK and Marilyn Monroe, Kendrick Lamar and Taylor Swift.[23]

---

[23] How is the position sketched in this section related to Quine's ideas about referential inscrutability?

Quine thought that translation is grounded by nothing more than 'what is to be gleaned from overt behavior in observable circumstances' (Quine 1992, 38). This sort of thing determines acceptable translations of 'observation sentences'—'sentences that are directly and firmly associated affirmatively with some range of one's stimulations and negatively with some range' (Quine 1992, 3)—as well as the logic of 'and', 'not', and 'or'. But even if we know that we can adequately translate another's sentence 'Pupkins' with our 'Lo, a dog', we don't have a basis for thinking that the other speaks of dogs when she uses the sentence. For the 'range of stimulations' which we directly and affirmatively associate with 'Lo, a dog' is identical with the range we directly and affirmatively associate with 'Lo, a temporal stage of a dog' as well as with 'canine-ish appearance at 12 o'clock'. Because of this, Quine claims, these two sentences are no worse as a translation of 'Pupkins' than is 'there's a dog'. Quine concludes that reference is indeterminate: 'it makes no sense to say what the objects of a theory are, beyond saying how to interpret or reinterpret that theory in another' (Quine 1969c, 57).

I think Quine's skepticism is overdone. I agree that there is a healthy indeterminacy as to whether, for example, samples of green tea are things of which 'water' as it's used in the everyday is true. But I reject Quine's linguistic behaviorism. Psychological structures like prototypes and schemata as well as (innate) psychological states involved in the analysis of perception and the generation of 'core concepts' are shared by all normal humans. They are associated in the course of language learning with both lexical items and more complex phrases. This association helps ground translation, I would say, in a way that supports our everyday practices of interpretation without offering support to the idea that 'Pupkins' means something like, 'Oh, lo, an animated piece of the sum of the canine world'. This and what I called in this section causal constraints on translation, I would say, reduces but does not eliminate referential indeterminacy.

It would be too much of a detour to defend the claims in the last paragraph. A good example of the sort of response to Quine's behaviorism I have in mind is Carey (2009), though not everyone agrees that Carey succeeds. The last section of this chapter gives a bit more discussion of referential (in)determinacy;

6. Referential Relativism?

Perhaps you are thinking the position just sketched is untenable. Didn't I just endorse all the following: I can say A's use of term t refers to R and be correct; you can say that A's use of t doesn't refer to R and be correct; so there's something (that A used t to refer to R) that's true for me, not true for you. Eew, relativism; that is *so* 2004. It's just too big a theoretical cost to pay, simply in order to endorse our happy-go-lucky homophonic practices of ascribing attitudes.

Actually, this isn't quite what I just endorsed, and the picture I'm sketching doesn't entail anything that deserves the epithet (or honorific) 'relativism'. The view I've been pushing clearly requires that something is relativized, for the view is that absent the purposes and intentions of a speaker, a theorist, or a collection of conversants, there is often no fact of the matter as to whether two utterances have the same semantics or say the same thing. If we think of a language as something that inter alia pairs utterances with semantics and sayings, a slightly bent version of the point is that absent interpretive choices, there is often no fact of the matter as to whether two utterances are to be understood as being made in the same language. This does not by itself imply anything like relativism, at least not if we think of my saying that A's use of t refers to R is saying something like: When A uses t, I understand her as speaking a language in which t refers to R.

What might seem relativistic in the above picture is what it implies about our talk about what others say and think. Suppose that you and I are interpreting A's utterance of the sentence, 'There's a dog in front of my house'. You and I, we may suppose, are coordinated in interpreting each other: we each interpret the other's use of 'dog', 'house', and so on with our own 'dog', 'house', and so on. But we differ on A: I interpret her 'dog' with my 'dog', but you do not, as you take her use of the term, but not ours, to apply to both *Canis familiaris* and doxes, dog–fox hybrids. So I take A to have said that there is a dog in front of her house, but you deny that; you say she said that there is dog-or-dox there. If each of our interpretive schemes is acceptable, I speak truly in my idiom when I utter

T: A said that there is a dog in front of her house;

you speak truly in your idiom when you utter T's denial. But, one might worry, doesn't T express the same thing in our respective idioms? So don't we have some thought (that A said there's a dog in front of her house) that's true for me, false for you?

No. Sayings are just that—they are assertive utterances of sentences. To say that A said such and such is a matter of interpreting her utterance in a particular way: my ascription involves one interpretation, I^{me} of A, yours another, I^{you}. What 'involves'

discussion of how the referential determinacy of terms like 'puppy' is consistent with things like the indeterminacy of the constitution and location of physical objects occurs in Richard (ms.).

means here can be cashed out in various ways. One might do this in terms of presupposition, or one might say that the best gloss of the syntax of *x said that S* is one on which it involves reference to or quantification over ways of interpreting. But on either gloss, whether what I or you say about A is correct turns on what interpretation of A we are using. So, yes, there is a kind of relativization here, but it is not a relativism on which some claim is true-for-me, false-for-you. We (may assume that we) both speak of the same person, A, and the same claim, that there is a dog in front of her house, when I say that the first asserted the second and you deny it; but there are different interpretive schemes involved in our assertions. Telegraphing the point: one can understand what is going on here in ways similar to the way in which a contextualist understands what is going on in certain cases in which people differ as to whether someone is rich. The contextualist tells us that claims that people are rich are claims that presuppose, refer to, or quantify over standards or scales, and so the difference is not one of incompatible beliefs, but over what scale of measurement is to be employed.

You may still be skeptical. From what position or perspective can someone coherently say that you and I are each correct about the interpretation of A's speech, though our interpretations are inconsistent? I can't say your interpretation is correct, since that would imply that my own interpretation is not. And some third party isn't really any better off, since they presumably will be committed to some interpretation of A.

Frankly, I don't see the problem. Theorizing about language and the humdrum business of deciding what A is talking about are different activities; I can suspend the commitments I take on in the latter while engaging in the former when I say that there are a variety of acceptable ways to interpret A's speech and thought, and that when someone speaks of what A says or thinks, they are to be understood as using or presupposing a particular way of interpreting her.[24] I can say that you used an acceptable interpretation of A and that relative to it, you said something correct about her without contradicting or otherwise undermining my own humdrum talk of what she said. You and I are 'speaking inconsistently' in interpreting A in the sense that we are using schemes of interpretation that can't be used simultaneously by a single interpreter. Big deal.[25]

---

[24] This is a little too strong, as it may not be determinate which among a class of interpretive strategies someone presupposes. It would serve no purpose beyond obfuscatory ones to qualify the text in this way.

[25] A caution: My purpose in this section wasn't to argue *against* a 'relativist' understanding of attitude ascriptions, by which I mean an understanding of sentences like T on which

(a) they express the same claim in different contexts (so you deny what I say if I use T assertively and you so use its negation), and;

(b) that claim can vary in truth across contexts (as it would if its truth-in-a-context turned on whether T's complement interprets an utterance of A's relative to the mode of interpretation used in the context).

My purpose is not to argue against this, but simply to show that the view I've sketched isn't *committed* to a relativistic understanding of what's said by sentences like T. For an exposition and defense of various sorts of relativism about what's said by sentences like T see Richard (2015) and Spencer (2016).

7. Referentialism

The announced topic of this chapter is change of meaning: the sorts of changes in the way a word is used and its semantic, social, and broadly causal properties and relations that suffice for its being apt to say that the word no longer means what it did. Given that this is our topic, the last few sections have been something of a digression. We digressed because we are thinking of meaning in terms of interpretative common ground and therefore as something constituted by presuppositions. It thus seemed apt to ask to what extent presuppositions persist through changes that may bring changes of reference in their train. Our verdict was that it is reasonable to think that, for example, both we and our recent ancestors presuppose that married people typically have children (and express this with the words 'married people typically have children'), even if it is also reasonable to think that 'marry' has enjoyed something of recent reference shift. That each of these is (separately) a reasonable way to think about things is a result of referential indeterminacy: it is indeterminate what the recipe for mapping diachronic use onto reference is; such indeterminacy is resolved on an ad hoc basis in interpreting others, typically by homophonous interpretation when cultural distance is not too great. Because of this, it is reasonable to interpret our forebears as talking about marriage with 'marriage'. This is not contradicted by the fact that it is also reasonable to interpret them otherwise.

Let us return to our announced topic. The received view in semantics and philosophy of language is that there is an analytic or quasi-analytic connection between meaning and truth. Scott Soames, for example, tells us that instances of

M: If s means in L that P, then s is true in L iff P

are 'obvious and knowable a priori', and that

> there is a conceptual or analytic connection between our ordinary notions of truth and meaning... This may be seen by noting that when no indexicality is involved and a sentence expresses the same proposition on different occasions of use, talk about its meaning is, for all intents and purposes, interchangeable with talk of the proposition it expresses.... The 'analytic connection' between truth and meaning is the result of three facts: (i) to say that a sentence s means in L that P is to say that s expresses the proposition that P in L; (ii) to say that s is true in L is to say that the proposition expressed in L is true; (iii) instances of the propositional schema
>
> PT: The proposition that P is true iff P
>
> are trivial, a priori, and necessary.   (Soames 1999, 105–6)

If we go along with Soames here, we may seem to have a partial answer to the question, 'Under what conditions does a word undergo change of meaning?' For suppose—as Soames does in this passage—that what's picked out by a use of the complement *that S* is individuated (in part) in terms of propositions à la Russell—structured entities composed of the objects, properties, and relations picked out by uses of the words in S. Then any change in what a word picks out—any change in reference—is a change in the propositions expressed by sentences in which the word is used. So changes in reference are changes of meaning.[26]

Even if we don't accept (i) or the idea that what is said is well thought of in Russell's terms, we may well think that M is trivial. And if we do, we will probably be sympathetic to the idea that a change in reference (or in possible worlds intension) suffices for a change of meaning. For given M, a change in the meaning of a word that results in a change of truth value in some sentence in which the word is used must be a change of the sentence's meaning. If meaning is determined compositionally, this means that the change of meaning of the word is responsible for the change of meaning of the sentence. It seems rather unlikely that only changes of reference that result in changes of truth value occasion change of meaning. M implies that referential shift is meaning shift.

A natural generalization of this idea—one that allows us to stop ignoring such things as tense and indexicality—uses David Kaplan's (1989) idea of an expression's character, the rule that assigns to a potential use of the expression in a sentence what the use contributes to what the sentence says. In the case of a word like 'marry'—ignoring whatever polysemy and homophony it might have—the word's character today is the rule that assigns the word's use (today, yesterday, or tomorrow) the relation we (today) pick out with the word.[27]

Kaplan proposed that character be identified with meaning, so that for him change in character is not only sufficient but necessary for sameness of meaning. If we think of meaning as species-like—so that meanings are population-level entities, reifications of historical patterns of communicative language use among speakers—we won't go quite this far, since words in different linguistic communities, communities quite unable to communicate with one another, may have the same character. But one might still entertain the idea that within a linguistic community, diachronic constancy of character is necessary and sufficient for identity of meaning. The next few sections are devoted to a discussion of this proposal, a proposal that I'll refer to as referentialism.

Before I begin this discussion, I want to recur to the issue of how those of us who theorize about language use the word 'meaning'. I have said several times that talk about meaning serves several purposes. People say they are talking about meaning when they are theorizing about properties and relations of phrases that determine: conditions of competence and comprehension; truth conditions of sentence uses; how sentences can be used to characterize attitudes like saying and believing. This book is primarily an attempt to say something useful about meaning in the sense of what

---

[26] This way of putting things requires taking relations to the referents of predicates. If that bothers you, you can probably see how to rephrase this to eliminate that presupposition.

[27] I'm assuming here that (tense ignored) 'married [to]' is not contextually sensitive—that it has a constant character in Kaplan's terminology. If so, then the character of 'marry' maps every context to the same function from pairs of a world and a time to an extension; if so, then, if some actual use of 'married' is true of the pair <a.b> at t, any actual use of 'married' is true of <a,b> at t. Section 9 discusses the idea that 'marry' is contextually sensitive in the sense that it picks out quite different relations (i.e., functions from times to extensions) in different contexts.

determines whether one is a competent speaker, someone who is able to participate in quotidian conversation in a more or less seamless manner. I acknowledge that there are senses of 'meaning' in which someone who is doing truth-conditional semantics or is giving an account of how sentences are associated with (things that can be used to characterize) the contents of our thoughts, assertions, hopes, and dreams is doing something that is and should continue to be called semantics. But it is not trivial or obvious that semantics in this sense gives us an answer to questions about what it is to be a competent speaker. Competence is not explained or well theorized by saying something like: To be a competent speaker of a language L is a matter of knowing, for each sentence s of L, what's expressed by an instance of a use of *S in L says that P*. Much of Chapter 3 is an argument for this claim.

Soames, it is worth observing, agrees. In a discussion of the relations of semantics and semantic competence, he observes that much of what we are able to think or dream we are able to think or dream only because we speak a language in which it is expressible. We do not become competent speakers of a language in which there is a sentence that expresses the proposition expressed by

C: Consumers strive to achieve the mix of purchases that maximizes the utility that can be achieved given their income

by having a prior grasp of the proposition and then associating it with C; most of us acquire the ability to think what C says by becoming competent in our language. In particular, we do not come to understand 'utility' by having a prior grasp of relation of utility and assigning it to the word; we come to understand sentences in which the word is used and (thus) the word; once understanding is achieved, we are able to think about utility. As Soames notes:

If this is right, then a natural and seductive picture of language acquisition and linguistic competence is fundamentally mistaken. According to this picture, we have the ability, prior to the acquisition of language, to form beliefs and entertain propositions. In setting up a language, we adopt certain conventions according to which sentences come to express these antecedently apprehended propositions. Learning the language amounts to learning for each sentence, which antecedently apprehended proposition it expresses.

The most fundamental thing wrong with this picture is that in the case of many sentences, we do not grasp the propositions they express prior to understanding the sentences themselves. As a result, coming to understand these sentences does not consist in searching through our stock of propositions to find the ones assigned to them. Rather, coming to understand the sentences is a matter of satisfying conventional standards regarding their use. Just what these standards are is not well understood. However, whatever they are, once they are satisfied, one is counted not only as understanding new sentences, but also as grasping new propositions. As a result, learning a language is not just a matter of acquiring a new tool for manipulating information one already possesses; it is also a means of expanding one's cognitive reach.   (Soames 1989, 589)

Part of what I am trying to do in this book is to give some articulation of what it is to 'satisfy conventional standards regarding [the] use' of our terms and thereby come to understand them.

I say this in part to forestall certain objections to what follows. I will express a good deal of skepticism about referentialism—about, that is, the idea that sentences change their meaning when (and only when) they change their character, their truth conditions, or what they say. When I do this, I am not objecting to the claim that there is a way of using 'means' on which instances of M are obvious and trivial. What I am objecting to is the idea that it is obvious or trivial that meaning in the sense of what we must absorb in order to be competent speakers is well theorized simply in terms of (knowledge of) reference, satisfaction, truth conditions, or propositions-cum-what-we-pick-out with complements of the form that S.

8. Meaning (Sort of) Divorced from Reference

One might argue that sameness of meaning requires sameness of reference—arguing, as it were, for half of referentialism—as follows. A grasp of reference is required for understanding particular utterances: to understand an utterance of 'Julia est française', I must know who the speaker is referring to with 'Julia' and what property is ascribed to her with 'est française'. Surely this generalizes from particular utterances to group usage: one understands 'Julia est française' as it is used by a particular group to the extent that one knows, for the range of references that are standard in the group for its parts, that those are the standard references for those parts. In fact, one needs the ability to more or less reliably suss out in normal contexts of use which use of the parts a speaker is making. But now suppose the reference of a word shifts. If there isn't a change in the knowledge and abilities that enable me to know what the word's reference is, I will no longer understand the word, as I won't be able to (reliably) determine its reference. So a shift in a word's reference entails a shift in what one must know in order to understand the word, and thus a shift in its meaning.

One relatively minor problem with this argument is that the sort of 'knowledge of reference' required for understanding is not one that precisely articulates the bounds of a predicate's extension. To understand an East Hampton native's utterance of 'The rich people who come here in summer have ruined the town', there's no need to know how the native draws a line between the rich and the rest. What the competent auditor does in understanding—what in some sense reflects her competence—is to suss out, given some clues from the context, a rough delimitation of the area in which the speaker would lay a line separating the have-a-lots from the rest of us. But if understanding a use of 'rich' is a matter of circumscribing a reasonable area within which lies its extension, shifts in the extension of the word don't have to be accompanied by shifts in the way I circumscribe the area within which the reference is to be found in order to preserve understanding. To put the point crudely: The target for understanding is a red line bisecting the scale that measures resources; the ability to understand is an ability which, given a use, draws a circle around a portion of the scale; understanding is achieved when the ability enables me to reliably enclose the red line in a reasonably sized circle. A shift to, say, the right of the red drawn by a use of 'rich' need not be accompanied by a shift in the rule that draws the circle in order for the circle to reliably indicate a reasonably sized area in which the red occurs.

This is a problem, but not the primary problem, with the argument. The argument correctly claims that understanding a word involves an ability to suss out what it is used to talk about. How is such an ability realized? This is an empirical matter, and a one-size-fits-all answer is unlikely. That said, presumably central to the answer is something like this. Focus on the word 'rich'. To have the ability needed to understand it involves being able to reliably determine what sorts of assumptions about wealth accompany a use of the word, and, on the basis of one's assessment of them (and perhaps some other input), being able to draw the sort of circle on the line of wealth mentioned in the last paragraph. How, in turn, would this ability normally be realized? One thinks that crucial to such an ability is 'being in touch' with what assumptions about wealth are commonly made by speakers—one needs, after all, a place to start in interpretation. What grounds the ability to understand uses of 'rich' in a group is, in part, one's ongoing monitoring of the ICG that surrounds the use of the word in the group.

Grant for the moment that this is correct. What would then be involved in understanding 'rich' as it is used by a group G? Well, the normal route involves something like this: one tracks the ICG surrounding the word in G more or less reliably, registers the ways it changes, and makes use of the information this monitoring provides in interpretation. Understanding the word is thus in good part a matter of tracking a process (the evolution of ICG) and, at various times, making use of the information such tracking provides. It's an ability, something that endures as the contents of ICG fluctuate, that provides a somewhat stable but shifting bank of information which constitutes one's understanding of the word.

If this is correct, what constitutes understanding—'knowledge of meaning'—is in part a persisting ability to track a process, in part a fluctuating store of information garnered by the ability. It is not having some particular nugget of knowledge—a small chest of propositions or an immutable rule for placing an oval over a line. But the argument we are discussing seems to presuppose that this last is what understanding is: the picture is that understanding the word is something keyed to a particular target (reference), and that it has to shift as the target does. At this point it shouldn't be necessary to observe that thinking of things in this way is pretty much of a piece with thinking that species are defined by a set of morphologies or ecological niches or genetic variants, so that change in shape, habitat, or bone density is destructive of a species.

All this suggests an argument against referentialism. Meaning as we are conceiving of it is what grounds linguistic competence. The natural measure of such competence is the ability to engage in fluid conversation. If this measures competence, then insofar as a change in a property or relation of a word does not by itself impede fluid communication between the word's users and their audience, that change shouldn't count as a change of meaning. But the fact that we are able (effortlessly!) to understand texts from the not terribly distant past without tutoring, even when changes that can be understood to be reference-changing have occurred—this fact argues strongly that meaning (in the sense we are discussing) can persist through reference change. When a change does not stymy conversation or seriously inhibit interpretation, it is not a change of meaning.[28]

I should perhaps say something to answer the question, 'What is it for fluid conversation to be stymied by a difference in the way speakers understand a word?'[29] To give a tolerably clear answer, we need a bit of groundwork. Individual conversations are fluid to the extent they involve successful interpretation of individual sentences.[30] Successful interpretation of a sentence utterance is a matter of two things: applying an ability to, given the semantic values of its simple items and of its syntactic modes of combination, work out what would and would not make the utterance correct; more or less correctly picking up on the things associated with individual words which the speaker expects you to recognize she wants you to recognize her as assuming.

Reasonably fluid conversation is projectably the norm within a language community: people generally know how utterances represent the world as being and what the speaker presupposes in speaking; the norm is that in normal situations people in a language community who have not been in conversational contact with one another immediately understand one another when they speak. We thus generalize from the fluidity of individual conversations to community conversational fluidity. Such fluidity is the most obvious manifestation of what makes it correct to speak of a shared language in the first place. It stands to the fact that a community shares a language much as reasonable reproductive fecundity stands to the fact that a population consists of conspecifics.

I have been assuming that when a speaker speaks, she makes presuppositions that are associated with the words she uses, presuppositions she expects her audience to recognize that she (wants them to recognize that she) makes. Call those such assumptions a speaker associates with her use of *e* in an utterance u u's *passing e* assumptions. And call the presuppositions which a speaker S thinks it is common knowledge that users of *e* expect their audience to recognize that they (want the audience to recognize that they) make S's *take* on *e*.[31] The norm will be that when there is conversation among members of a group G whose members share a language, there is a pretty strong overlap between the passing *e* assumptions in the conversation, the conversants' takes on *e*, and the ICG that surrounds *e* in G: if that weren't the case, it would not be the case that within G its members mean the same thing with *e*.

---

[28] More precisely: when a change that is not the introduction of a new usage of a word does not stymy or seriously inhibit interpretation, it is not a change of meaning. Changes that are introductions of new usages are discussed in Section 10.

[29] I am indebted to readers for the Press for insisting that I do so.

[30] Well, of course it involves more than that. One needs to pick up on what illocutionary acts are being performed and on what dialogic, narrative, rhetorical, and other relations sentences uses have to one another. But for the purpose at hand, which is discussing change of meaning of lexical items, we can use a notion of interpretation that rests at the sentential level.

[31] The notion of a take on an expression by a speaker needs various relativizations, but making them would at this point be only obfuscatory.

So what is it for fluid conversation to be stymied in a community by a difference in the way speakers understand a word *e*? Such a difference stymies conversation to the extent that, because of it, the passing *e* assumptions in the community are misidentified with the result being one or another sort of incomprehension—as in, 'what do you mean "his husband"?? He's a man, he can't have a husband!' Clearly, such stymieing is a matter of degree: a change in one person's use of *e* may hamper only a few, a good number, or an overwhelming majority of community members' comprehension of that person's use of *e*. Clearly, the extent in which a change in one person's use of a word stymies communication may be only transitory: at first, uses of 'gay' to pick out people who are gay might have been met with blank stares; as the use became entrenched and widely recognized, not so much.

Stymieing in the first instance is a concept of a synchronic effect: a change in the way I use 'marriage' makes my uses right now incomprehensible to you right now. But as I intimated above, we can make a certain amount of sense of diachronic stymieing and take it as a sufficient condition for change of meaning. We do in a straightforward sense engage in attempts at (one-way) communication when we try to interpret inscriptions, films, and YouTube videos from the past, and such interpretation can be difficult or impossible because of shifts in interpretive ground.

One might be tempted to generalize here to solve the linguistic version of the species problem with a 'counterfactual stymieing criterion', much as a fan of the biological species concept might be tempted to say that temporally separated members of a lineage are of a species provided that were their biological duplicates to be temporally and spatially proximate, they would be potentially fecund or recognize one another as rivals or as potential mates. Though I don't think such a criterion can be made to work, some discussion is in order.

A counterfactual criterion for a word's changing meaning in a lineage of speakers might go as follows. We imagine users from the earlier time transported forward in time in such a way that they have no inkling of the change and ask if ceteris paribus that ignorance would impede attempts to interpret and communicate at the later time. We imagine speakers from the later time to be transported backwards in such a way that they have no inkling of the difference and ask the same thing. If no impediments are found in either direction, that is reason to say that there is no change of meaning.

The proposal seemingly agrees with what I suggested above, that a shift in the reference of a predicate in a population need not impede fluid communication. Consider the word 'pasta' as used when it entered English in the mid-nineteenth century.[32] The word was appropriated from Italian, and (so far as I can determine[33]) the Italian word was applied only to wheat-based food. My guess is that in 1890 the suggestion that

---

[32] There seem to be uses in the 1840s of the term as a word of English in the OED, though as the uses are in discussions of food in Italy, they could be interpreted as a kind of word poaching that falls short of expanding the lexicon.

[33] But I have not made an attempt to cull Italian nineteenth-century writing on pasta.

there could be rice pasta, agar or seaweed pasta, bacon-infused agar pasta,[34] acorn starch pasta, or Konjac pasta[35] would have been met by many, perhaps pretty much all, Italians as roughly as plausible as the suggestion that Lutheranism or Calvinism was a variety of Catholicism. Likewise, I suspect, for most or pretty much all English speakers. Today it easy to find internet references to all the above-mentioned pagan pastas.

Consider now a nineteenth-century chef from London transported to Yotam Ottolenghi's Islington kitchen who witnesses him teaching a class on making squash pasta. She might be surprised and distressed by what she heard, but she would immediately, effortlessly understand what was being said. (That she might think, 'but the spotulism he's making isn't pasta' doesn't show that she doesn't understand; we do not misunderstand simply because we disagree.) Something similar would be true of time travel in reverse. To the extent that such counterfactuals generalize across the relevant populations, we do not have meaning change.

There are many objections you might make to this proposal, some more telling than others. On the less telling side, you might object that it doesn't follow from the fact that the chef automatically understands Ottolenghi and vice versa that 'pasta' means the same in the chef's mouth as it does in Yotam's. The chef, you might say, can see—any nineteenth-century speaker competent with 'pasta' could see—that the word is being used for edibles shaped, cooked, and probably dressed like traditional spaghetti, macaroni, fusilli, and so on. The chef draws an inference, from her knowledge of how 'pasta' was used in the past and the particulars of her situation, to the word's meaning in that situation.

Quite so: what the nineteenth-century chef knows about the use of 'pasta' puts her in a position to effortlessly grasp Yotam's use. Coming into the conversation, the chef knows that people use 'pasta' for edibles shaped in certain ways (as tubes, strings, corkscrews, etc.) that are cooked in boiling water, are typically served warm and dressed with certain sauces (tomato, olio e aglio, etc.), and which are made by combining durum wheat, water, and salt, sometimes with the addition of eggs, squid ink, herbs, etc. Analogously for Yotam's knowledge under projection back in time to watch the chef train her underlings in the proper way to make pasta.[36] The question is not whether Yotam and the chef are required to make inferences, from what they know and the situation they find themselves in, in order to interpret. One always needs to draw inferences from one's linguistic knowledge and the situation to arrive at an interpretation. Rather, the question is whether Yotam and the chef's linguistic knowledge enables each of them to seamlessly construct the ICG the other's use occupies. If it does, we have the sort of continuity in ICG and similarity in ability to track it that can be said to constitute sameness of meaning.

---

[34] It's a thing. See http://www.instructables.com/id/Molecular-Gastronomy-Bacon-Agar-Spaghetti (this article speaks of agar pasta as well as agar spaghetti).

[35] http://www.amazon.com/Konjac-Shirataki-Angel-Pasta-Noodles/dp/B001IQ1ITM (konjac comes from the root of something sometimes called a yam plant, though it's not related to the yam).

[36] What counterfactual scenario should be considered here is tricky; we presumably don't want Yotam to bring with him historical knowledge about past use.

In this case it's possible to appeal to a bit of cognitive psychology to buttress the idea that there is conceptual continuity. It's a commonplace that a good deal of our expectations and knowledge are stored in what are often called schemata: cognitive structures which allow us to organize information in a way that is easily accessible and easily modified. One sort of plausible schema is that of a template that can be used repeatedly to structure and store information about various determinations of a kind. Take, for example, the kind foodstuff. We have concepts of various foodstuffs—pasta, salad, pickle, dessert, and so on. Our various individual conceptions have a good deal in common, in part one thinks because those conceptions share a common structure. They are all in part the results of filling in (at least some of) the blanks in a schema that looks like this:

Name of foodstuff: _____
It is made out of _____
It is served cooked/uncooked _____
If cooked, cooked as follows: _____
It is a part of a meal/eaten outside of meals _____
If part of a meal, served when: _____
It is associated with such and such a cultural tradition: _____

...

If the ICG surrounding a term for a foodstuff is in good part a matter of information that is generated by filling in such a schema, then the meaning of the term has a particular structure. This structure—and most of its filling—persists through relatively small changes in individual conceptions—it persists when people change the entry in the first slot from wheat, salt, water (and sometimes egg) to a disjunction of this with such things as flavored agar. And so we have at least two reasons for saying that relatively small changes in the presuppositions that constitute an individual's conception of a foodstuff do not generally make for a change in concept, even if they do make for a change in reference. First of all, such changes do not result in the enduring mental structure realizing the concept—that constituted by the schema and the way in which its slots are filled in—passing out of existence or even changing in a radical way. Given that the presumption is that the persistence of this structure and a good deal of its filling is the persistence of the concept, the presumption is that such changes do not drive the concept out of existence. Secondly, such changes can be reliably predicted not to inhibit comprehension. If all that has changed in speaker S's pasta concept, between the time auditor A last encountered S and her current attempt at interpreting S is adding the disjunct *bacon-infused agar*, A can be expected to quickly and reliably see that something along these lines is the case. And so comprehension will be immediate. Whether reference has changed is neither here nor there.

I've been responding to what I see as a misguided objection to the counterfactual criterion floated above, the objection being that it mistakes continuity in the ability to interpret given observable context for continuity of meaning. But there are more serious objections to the proposal. Unsurprisingly, it has problems kindred to those that plague many attempts to extend one or another synchronic criterion for conspecifics to a diachronic one. Take, as an example, the proposal that animals are conspecific provided that they share a system that allows them to recognize each other as potential mates. Mate recognition systems are, like other biological systems, subject to evolution. Would today's black rhinoceroses recognize their black rhinoceros forebears in the Miocene as potential hook-up partners? It's not clear, but it is clear that biologists speak in ways that imply that there is a single species, the black rhinoceros, that arose in the early Miocene and persists today. Even more troubling is the fact the counterfactual criterion is liable to generate paradox: why, after all, couldn't a mate recognition system (or a biological system for breeding, or . . .) evolve as follows: For some times t, t', t", t earlier than t', t' earlier than t", members at time t of a population lineage l can counterfactually recognize (interbreed with, . . .) members of the lineage at t' and vice versa; members of l at t' can counterfactually recognize (interbreed with, . . .) members at time t" and vice versa; but this is not so for the t and t" members of the lineage. But one would have thought that *is conspecific with* was an equivalence relation on the birds, the bees, and the beasts. So, one thinks, if we are going to stick with individuating species in terms of mate recognition systems, we will have to say something like: that temporally contiguous parts of a lineage can in principle recognize one another as potential mates suffices for conspecificity. This, of course, threatens to over-extend species, with birds potentially conspecific with certain dinosaurs. Obviously the same sorts of worries can be pressed against the counterfactual test above.

One could swallow the paradoxical upshots of the use of mate recognition systems as diachronic species criteria by pleading that one is simply looking to elucidate the everyday notion of species. It is pretty firmly entrenched in everyday thought, after all, that progeny are conspecific with their progenitors, and that if x is of the same species as y, and y of the same species as z, then x and z are of the same species. But it is also firmly entrenched in everyday thought that evolution can bring new species into existence. If you put all this together, you have—well, you have a mess. That extending the mate recognition for being conspecific diachronically produces more or less the same mess can hardly be an objection to the claim that the extension is an inaccurate analysis of the everyday notion of species. One could say much the same of the counterfactual interpretation criterion of sameness of meaning and the everyday notion of meaning.

Frankly, I don't think this is a terribly charitable thing to say about either the ordinary concept of species or meaning. But in any case, the search here is primarily a search for notions of meaning that can do some work in theorizing about natural language. Dialetheism notwithstanding, a notion that yields contradictory judgments on whether things are synonymous is not a promising candidate.[37]

---

[37] My discussion of the counterfactual criterion for sameness of meaning has benefited from comments and kvetching by two of the Press' readers.

One *could* modify that criterion in ways that might avoid paradox. The criterion provides a test for when it is apt to say that a phrase as used at different times has the same meaning. Note there are three temporal

9. Referentialism and Indeterminacy

I have been free and easy, going back and forth between talk of a word's meaning and of the concept it expresses. But there are differences in the way we use 'meaning' and 'concept'. Many find it hard to hear, 'Tim and Tom mean the same thing by the word "poem", but they use it to refer to different things' as saying something sensible. We don't blink when we hear things like

A.   The German sentence 'Bodo hat noch nicht gegessen' means that Bodo hasn't eaten yet;

we find it obvious that

B.   If the German 'Bodo hat noch nicht gegessen' means that Bodo hasn't eaten yet, then (a current use of) the sentence is true iff Bodo hasn't eaten yet.

We thus tie talk of meaning to truth and reference. Even if we bear in mind that we are talking about meaning in the sense of what grounds competence, it can be an uphill battle to convince oneself that something like referentialism might not be correct.

Here it is illuminating to shift ideology. For the nonce speak not of meaning and understanding, but rather of concepts and their grasp. To understand the word 'pasta', one needs to associate the concept *pasta* with it. It is not odd to say that what one needs to have the concept *pasta* is different today than it was century ago. Nor is it odd to

---

players here: we are looking at a test for the aptness of saying something—an event of saying, and as such, something that occurs at a time t*—about use at t and t'. It is perfectly possible that in one situation, relative to one time, it is apt to say something while at another time it is not. It might be apt for Ottolenghi in 2015 to say that the nineteenth-century chef and he meant the same thing by 'pasta', and apt for the chef in 1897 to say she and Ottolenghi meant the same by the term. It might be apt for Ottolenghi in 2015 to say, of a projected evolution of the word's meaning, that it would not change the term's meaning, but not apt for the nineteenth-century chef to say this. In judging sameness of Fness for an evolving system, it will at least sometimes make sense to understand such judgments as relativized to a particular point in the system's evolution. If, for example, we want to make judgments about whether evolution has given a species a new way of mating, or digesting, or whatever, we will probably (implicitly) take some point in the evolution of the species as a reference point—whether later developments are developments of a new way of mating or digesting is a matter of the degrees of difference between them and the reference point.

Taking Ottolenghi in 2015 as the point of departure, both the nineteenth-century chef's use of 'pasta' and the use of a denizen of the twenty-second century who rejects the idea of wheat-based pasta may aptly be said to be uses of 'pasta' with the same meaning, given that both the twenty-first-century use paired with the nineteenth-century use and the twenty-first-century use paired with the twenty-second-century use pass the counterfactual test. If we think of things in this way, no puzzles about failures of transitivity of identity arise.

One way to spell this out is to say that the proper notion for theorizing about meaning is not the binary, atemporal *use u of word w shares meaning with use u'* relation, but the three-place, temporally relative *from the perspective of the way w is used at t, uses u and u' of w share meaning*. A natural way to spell this out would be to require a certain sort of continuity of use: Relative to Ottolenghi in 2015, the use(s) of the chef (and her contemporaries) share meaning with Ottolenghi's only if all temporally intervening uses of the term do.

Whether playing this game is worth the cost of illumination I leave to others.

say that the concept *pasta* is now applied to or is now true of things it was not applied to or true of a century ago. Why there is this difference I do not know, but I do not think my ear is idiosyncratic in this regard. If we take the definite article seriously—*the* concept *marriage* has different application conditions now than it did before—we seem to be rejecting referentialism. Anti-referentialism about concept identity is just easier on the ears than it is about meaning identity.

I expect resistance from referentialists. Some forms of resistance are less interesting than others. One might say, for example, that 'pasta' is a context-sensitive term, its character the function that takes a time to the property of foodstuffs that speakers at that time use the word 'pasta' to pick out. In 1900 the word was used to pick out something like the property *foodstuff whose primary ingredients are wheat, salt, and water which is made by combining this into a dough which is divided, shaped, and dried*; today it picks out another property whose possession does not entail being composed from wheat. But this is not a change in character, and so isn't a change in meaning.

Such a proposal can be understood in various ways, depending on what's meant by talk of properties. A property might be something with a modal profile—it is or determines a function that takes a possible world at a time to an extension. Or it might simply be a function from times to extensions.[38] My own feeling is that if we adopt either proposal or anything much like them, we have thrown in the towel on the linguistic version of the species problem. After all, it's not clear why we should adopt such a proposal about 'pasta' unless we're prepared to say the same sort of thing about every other seemingly non-context-sensitive term. And if we say this about the word 'pasta', we are in effect saying that the word 'pasta' can't change its meaning. For what we are saying is this: Speakers at some point started using 'pasta' to pick out a property, accompanying the use of the word with a set of common presuppositions and criteria of application. The latter change; those changes may (or may not) cause changes in the property picked out. But neither change in presuppositions nor in criteria of application nor in property picked out counts as a change of meaning. One can say this, but it's really just a sneaky way of saying that the notion of meaning has no descriptive or explanatory oomph.

A more interesting attempt to defend referentialism begins by acknowledging what I said above about diachronic referential indeterminacy. It is indeed, the defense begins, indeterminate whether (for example) the reference of 'pasta' in 1917 and 2017 is the same. Indeed, it's indeterminate whether we are still using the concept that

---

[38] Assume for simplicity that at any time t at which 'pasta' is used in a (diachronically extended) population, it's associated with tolerably precise criteria P_t that determine how it is supposed to be applied, criteria that can be identified with a function from a world (at a time) to the things that satisfy them. Then one way of understanding the first suggestion is that the meaning-cum-character of 'pasta' is the function f from world times to extensions such that $f(<w,t>) = \{x | x$ as it is in w at t is in $P_t(<w,t>)\}$. The second suggestion can be developed in various ways, depending on whether or not one is skeptical of the modal idioms. If one is not skeptical, one might say that it a contextual matter, something somehow determined by the intentions of the user, as to how a use of 'pasta' under a modal is to be understood.

speakers in 1917 were expressing when they used 'pasta'. These two indeterminacies can be expected to go hand in hand, since there is considerable overlap in the properties of use that contribute to determining reference and those that contribute to determining meaning. Given this overlap, though, it's natural to think that conceptual and meaning identity should go hand in hand, or almost hand in hand, with referential identity. ('Almost' here is an acknowledgment that environmental factors may cause a shift in reference that some might say does not bring about a shift in concept.)

I agree that the two indeterminacies—of whether former and current use are coreferential, and of whether they are co-conceptual—are tied to each other. Indeed, they are tied to one another because the facts about use relevant to the question, 'what does this word refer to?' tend to include those relevant to the question, 'what does this word mean?' and vice versa. Indeed, I agree that it is possible—common, in fact—to talk about meaning and reference in such a way that when a phrase is not an indexical or demonstrative, our talk conforms to the dictum *words that mean the same are used to talk about the same thing*. What I do not see is that this means that there is an unbreakable connection between conceptual and referential continuity. An example:[39] 'tall' entered the language as a term of praise for men meaning (among other things) *strong in combat, brave, valiant*. By 1500 it acquired the meaning *more than average in height, long, lofty*, but was applied only to men and ships; in the 1600s it came to be applied in this sense to women and objects other than ships. The first shift seems like a change in meaning, a kind of property synecdoche. But it is natural to look on this last shift—the development between 1500 and the 1600s—as a case in which meaning is preserved but because of a lifting of a restriction on application, reference is shifted.[40]

It will be said by the defender of referentialism that this isn't really a counter-example: Agree, the defender says, that the meaning of 'tall' in England throughout the period is the ICG surrounding the word. Obviously this shifts: in the beginning of the period it's common knowledge that women and trees are not things that are ever tall; but by the end it's common knowledge that many women and trees are tall. In response: it doesn't follow from this that there has been a change of meaning in 'tall'. At least it doesn't follow if there is a genuine difference between change in meaning—change in the aspects of use and common ground presuppositions that constitute the meaning of a word—and change of meaning—change in those aspects of use and presupposition that result in one concept or meaning being replaced by another. The argument the defender of referentialism gives here is in about the same league as the argument: The average height of a human in the seventeenth century was 167cm;

---

[39] I lift the details from Steinmetz (2008); evidence for his judgments can be found in the OED entry for 'tall'.

[40] A natural way to think about this last sort of change structures the meaning of 'tall', so that it consists of a principle for sorting a domain (in this case humans, artifacts, and plants) into two sets (the tall and the not tall) and a presupposition about what part of the domain the principle can be applied to. The audience is supposed to recognize both the principle for sorting and the presupposition about what part of the domain is being sorted. What shifted in the sixteenth century was not the principle but the presupposition.

the average height of the twenty-first-century descendants of seventeenth-century humans is 178cm; so today's humans are of a different species than are seventeenth-century humans.

10. Conceptual Evolution

Species often arise because of highly contingent events. Because of this, the properties that differentiate one species from another may do so contingently. Suppose, for example, that something isolates a subpopulation c of a variety of the ladybug species *Coccinella septempunctata* (C, for short) from the rest of the members of C. There are changes in the ecologies of (the descendants of) c and of C-c—aphids, let us say, acquire different habits in their environments of each. These changes result in selection of differing traits in the two populations; over time, there are enough changes in each population that their members won't interbreed. At this point—or long before—speciation has occurred.

Suppose that among the most salient traits that differentiate descendants of c from those of C-c is novel spotting and banding in c descendants.[41] Was it impossible for Cs to develop the relevant traits while remaining Cs? Presumably not: if all of the members of C had moved to the location of the c's to begin with, there would not have been speciation, and they all would have come to look as the c's eventually did. For that matter all of the Cs, if they had found themselves in the c environment, might have gradually evolved in a way that would have made it impossible for them to interbreed with creatures like those that the C-c's eventually became.

The example is, of course, schematic, and one would need to fill in details in order to lean very heavily on it. But the idea—that it is not a population P's (more or less) intrinsic traits that determine whether it is conspecific with an ancestor populations P*, but rather relational facts about whether and how P diverged from other descendants of P*—is fairly standard in evolutionary biology.[42] On many ways of thinking about speciation, even the development of traits that affect gene flow—for example, those that equip an animal to recognize potential mates—need not precipitate a new species. In the schematic example above, were all of the Cs to undergo the actual ecological fate of the c's, and develop a mate recognition system that wouldn't recognize ancestor Cs as mates, that would not speciate—though if just the c descendants developed it while the C-c descendants evolved one that didn't jibe with the other, that would (on standard thinking) be an occasion of speciation.

What does this tell us about reference and meaning identity? Well, it doesn't tell us—that is, entail—anything. But it is certainly suggestive. The use of a word is an

---

[41] If spotting and banding were somehow tied to potential mate recognition, this difference would contribute to reproductive isolation and thus, on many accounts of species, a difference in species.

[42] A readable discussion that bears this out—while airing opposing views—is given in chapter 9 of Sterelny and Griffiths (1999).

event-like sort of thing. How a word gets applied, what people expect on the basis of its occurrence in various contexts, what its emotive and other connotations are: these are things that are best described not in static terms, but in terms that recognize their dynamic qualities within the practice of both individuals and populations. Meaning qua what one grasps in understanding is an abstraction from such practice, and thus, one thinks, is also something dynamic. If we ask how to individuate uses or meanings, the natural answer is kindred to the kind of phylogenetic answer biology tends toward in the case of the species. Species arise not simply because of incremental changes that are reflected in the traits of individuals, but because of historical contingencies that put a (sub)population on a historical course that is in an important way directed differently from, and in potential competition with, the ancestor population. If we think of meaning in this way, we will say that a new meaning arises 'from' an older one when events give rise to a way of using a term that is in an important way different from, and in potential competition with, the old way of using the term.

If you think about it for a minute, the idea that the reference (or the conceptual or the inferential role) of a word is essential to its meaning seems just plain crazy. The underlying practices that determine word meaning are messy, vague affairs that don't have crisp identity conditions. Use and practice, after all, are processes. The way a word is used is something that we are all, for all of our lives, in the midst of learning. Use is a moving target, and as such something that is elastic enough to survive small, slow changes. It seems worse than artificial to say that small changes from year to year—a change that adds a paradigm or two to the paradigms of pasta, or the gradual change in the doyens of ditalini from Chef Boyardee and Emanuele Ronzoni to Jose Andres and Stephanie Le—must amount to meaning change. The shapes and role of pasta do not (much) change from 1890 to 2015; the modes of manufacture are modernized but more or less continuous with the older ones; new raw materials are introduced, but—well, why think that this changes the meaning of 'pasta', as opposed to marking the advent of new sorts of spaghetti? But as suggested above, such incremental changes in use can result in what one can use the term 'pasta' to pick out. And this implies that meaning can survive referential shift.

In a way, this is just a generalization of observations that can be attributed to the Quine of 'Two Dogmas'. Quine says, or can be understood as saying, that changes in such things as inferential or conceptual role need not be changes in meaning, even if the bits of the role that change ('it's a pasta, so it's made of wheat') seem very, very important. We should accept the truism that inferential and conceptual role are linked to reference, even though the link is not direct but holistic. But it's hard to see why we would want to go on to insist that the preservation of reference—or conceptual role, or inferential role—is necessary for preservation of meaning. After all, if the inference *pasta, so wheat-based* can be given up without meaning change, and the inference was part of what was making the word 'pasta' refer only to wheat-based stuff, why exactly do we have to suppose that once 'pasta' refers inter alia to bacon-infused agar slammed out of a tube with a gush of nitrogen that the word has changed its meaning? This is not to say that preservation of meaning is consistent with massive change in reference or conceptual or inferential role. But at the moment we are wondering whether there is a solution to the linguistic analog of the species problem. To solve it, one thinks, we need to locate something that provides a way of locating a particular point or relatively small temporal interval within the history of a linguistic form at which we can gesture and say, 'there, that's where the word changed its meaning'.

We need to seriously consider the suggestion that in searching for necessary or necessary and sufficient conditions for change of meaning (or, for that matter, for speciation), we are thinking about things in an unprofitable way. Speciation itself is a process in which succeeding groups in a lineage become more (and more) separated from earlier groups or simultaneous groups with which they lack the possibility of reproductive encounters. Speciation occurs when one group gets separated enough from others. What makes a certain degree of separation enough is in part a matter of our interests (are we interested in equilibria for allele distribution? are we interested in morphological similarity?), to some extent a matter of stipulation. It varies with historical contingencies—what constitutes separation in one environment may not constitute it in another. This does not mean species talk is not based in fact—once we fix a measure, it will be pretty objective whether x is or is not more separated from y than from z. And it doesn't make species talk unuseful for (many) descriptive or explanatory purposes.

Meaning is an aspect of vocabulary items and constructions used by populations whose members are in actual and potential communication with one another. One assumes—the assumption, of course, is a theoretical bet one might lose—that there is something in the way vocabulary and constructions are realized in the mind of the individual speaker that corresponds to the way lexical entries in the dictionary are divided: the entry for 'hit', for example, is divided into two subcategories—nouns and verbs—with each subcategory constituted by sub-entries (hit, v. 1. to strike with (something held in) the hand; 2. to impact; 3....). Call these divisions in the lexical knowledge uses. Make another theoretical bet with me, and assume not only that there is such a thing as the relation of coordination discussed earlier in the chapter, but that it is uses that are the relata of coordination.

Uses so conceived are repositories of such things as dispositions to insert a term in certain loci in phrases of certain kinds, assumptions about what others assume when they use a phrase, emotive associations, etc., etc. And thus like many repositories, they are process-like: just like the town dump, the contents of a use of 'hit' can be expected to change over time as a result of what those in the surround throw into it. Uses so conceived are the uses of an individual: they are the hypothesized mental structures that people invoke in interpreting the speech of others. But use so conceived is an aspect of something inter-subjective—use is the locus of coordination. My use—especially as it changes—can produces changes in the use of others. Indeed, it can produce changes that may be accompanied by, or that lead to, changes in patterns of coordination within a population.

If you think of matters this way, the possibility of something that looks not just a little like an evolutionary process suggests itself. Take a population in actual and potential communication at a time; the individual uses of phrases in the lexicons of its members will be coordinated at that time. Idealizing, we assume that this coordination more or less groups the community's uses into equivalence classes; call such equivalence classes concepts. The uses that go to make up a concept at a time will vary, of course, but there will be a rough uniformity in them—too much divergence will, at least over time, result in coordination disappearing.

Changes either in the uses that constitute a concept or in the relations those uses have to other uses may lead to changes in patterns of coordination. Some examples.[43] (1) 'Gay' has come to be the commonly used non-derogatory term for...well, for people who are gay. While it can still be used to mean bright or lively looking, outside of Christmas carols this use seems to be dying pretty quickly. One hypothesizes that it is heard, or at least that people fear it will be heard, as insulting in much the way that the middle school use of 'gay' to mean lame is heard by some people;[44] this, in turn, makes using 'gay' with its original meaning feel taboo; and this makes people avoid using it this way.[45] In this case, a new use and social facts lead not only to a concept separate from—i.e., uncoordinated with—other concepts associated with 'gay', but to a process that threatens to extinguish concepts that were associated with the word. (2) 'Gay' is sometimes hypothesized to originally have become an adjective for people who are gay in virtue of its having had a use that applied to a person who 'had loose morals'; one version of the hypothesis is that this is the upshot of a commonly held generic belief that 'homosexuals are gay-in-the-sense-of-having-loose-morals'. The use of 'gay' from which the new concept arose subsequently 'died out'; it is not clear (assuming the hypothesis is more or less correct) whether the new use of 'gay' had anything to do with this.

In each example, a phrase (which in these examples already had concepts associated with it) gains a new use that comes to be differentiated from others insofar as the new use is established in the population via coordination—people recognize the use and coordinate lexical entries with it. This, in turn, opens the possibility of 'independent evolution'. For example: use of 'gay' in the mid-twentieth century as a derogatory term for homosexuals is coordinated with other such uses, (typically) not coordinated with other uses of the word, and tends to give rise to uses in others that are coordinated with those with which it is coordinated.[46] This 'isolation', in turn, means that it is

---

[43] Unless otherwise indicated, examples are drawn from the OED's accounts of the evolution of use.

[44] Though those who use 'gay' in this way seem often enough not to have an animus against gay people, nor do middle schoolers typically hear it as insulting to gay people. See, for example, 'How "gay" became children's insult of choice', http://news.bbc.co.uk/2/hi/7289390.stm.

[45] This alone marginalizes the use of 'gay' with its original meaning. The decline in exemplars of this use, in turn, can be expected to contribute to a change in the form's use.

[46] Insofar as reliable coordination is a synchronic mark of sameness of meaning, this seems to imply that 'gay' used as an epithet has the same meaning as 'gay' used as a badge of pride. I don't think this is a bad result; it seems to me of a piece with the idea that in a community in which the meaning of 'marry' is fiercely contested

possible for this lineage of uses to develop in ways that are different from the ways in which other lineages—including the 'parent lineage'—develop.

This sort of process is analogous to the biological process of speciation: a population (of uses) arises that is isolated from other populations (because the members of the population are coordinated with one another but not with others); the way in which the population is isolated facilitates its evolving independently of other populations. It is different from other processes of linguistic change. Consider, for example, (what one imagines was) the process by which 'skyline' came to be used, not as a term for any horizon but for cityscapes: in this process, one suspects, it was not the case that a use of 'skyline'-cum-cityscape arose that was uncoordinated with the older use; rather, sequences of coordinated uses of 'skyline' became increasingly unlikely to be accompanied by a disposition to apply the term to non-metropolitan skylines. This looks more like evolution without speciation.

One doesn't want to make too much of a couple of examples.[47] But the examples do suggest a way of thinking about concepts on which preservation of reference is neither necessary nor sufficient for 'conceptual identity'.

11. Deflationism about Reference

Meaning-cum-ICG is meaning characterized without reference to truth or reference.[48] I argued in the middle of this chapter that the reference of our terms—and thus the truth conditions of our utterances—is indeterminate. It is not that there are no facts about reference: Someone who proposes that my everyday uses of 'pup' are true of my wife, or of all of the cohesive collections of molecules on Venus, is simply, determinately in error. That such claims about reference are determinately false doesn't mean it's even close to determinant whether 'dog' as I use it is true of certain ancestors of my pet Sheltie. On the story I sketched mid-chapter, what is more or less determinate is not

(D)   My use of 'dog' is true of exactly the protoplasmic hunks h1, h2, . . . hk.

What is determinate is that (a) an interpretation of my speech and mentality is acceptable if it is among those which best conform to certain causal and interpretivist constraints, and (b) for a certain set of hunks of protoplasm H, there are ways of interpreting me among those that best conform to these constraints on which my use of 'dog' is true of exactly the members of H.

(in the sense that some take it as obviously impossible for two men to marry while others take it as obviously possible), there is a single meaning of the word as it used in the community. This, of course, is consistent with saying that there are many conceptions of marriage in the community, just as there are many (emotively tinged) conceptions of being gay.

Chapter 6 discusses how a word may be univocal—may in a significant sense have a single meaning—even when there are differing conceptions associated with it.

[47] Unless one is a philosopher.
[48] Thanks to Patrick Greenough for questions that sparked this section.

If you accept this picture, you should think that the sorts of facts usually offered as determining reference and truth—facts about causal and social relations between patterns of usage and the environment—have a role in explaining why meaning claims like

Mark's utterance of 'Sparky's a big dog' meant what Odile's utterance of 'Sparky, c'est un chien énorme' meant

are correct. So facts about causal and social relations between use and the environment contribute to determining the adequacy of ascriptions of meaning, assertion, and belief. But such facts alone do not determine what words mean or what their uses refer to; one can't get from facts about causal chains, social deference, causal covariance, and proper function (or all this and such things as cognitive role) to facts about truth conditions or facts like the fact that Odile's utterance was an assertion that Sparky is really, really big. What is explanatorily basic is not that x is referring to object y with (the utterance of) the word z; rather, it is that given x's social and environmental relations, her current linguistic behavior is well interpreted as behavior in which she refers to y with z.

Some might describe this as a view that denied any explanatory utility to reference whatsoever—a kind of closet deflationism. A deflationist like Hartry Field allows that our linguistic behavior is in one or another way connected to objects in and aspects of the environment: Perceiving a dog tends to cause Odile to be disposed to assent to 'c'est un chien'; by and large perceptual encounters with non-dogs don't cause this; so Odile's 'chien' indicates dogs. Of course it indicates lots of things—undetached dog parts, temporal dog slices, parts of a canine-ish scattered object, etc. And even waiving this sort of indeterminacy of indication, indication relations, as Field observes, often distort reference: Bobo might systematically misestimate height so that his use of 'his height is 5'11"' indicates that the relevant person is 5'7"; Jeff's use of 'And surely that is a miracle' may indicate not the presence of a miracle but that Jeff does not understand how an event occurred. Field allows that indication has an explanatory role to play, since along with facts about things like similarity of functional role, it helps explain why we can use others' linguistic behavior to gain information about the world. But facts about indication are not facts about reference (Field 1994, 2005). One might well say that even when we add what I called the facts about the three Ps mid-chapter—the facts about paradigms, projection principles, and deference patterns—we only get facts about (cognitive role and) social relations among individual indication relations. So such facts don't add up to a relation of reference that relates 'dog' to dogs. If the word–world relations available to describe and explain facts about meaning are exhausted by these, then reference and truth conditions have no explanatory role to play—at least not on a view like mine—in accounts of mind and language.[49]

---

[49] Deflationists like Field of course allow that there is a role for deflated notions of reference and truth, notions that can be obtained by, say, *stipulating* that (non-paradox-inducing) instances of

I'm not much enamored of this line of argument. First of all, it overstates the gap between the properties and relations that make sentence use an intentional activity and 'ordinary' reference. Bobo's uses of 'he's 5'11"' are connected by social practices of translation to the uses of that sentence by others: Bobo interprets others' uses homophonically, and this practice acts as a corrective on his own uses; how others interpret Bobo depends on whether they are aware of his misestimations. Bobo's uses of the sentence are accompanied by robust beliefs about and dispositions to defer to measurement using yardsticks and the like; this means that he has physical, more or less non-social relations to the environment that act as a corrective to his height estimations. The first fact makes what other people indicate with the sentence relevant to how we assign semantic relations to Bobo's sentence; the second fact (along with facts about how the beliefs and dispositions of others function to correct their ascription of height) means that there is much more relating a speaker's speech to his environment than uncorrected indication.

I do not say that these sorts of facts narrow down the acceptable interpretations of Bobo to a small number of closely related schemes of reference. For one (among many) thing(s), it will often be indeterminate as to when and how we should allow community patterns of use to decide the interpretation of Bobo's sentences: nowhere is it written that Bobo's use of 'this is a vegetable' is to be interpreted in accord with community standards iff, given evidence that 65 percent or more of the community use the sentence in a particular way, Bobo will try to use the sentence in that way. Nonetheless, the sort of facts mentioned above make it reasonable to think (for example) that interpreting Bobo as meaning 5'7" with his uses of '5'11"' while interpreting everyone else as meaning 5'11" with their uses of '5'11"' will be unreasonable. Indeed, the norm with a person like Bobo in a community like ours will be that interpreting him and everyone else as meaning 5'11" with '5'11"' is to give an interpretation at least as reasonable as any other.[50]

The second reason I am not enamored with the above line of argument is this. I concedes (well, it should concede) that there are robust causal and social relations between linguistic behavior and objects in and aspects of the non-linguistic world: indication, various feedback relations that calibrate indication, as well, presumably, as relations grounded in the three Ps. These relations have an explanatory role in accounts of meaning and mind: it is by appeal to them (and principles about interpretation) that we should explain why it is correct to say that Odile was talking about dogs and not

> My uses of 'F' are true of Fs and only Fs
> If t exists, then my uses of 't' refer to t
> My use of 'S' is true iff S

are to be accepted. But such notions can't be used to *explain* why our use of 'cow' refers to cows and not dogs.

[50] In fairness to Field: I suspect that he might allow that there is more to word–world relations than simply indication relations. That said, the work pointed to above reads as if only indication could be relevant to fixing reference.

donkeys or doxes when she name-checked Sparky, or to say that she walked to the store because she wanted some Nicorette and thought it was for sale there. But then there are robust, significant facts about the relations between linguistic behavior and the world that contribute to determining what we are talking about when we speak and that thus have an explanatory role in accounts of language. That very much sounds like a view on which reference has an explanatory role. Indeed, so long as it's conceded that we explain Odile's behavior by saying that she (had a) thought (true iff) that there was Nicorette at the store, and concede that such things as indication and the three Ps ground the fact that (on a reasonable interpretation of her) her thought had those truth conditions, we appear committed to (claims whose truth require ascribing) truth conditions (to mental state) having an explanatory role.

Now, it will be said that this is obviously not a case in which the notion of reference or truth conditions plays an explanatory role. Suppose that there are two accounts of Odile's reference and walking, one on which her uses of 'dog' refer to dogs (but not doxes) and 'store' to refer to stores; one on which the one refers to dogs and doxes while the other to something other than just everyday stores. Suppose those accounts are maximally good as interpretations of Odile. We can explain why the two accounts are maximally good by pointing to principles of interpretation and physical facts. But nowhere in such an explanation will we invoke a relation of reference that holds between Odile's words and world; we will invoke facts about indication relations (hers and others), her dispositions to be corrected by environmental interactions and to project usage (hers and others), and so on. These do not add up to reference, and so the explanation does not make use of the notion of reference. And certainly no other (good) explanation will or could employ a non-empty, non-stipulated relation of reference; it has, after all, already been conceded, when referential indeterminacy was embraced, that there is no such relation.

Short response: Such an argument assumes that an explanation that cannot be recast in physical/chemical/biological terms 'without loss' is not an explanation. But—assuming that *E can be recast in physical (etc.) terms without loss* means *physical (etc.) facts alone entail E*—we should respond by asking why we should assume that an explanation which is not determined to be correct by nothing more than physical, chemical, and biological facts is not an explanation.

Do not say that to deny this is to contravene some plausible version of naturalism, the view that the only facts there are are facts that supervene on the physical, chemical, etc. facts. There are good reasons to think that we can and do describe and explain the world using the vocabulary of economics, history, and so on, but that descriptions in the vocabulary of physics, etc. do not by themselves entail descriptions in economic and historical terms; the physical descriptions determine the economic and historical ones, but only relative to one or another way of projecting from physical descriptions to economic ones. When there are multiple ways of projecting from the physical vocabulary to the richer one, one can reasonably require that relative to a particular way of projecting from the physical to the economic, the physical determines the economic. But surely no more than that is necessary.

Elaborating: Think of an explanatory scheme E as something like a practice of giving explanations in a particular language of what one could (in principle) observe. Such a practice may confine itself to an austere language A involving only (broadly logical, mathematical, and) physical, chemical, and biological terms. But if we are concerned with schemes that humans with human interests might actually employ, the language in which explanations are cast will also include vocabulary that allows for the sorts of explanations given in economics, cognitive psychology, and history. As such, it will involve an explicit or implicit way W of projecting from matters described in a language like A to descriptions couched in an expanded vocabulary. A reasonable supervenience thesis is one that requires that relative to whatever way W of projecting from descriptions in A to ones couched in the expanded vocabulary, an explanatory scheme is acceptable only if fixing the description of a situation in the vocabulary of A fixes how we can describe it in the expanded vocabulary.[51]

If this is correct, then the objection we have been considering does not show that when we (correctly) say that Odile went to the store because she thought she could buy Nicorette there, we do not give an explanation of her behavior. Whether we do turns not on whether the notions of reference and truth conditions have reductions to the austere notions of physics, chemistry, and biology, but on whether (relative to whatever way of projecting from the physical, etc. facts to the intentional idiom we are employing) the truth of our claim is tied to mechanisms (realized in Odile's mentality) that contributed to bringing about her journey.

I don't think that the view I've been elaborating commits me to a deflationism about reference and truth; what I've just said should make it clear that I'm not terribly sympathetic to such views. That said, I'm not convinced that a lot of interest, philosophical or otherwise, is to be uncovered by trying to find 'the correct account of the meta-semantics of our terms'—that is, 'the correct' account of the causal and social relations and interpretive principles (Davidsonian charity versus a principle of evidence maximization versus 'knowledge maximization' versus 'reference magnetism' versus

---

[51] More exactly: Suppose the language A to be sufficient for 'stating the physical, chemical, and biological facts'. I am assuming that practices of describing the world using the intentional idioms involve (idealizing a good bit, I admit) one or another way of projecting from the physical facts (equivalently, from descriptions in A) to claims in the intentional idiom. Such ways of projecting correspond to one or another account of the reference of ourselves and others, and are adequate to the extent that they are in line with what I've called causal and interpretive constraints. I am assuming that *relative to such a way of projecting*, claims cast in the intentional idiom can also be taken to be 'fact stating'; their indeterminacy is a matter of there being many equally good ways of projecting. The reasonable supervenience claim is something like this: (There are maximally adequate ways of projecting from physical, etc. facts to intentional claims and) relative to any maximally adequate way of so projecting, it is not possible for there to be a difference in the truth of claims made in the intentional idiom without a difference in the truth of claims expressible in the physical idiom.

some other principle).[52] The argument in the middle of this chapter is predicated on the belief that there is no such account to be found, because nothing fixes that only such and such a set of principles can be used to generate an adequate understanding of the speech and thought of others.

Does that mean I think that (compositional) semantics is uninteresting or not worth pursuing? Not at all. What seems fairly indeterminate—and to the extent that it is determinate subject to change without our being aware that it has changed—are the semantic values of the simplest expressions that make up our sentences. What is arguably not very indeterminate—and to the extent that it is determinate typically does not change very much across generations—are the compositional principles which, supplied with semantic values for the simple items in a sentence, compose them to arrive at values for complex phrases. Even if it is indeterminate just what groups 'racist', 'pond scum', and 'racist pond scum' pick out, it is pretty determinate what the rule for getting from the extensions of the first two to the last is. The indeterminacy of reference is no more a threat to the (usual synchronic) determinacy of principles of compositional semantics than the blurriness of species boundaries is a threat to the objectivity of genetics. That's not to say that it's invariably determinate what compositional mechanism is to be associated with a construction. We have a pretty good idea what are the range of not implausible assignments of extensions to 'Mitt Romney' and to the phrase 'thinks it a good idea to keep one's pet on the top of a moving car'; we thus have a tolerable idea of what are reasonable opinions about when it is apt or even true to say, 'Mitt Romney thinks it a good idea to keep one's pet on the top of the car'. We are less than clear about what is a reasonable account in this case of how the extension of the whole is a function of the semantic values of the simplest parts.[53] That said, there are more and less reasonable accounts of the matter; it is an area where data can, at least occasionally, be turned into evidence.

I say all this because you may well wonder whether I am a closet radical, one who wants to forsake over a hundred years of compositional semantics. I don't. I do think there are dimensions of meaning that we have pretty much ignored in the last hundred or so years. Time to broaden our gaze.

---

[52] This is not to say that there is nothing interesting involved in the project of articulating *a* set of hypotheses that could or do govern interpretation in one or another sort of situation. It's the idea that all such projects must converge on a single set of principles that I am objecting to.

[53] If the point is unclear, think of the range of (not implausible) stories told about the semantics of attitude ascriptions, some of which invoke syntactic elements not obviously present on the surface.

5

Meaning, Thought, and Thought Ascription

Suppose it is common knowledge among you and me and Grace that we speak the same language. You say to Grace, 'You can ride inside our car'; Grace asks, 'What did she say?'; I say, 'She said that you can ride inside our car'. How, if at all, does the interpretive common ground (ICG) of the words 'ride' and 'car' in our group enter into to 'the proposition expressed' by your utterance? How, if at all, is that ICG related to what's picked out by the complement 'that you can ride inside our car'? Exactly what determines whether my comment about what you said is true or false?

Chapters 3 and 4 touched on these questions, but you may feel that more detail than I've given is called for. This chapter gives some of that detail, concentrating on the ascription of propositional attitudes. Section 1 sketches a view of attitudes and attitude ascription. Section 2 addresses how truth conditions and linguistic meaning do and do not help to individuate 'the objects of the attitudes'. Section 3 returns to the last chapter's discussion of how the reference of another's words or concepts bears on the truth of an ascription of saying or thought to her.

All this is something of a digression from our primary topic, setting out a picture of meaning as a population-level process. Nothing in Chapter 6 depends on the discussion in this chapter; if you're more or less satisfied with the discussion of propositions and attitude ascription in the last two chapters, feel free to proceed directly to Chapter 6, which returns to discussing the ways in which meanings are like segments of population lineages.

1. Attitudes and Their Ascription

The last four chapters sketched a picture of meaning-cum-the-anchor-of-linguistic-competence. Meaning in this sense is, as I have said, relevant to reference and truth conditions, but is nonetheless independent of it. When we turn to discussing attitudes and their ascription, meaning-cum-semantic-value—what (uses of) phrases contribute to determining truth conditions—becomes important. For it is more or less built into 'the logic of clausal complements' that both what sentence uses say and attitudes like belief are partially individuated in terms of truth conditions. After all, the following arguments are pretty obviously valid:

Selina said/believes that Cluzot admired Desclos.
It's true that Cluzot admired Desclos just in case Cluzot admired Desclos.
So, Selina said/believes something that is true just in case Cluzot admired Desclos.

The proposition/belief that Donald resigned is of necessity true iff Donald resigned.
The proposition/belief that Rex resigned is not of necessity true iff Donald resigned.
So, the proposition/belief that Donald resigned is not the proposition/belief that Rex resigned.

If anything is clear about propositions—about, that is, whatever it is that is invoked by the use of a complement clause like 'that Rex resigned'—it's that they are representational in the weak sense that they can be said to be true or false. If anything is clear about what we are doing when we ascribe a propositional attitude like belief—when we say something like 'Shannon believes that Rex resigned'—it is that in doing it, we are saying that someone is in a state that is representational in the sense that it is to be individuated in part in terms of a proposition and thus in representational terms. The purpose of this section is to discuss what else we might be doing in ascribing an attitude.[1]

According to Frege, mankind has a common store of ways of thinking of objects and properties. Our thoughts are constituted by these common ways of thinking; we associate them with our words and sentences. We understand another's utterance when we know what way of thinking it expresses; to say what the other said or thinks, we find a sentence S which in our mouth expresses what she said or thinks and then say that the other said that S or the other thinks that S. The early Russell had a similar view, minus the ways of thinking. According to Russell, there is a world of objects and properties about which we all talk and think; our thoughts—the propositions we say and think—are constituted by these objects and properties. To understand another is to know what propositions his utterances express; to say what the other said or thinks, we find a sentence S which in our mouth expresses what she said or thinks and use it to ascribe the attitude.

On these views, the contents of our thoughts are shared. And so the process of attitude ascription can be, as we might put it, algorithmic. Presented with an utterance, we decode it, finding the thought constituents and thought expressed; then we find words that express the constituents and thus, when properly put together, express the attitude's object. We may not be presented with another's thought in a way quite as

---

[1] The balance of this section borrows from the second half of the introduction of Richard (2013); if you have a sense of déjà vu, that's probably because you have déjà lu.

Among my goals in this chapter—indeed, in this book as a whole—is to suppress technical complications. So I have avoided laying out the ideas developed in this section in a way that makes explicit the compositional mechanisms that determine the truth conditions of a use of a sentence like 'Shannon believes that Rex resigned'. The introduction and chapters of Richard (2013) do this in considerable detail.

straightforward as we can be with his utterance. But we can usually dope out what the other thinks, in good part because we can dope out how she would express her thought.

An obvious worry, particularly about Frege's view, is that thought content isn't shared, at least not in a way that makes it reasonable to think that attitude ascription proceeds by content matching. As Frege himself observed, different people think of objects in different ways. And as should be obvious once this is pointed out, we often don't have a clue, and don't care to have a clue, about how another thinks of the objects of which she thinks or speaks. The other says

Paracelsus was a chemist;

we do not pause to see if the other's store of Paracelsus information—or the other's conception of what makes one a chemist—resembles our own before saying

The other thinks that Paracelsus was a chemist.

Well and good, you say. This shows that Frege's picture of attitudes and their ascription was wrong. So let us dispense with sense and adopt Russell's view, on which what the other thinks is not made up of ways of thinking of Paracelsus and the set of chemists, but of Paracelsus himself and the property of being a chemist. Given that content is Russellian, there's every reason to think that it's shared, every reason to think that attitude ascription may proceed algorithmically.

Now, there are two reasons to worry about this response. The first—which I want to put aside for a bit—is the well-known worry that our practice of attitude ascription is not well interpreted as one of simply ascribing Russellian content. We say, for example, that Mary may fail to know that Twain is Clemens, even though she knows that Twain is Twain; but (assuming as neo-Russellians do that the Russellian content of a name is its bearer), the Russellian thought that Twain is Twain just is the Russellian thought that Twain is Clemens. I want to concentrate for the moment on the converse worry, that (my use of) *the other thinks that S* may be true even though none of the other's thoughts has the Russellian content of (my use of) S. The ur-version of this objection goes something like this: I pretend to throw a ball and Diva the dog runs across the yard. Why? Because Diva thought that I threw a ball. The ascription is surely true. But the dog can't think what I say when I say, 'I threw a ball'—that is, she can't think something with the Russellian content of that sentence. The dog isn't disposed to group tennis balls, ping pong balls, footballs, and ball bearings together. But she would have to be able to do something along these lines in order to have the concept of a ball, which she would have to have were she able to think the Russellian content that I threw the ball.

The objection is prima facie incoherent. If it's true that the dog believes that S, how can it fail to be true that the dog has a belief with whatever semantic properties the sentence S (as I use it in ascribing belief to the dog) has?[2] But—at least given that we

---

[2] When I speak in this chapter of semantic values, semantic properties, and semantic content I intend (unless I say otherwise) that which determines the truth conditions of an utterance or mental state. The semantic content of an utterance, for example, is constructed from the semantic values of the constituents

have eliminated a Fregean account as an alternative—the semantic properties of the sentence I use are Russellian. Or at least they are referential. When I use the sentence, 'I threw a ball', the sentence has a part that refers to me, a part that refers to the property of throwing a ball. We may, of course, debate about what the property of throwing a ball is. It might be an abstract entity of some sort, or a function from worlds to sets of ball throwers, or just the set of this worldly throwers of ball. No matter: if the dog believes that I threw the ball, the dog has a belief that can be reported as having the content of my use of 'I threw the ball'. But that content is Russellian, or at least referential.

Note that to respond in this way is not—at least not obviously—to say that the dog has our concept *ball*, or that the dog has a representational ability that is on a par with that of users of the English word 'ball'. Rather, it is in effect to concede that the dog doesn't need anything much like our concept *ball* to think that I threw a ball. Insofar as the original objection was that the dog's believing that I threw a ball can't be a matter of its being in a state that, independently of and prior to my interpretation of it, has the content of my use of 'I threw a ball', the response concedes the point of the objection.

The ur-objection's point can be made without resort to animals or children. Recall Putnam's discussion of the word 'water' (Putnam 1975). The way Putnam seeks to establish that 'meaning ain't in the head' involves three claims: the reference of the word 'water' on earth today is not its reference today on Twin Earth; the reference of the word 'water' on earth today is the same as its reference on earth in the eighteenth century; the reference of the word 'water' on Twin Earth today is the same as its reference on Twin Earth in the eighteenth century. The latter two claims, I think, tend to be treated as if they go without saying—after all, when an eighteenth-century Englishman—Boswell or Dr. Johnson, say—said 'I want a glass of water', didn't he say that he wanted a glass of water?

Indeed he did. But to agree to this is not to say that the semantic properties of Boswell's utterance, independently of and prior to my interpretation of it, are identical or even all that close to those of the sentence I use to interpret it. It is (arguably) determinate today that 'water' is not true of more or less pure samples of D_2O, aka 'heavy water', which though visually indistinguishable from H_2O is lethal to fish and (in large doses) humans. It is hard to believe that this was determinate before the advent of modern chemistry.[3] The semantics of Boswell's words, independently of and prior to my interpreting those words with my own, are just not the same as the semantics that my words have, independently and prior to my using them to interpret Boswell. We sharpen the content of Boswell and Johnson's utterances when and by saying what they said in our idiom. In ascribing an attitude to them, we are not, or not merely, giving

---

of the sentence uttered along with whatever rules of composition are associated with the sentence's syntactic structure. As should be clear, I think of such content in a broadly Russellian fashion: names and demonstratives have their referents as contents; (syntactically simple) predicates have properties and relations as contents; syntactically complex phrases have structured entities, whose parts are the contents of their simplest constituents, as contents.

[3] Here I echo thoughts of Joseph LaPorte. See the discussion in LaPorte (2004).

a report of a pre-existing identity of content. We are interpreting them, and thus forging an identity.

The fact that Boswell's words do not, prior to our interpreting him, have the content we ascribe to him does not mean that our ascription of that content is incorrect. Why shouldn't we say the same thing about the dog? The fact that the dog's belief state does not have, prior to and independently of our ascribing the belief that I threw a ball, the content of the sentence we use in the ascription doesn't mean that our ascription of that content is incorrect. Of course, this response raises a question: If the truth of my report *a believes that S* doesn't require a match of content between the sentence S as I use it and the content that some state of a's has independently of my ascription, what does the truth of the ascription require?

Consider again the example of Boswell and the water. There is a certain semantic isomorphism between what is reported and what is used in the report. Boswell says, 'I want a glass of water'; I report him with 'Boswell said he wanted a glass of water'. Ignoring some subtle issues connected with tense, the reporting sentence recapitulates the term–verb–quantifier structure of the vehicle of the attitude.[4] Here something of the algorithmic flavor of the content-matching picture of attitude ascription seems correct. Whether my report is accurate is in part a matter of whether there is a match— at a certain level of semantic structure—between attitude vehicle and the representation of that vehicle in the report. Given such a match, the report's accuracy then turns on whether there is the 'right sort' of relation between the parts of the attitude vehicle and the parts of the sentence in the report—each part of the sentence in the report has to be a 'good interpretation', in a sense that needs specifying, of the corresponding part of the vehicle.

Considerations that have nothing to do with mismatches of referential content suggest that part of a correct account of attitude ascription will invoke the idea of the words in a report being a 'good interpretation' of the vehicle of the attitude being reported. Consider a homely example.

Eleanor Jane (=EJ) is Jane to her friends, Eleanor to others; her friends are well aware of this. You and I are her friends. I see that Bob and Ray, who know EJ but are not her friends, see her leave; I see that only Ray recognized EJ. (Of course, what Ray thinks is 'there goes Eleanor'.) I say to you, 'Bob and Ray saw Jane leave, but only Ray knew/realized that it was Jane who left'.

The way I speak in this example is quite natural. What information, exactly, would I normally convey by speaking in this way? How is it conveyed?

It is surely not conveyed that only Ray knew the Russellian content that Jane left. For Bob, knowing that that woman left, knew that too. Appeal to Fregean senses does not seem to be helpful—why think that the sense of my use of 'Jane' is a part of any thought known by Ray? Appeal to the idea that I am conversationally implying that Ray's belief

---

[4] Some think that 'wants' actually takes a sentential complement in both vehicle and report. This doesn't affect the point.

is associated by him with the sentence 'Jane just left' is no help—it's part of the story that Bob and Ray don't know Jane is so-called.

It would be natural for me to speak as I do even if I didn't expect you to know whether Bob and Ray know EJ. So it would be natural for me to speak as I do even if I have no expectations about what you might assume about how they refer to EJ when they recognize her. What I convey in this example, roughly put, is that Bob and Ray saw Jane leave, but only Ray recognized her: Ray had a bit of knowledge realized by something along the lines of *a just left,* where *That's a* would, for Ray, be a good answer to the question, Who's that?; Bob had no such knowledge.

If that's what I convey, how exactly do I convey it? Here, the idea that attitude ascription requires that the words of the ascriber be a 'good interpretation' of the representations of the ascribee can do some work. Suppose that when we ascribe a belief saying *a believes that S,* we offer the sentence S as a representation or translation of what realizes one of a's beliefs. If we suppose this, we may suppose that attitude ascription presupposes something like a 'translation manual', one keyed specifically to the individuals to whom attitudes are ascribed. In our story, I intend—and, if you understand me, you understand me to intend—that my use of 'Jane' in 'Ray but not Bob realized that it was Jane who left' represents representations of Jane that identify her to the subject of the attitude. The semantic rule governing belief ascriptions is then something like: the ascription *a believes that S* is true in a context just in case the sentence S, relative to context's translation manual, translates some belief-realizing state of a.

We may assume that translation requires the preservation of referential content. But we may also assume that another's words or representations may, within limits, acquire content by being interpreted, as Boswell's word 'water' acquires the content of our word 'water' when we interpret his speech. Within a particular context, our interests can impose further, non-referential constraints on translation, typically keyed to particular individuals. When this happens, context contains rules of the form:

When ascribing an attitude to A, the use of phrase p may only represent representations of A's with property P.

If, for example, we are concentrating on how the ancients might have expressed their astronomical beliefs, our context may presuppose the rule:

When ascribing an attitude to Sumerians, 'Hesperus' may only represent representations associated with the Sumerian word it conventionally translates; ditto for 'Phosphorus'.

Given the conventional account of what the Sumerians did and didn't know, this insures that while 'Hesperus = Hesperus' translates a Sumerian belief, 'Hesperus is Phosphorus' doesn't. So we speak truly when we say that the Sumerians believed that Hesperus was Hesperus, but didn't think Hesperus was Phosphorus.

In our story, Ray thinks to himself, 'That's Eleanor who just left'; Bob, on the other hand, doesn't think anything like this, but just thinks 'that woman just left'. The operative translation manual is:

When talking about what Ray thinks, 'Jane' represents only Ray's standing representations of Jane. When talking about what Bob thinks, 'Jane' represents only Bob's standing representations of Jane. Otherwise, any translation that preserves referential values is fine.[5]

Given all this, it's easy to see why it's true that Ray but not Bob realized that Jane left. Translating Ray's thought 'Eleanor left' with 'Jane left' doesn't violate the translation rules, as 'Eleanor' is one of Ray's customary ways of thinking of EJ, and so the translation rules allow 'Jane' to translate it. So it's true that Ray realizes that Jane left. But since Bob doesn't recognize Eleanor, there's no belief of his that can be translated with 'Jane left' without breaking a translation rule. So it's not true that Bob realizes that Jane left.[6]

On this picture, attitude ascription is partially algorithmic—it involves something like a loose isomorphism of content. And it is partially artistic—it involves contextually variable decisions about how to render the simple bits and pieces of a thinker's thoughts. Now, it will be said that in the general case, we can't hold on to even this much of the algorithmic picture of attitude ascription. Return to the ur-objection. The semantic structure of the complement in the report *Diva the dog believes that I threw a ball* is term–verb–quantifier. Are we to suppose that the dog is in a state with an aspect or part that can be identified as a quantifier? Is the dog a candidate for a logic course?

I have mixed emotions about this challenge. On the one hand, I think that it is probably wrong to say that there is nothing in the dog that corresponds semantically to the phrase 'a ball'. After all, the dog surely has something aptly described as 'a plan to find a ball'. There is no particular ball that the dog represents in this plan. But it's not implausible to think that such a plan involves something that deserves to be called a representation of a ball—if not, why does the dog plan to fetch a ball, as opposed to a

---

[5] By *x's standing representations of Jane*, I mean those of x's representations of a type that x customarily employs to think about Jane.

[6] I said above that I didn't want to get into the gory details of the compositional semantics for attitude ascription I have in mind. But here's an indication of how it goes.

I assume that the semantic value of a complement *that S* is a fusion of Russellian semantic values and the representations in S. For example, the Russellian semantic values of 'Jane' and of 'left' are EJ and the property of leaving; the Russellian proposition that Jane left is (something that can be represented as) the ordered pair <the property of leaving, EJ>; the semantic value on my view of the complement 'that Jane left' is what you get if you fuse the bits of the Russellian proposition with the relevant parts of the sentence—it is (something that can be represented as) <<'left', the property of leaving>, <'Jane', EJ>>.

Call this sort of thing an *articulated proposition*. I assume that (on a first approximation) mental states that determine beliefs, desires, as well as linguistic acts like promises, statements, orders, and so on involve things that represent/can be interpreted as representing, and so also determine articulated propositions. For example, Ray's mental state in our example determines the articulated proposition <<'left', the property of leaving>, <'Eleanor', EJ>>.

The semantics I'm presupposing—developed, discussed, and defended in Richard (1990, 2013)—has it that when I utter something of the form *x believes that S* I am offering the articulated proposition determined by the complement *that S* as a good translation of some articulated proposition determined by a belief state of x's. Whether my offering p is a good translation of an articulated proposition q determined by one of x's belief states depends on whether, using a translation manual that conforms to the sort of contextually determined translation rules mentioned above, one can transform p into q. It is tolerably clear, I hope, how such a mechanism validates the judgment that 'Ray but not Bob realizes that Jane's left' in the example above.

screwdriver?[7] If this is right, why shouldn't we suppose that there is something 'in' the dog that is playing a role much like the role played by 'discourse referents' in various dynamic semantic theories? And if that's the case, then there is something in the dog that corresponds to the phrase 'a ball'.

On the other hand, I think we need to acknowledge that something looks to be out of whack about the epistemology suggested by the content-matching picture of attitude ascription. Most anyone who watches me and Diva the dog knows that the dog thinks that I threw a ball. We know it without reflection and on the basis of no more evidence than our familiarity with the dog's fetching behavior and our current observation of the dog. But given the content-matching account of attitude ascription, it can seem that in order for us to be justified in thinking that the dog thinks I threw a ball, we should be onto some fact that justifies our thinking that the dog has a mental structure that plays a role like that of the indefinite 'a ball'. But surely my observation of the dog justifies no such thing.

In the case of Bob and Ray, we have good reason to think that their beliefs about EJ are realized by states that involve representations of EJ and of the property of leaving the room—after all, we have excellent reason to think that those beliefs could be expressed by them with English sentences. In the case of Diva the dog, perhaps we don't have much reason to think that she is quantifying over balls, either those contextually available or otherwise. Still, we have reason to think that there is some state of the dog that is a belief and is a state that pictures the world accurately if and only if I threw a ball.

In fact, we have reason to think that the dog's state has some structure, even if it lacks the structure of the complement of

A.   Diva the dog believes that I threw a ball.

As we usually think of that complement, it has a hierarchical structure, something along the lines of

A'. $[[_{DP} I] [_{VP} \text{threw} [_{DP} \text{a ball}]]]$.

Surely we have reason to think that the state that realizes Diva's thought has an element M that represents me. Don't we also have reason to think that there is some canine cognitive mechanism—TAB, call it—that is involved in the dog's belief and is reasonably interpreted as representing the property of throwing a ball? The dog, after all, is plausibly thought to recognize my action as being of a kind with your actual throwing of a ball, and as of a kind with young children's underhand ball tosses, etc., etc. She does, after all, reliably respond to them in the same way. If the dog's ability to recognize this sort of action is implicated in her belief, then her belief involves something that is reasonably interpreted as a representation of the property of throwing a ball.

---

[7] This isn't to say that the representation needs to be one that, independent and prior to our interpretation, applies to just balls, as opposed to balls and Frisbees.

If all this is so, then the state that realizes the dog's belief has some of the semantic structure of the sentence I use to report the belief. My sentence is a combination of the phrases 'I' and 'threw a ball', with the latter predicated of the former, so that the whole has a referential content which, abstracting a bit, can be represented so:

<Mark Richard, the property of having thrown a ball>;

the dog's belief state is in some sense composed of M and TAB, with the latter predicated of the former so that the whole has a referential content that is reasonably interpreted with my sentence.

When I think to myself, 'Ha! Fooled her—she thinks I threw a ball', I do not have the sort of interests I have when I am focused on the Sumerians' beliefs about Venus or Bob and Ray's thoughts about EJ. So there are no special constraints, beyond the usual requirement of (approximate) match of referential content, on how my words are to represent a belief state of Diva. So in context, the complement of the Diva-ascription is indeed a 'translation' or representation of one of Diva's states of belief—'I' represents M and 'threw a ball' represents 'TAB'.

I have been pointing out that understanding attitude ascription as involving a kind of translation of representational states doesn't require supposing that those states recapitulate all of the semantic structure of the sentences in our reports. It will be said that I haven't addressed the deepest problems with this idea. Consider an example of Dan Dennett's (1971). A chess-playing computer running a certain program may play in such a way that it is correct to say that it thinks that it needs to get its queen out of the back rank early. But there need be nothing in the machine that could plausibly be said to represent this belief by representing its parts. That the machine has this belief is not something that is true in virtue of its having and appropriately combining representations of itself, the temporal stages of a chess game, and a certain strategy that involves moving the queen up. We would say this sort of thing, after all, simply if the machine has a pronounced tendency in playing to move the queen out early, even when it appears there is no immediate advantage to be had in doing so.

Let us, for the sake of argument, concede that the computer may have this belief, though it has no state that realizes it by having proper parts that are adequately interpreted by proper parts of

B.   The computer needs to get its queen out of the back rank early in a chess game.

Still, if the computer has the belief, it is in a state that realizes a belief and whose content is adequately rendered by that complement. If there are states that can have the content of this sentence without having its semantic structure, those states can be reported—and thus 'rendered' or 'translated'—using a sentence whose explicit structure makes the semantic structure of the state's content explicit.

It is no part of the ideas, that content is structured and attitude ascription is a kind of translation or representation, that the states that realize beliefs must themselves be structured like the sentences we use to report the states. A belief can be realized by a complex of dispositions—at least when those dispositions are embedded in the right sort of cognitive system—and dispositions often lack anything like sentential structure. Just as we may choose, in interpreting Dr. Johnson's utterance of 'water is tasty', to render it as involving the content of our term 'water', so we may choose, in interpreting the dispositions of the computer, to render them with our concepts of chess, the back rank, the queen, and so forth. In the case of the computer, this is a good rendering because there is a rough parity between the behavior controlled by belief-grounding dispositions of the computer and the behavior that is controlled by the belief of someone with an articulated belief about getting the queen out.[8]

Some will say that beliefs realized by such things as dispositions are properties of the whole organism. And they will say that once we grant that (at least some) attitudes are properties of the whole organism, and need not be recorded by substates with semantic structure, we should also (a) grant that the contents of those attitudes are unstructured, and thus (b) understand attitude ascriptions as ascription of unstructured contents. One argument for this conclusion goes as follows. Consider a case like that of the computer. It is fairly determinate what the computer believes. But determinacy in its belief does not extend below the level of truth conditions. After all, we can report the computer's belief using B's complement, or using

C.   One needs to get one's queen out of the back rank early in a chess game;

or using

D.   It is generally a good thing for a chess player to move her most powerful piece out before the mid-board is crowded.

Each of these is acceptable because each captures what the world must be like for the belief to be correct; there is, in the case of the computer, nothing more to capture about the content of its belief than its (modal) truth conditions; differences between C and D due to their differing semantic structure are irrelevant to saying what the computer believes. Thus, those differences must be irrelevant to capturing the content of the computer's belief. Thus, sometimes an ascription of an attitude is an ascription of something whose content is unstructured; the content is simply the truth conditions of the attitude. But surely we are ascribing the same belief to the computer and to Sandrine when we say:

Both Sandrine and her opponent the computer think that a player should get its queen out of the back rank early in a chess game.

So even when there is a sentential record of a belief, that doesn't mean that the belief's content is structured.

---

[8] If you've read my earlier work on propositional attitudes, you may wonder how the ideas in this paragraph combine with the machinery in Richard (1990). Technical details and philosophical commentary can be found in Richard (2013, 22–5).

It is true that we could use either C or D to ascribe a belief to the computer, and that the properties of the computer that ground the truth of one ascription are the same as those that ground the other's. It is true that the computer does not have an articulated representation of the semantic structure of these sentences. How does it follow—why is it even plausible—that differences between sentences that don't affect their possible worlds truth conditions are irrelevant to whether the sentences report a belief? It is not just that the computer behaves in a way appropriate just in case sentence C or D is true that makes an ascription with C or D in the complement true. It is also that the computer's dispositions are relevantly similar to the dispositions of people who have beliefs realized by these sentences that makes such ascriptions true. Like such people, the computer manipulates certain objects (picked out in the sentences) in certain ways (also picked out in the sentences) at certain times.

It is this difference between ascriptions involving C or D and ones involving the necessarily equivalent

E.   One needs to get one's queen out of the back rank early in a chess game just in case the total number of moves in the game will be less than or equal to a number that is equal to the product of some set of powers of primes

which explains why using E to ascribe a belief to the computer does not give us something that's true. It is simply, obviously, manifestly false that all that is relevant to the truth of an ascription of an attitude are the modal truth conditions of the content sentence. Beliefs and other attitudes are states that are articulated. Often enough the articulation in adults is linguistic. But there are more ways to have an articulate belief—and thus a belief with content that is structured—than by writing a token of a sentence in the belief box.

It is simply false that if a belief is realized by something—a set of dispositions, say—that itself lacks semantic structure, there is nothing more to the belief's content than what is given by the set of worlds in which it is true. The computer's belief about the queen is a belief about the queen and the early parts of the game; it is not a belief about how these relate to arithmetical properties of the number of moves the game might contain. That this is so, of course, is manifest in what realizes the belief in the computer—the computer has dispositions to respond to and manipulate the queen in the early stages of the game; it has none that relate number theoretic calculations of the likely length of the game to getting the queen out. There are more ways for the psychological facts about someone to make a structured content one that they believe than their simply tokening a sentence that expresses that content.

Robert Stalnaker gives a variant of the argument I have been criticizing in the first chapter of his book *Inquiry*. As I read Stalnaker, he argues as follows. What makes something a belief, desire, or another propositional attitude is that it plays a certain role in the production and explanation of rational action: it represents a possible state of the world, typically one that an agent sees as a possible outcome of action or something to take into account in acting. But, the argument continues, there's nothing more to the content of a belief than what's necessary for it to play the just mentioned role in the production of action. And taking a belief to have as its content the structured content that a is F does not make it represent a different state of the world than taking it to have an unstructured content, such as the set of worlds in which a is F. Thus, the extra structure found in the structured content that a is F is not part of the content represented in the belief that a is F. If this argument is on track, we should deny that any belief has a structured content.[9]

Stalnaker himself gives us reason to be suspicious of this argument. He writes:

> What is essential to rational action is that the agent be confronted, or conceive himself as confronted, with a range of possible outcomes of some alternative possible actions .... the primary objects of the attitudes are not propositions but...alternative possible states of the world. When a person wants a proposition to be true, it is because he has a positive attitude towards certain concrete realizations of that proposition. Propositions [qua objects of attitudes like belief and desire]...are simply ways of distinguishing between the elements of the relevant range of alternative possibilities.   (Stalnaker 1984, 7)

Observe that on Stalnaker's own view, what we represent and what is the 'primary object of the attitudes' isn't a set of possible worlds, but a 'state of the world', a 'concrete realization' of a set of worlds. I think Stalnaker is right about this. When I think that you are asleep, what I represent is not a set of possible worlds: to do that I would have to do something like picture a collection of worlds, spread out, as Larry Powers once put it, like raisins in a pudding. What I represent, when I think that you are asleep, is you being a certain way, asleep. What I represent, and what I have a concrete attitude toward, is a particular distribution of objects and properties. But in a quite straightforward sense of (possible) 'state of world', the state of your being asleep is a different state of the world than the state of your being asleep while $1+1 = 2$. Certainly to represent the latter state of the world is a different thing than representing you being asleep: to represent the second I have to represent the numbers 1 and 2; not so for the former.

The most straightforward sense of 'possible state of the world' is this: a possible state of the world is one or more objects having or being related by one or more properties or relations which the objects could have or be related by. Stalnaker himself allows that such states are the 'primary objects of belief'. So why shouldn't we identify the content of a belief with its 'primary object'? Why shouldn't we accept the first two premises of Stalnaker's argument while throwing out the third, saying that to take the content of a state to be an unstructured set of worlds is in a sense to deprive it content? Since contents are objects having properties and standing in relations, merely to ascribe truth conditions to something is not to ascribe a content to it at all, but merely a range of possible contents.

Now, it will be said that this can't be right. The dog has a perfectly determinate belief. Since the dog's belief is determinate, it must have determinate content. But since the

---

[9] There is a fairly compact statement of such an argument on page 23 of Stalnaker (1984).

dog lacks a sophisticated representational system, it is not in a position to represent the structured contents associated with sentences we can use to ascribe it beliefs. But if the dog determinately believes a structured content, it must represent it—else why think that it believes that content, as opposed to one of the many structured contents that are equivalent to it?

There are many things one might mean by saying that the dog has a determinate belief. I will assume that someone giving this argument means simply that

A.   Diva the dog believes that I threw a ball

is determinately true. Then the question is whether it can be, if it is interpreted as ascribing a structured content to the dog. I don't see why not. Let us grant that Diva does not represent the content of 'I threw the ball' in anything like the way we do. That doesn't imply that she lacks determinate dispositions to behave in ways that relate her to me and the activity of throwing a ball in such a way that it is correct to say that she thinks that I threw a ball. If she does, E is true, no matter what sort of content it ascribes.

It will be said that I have not addressed the point. The doggish dispositions that ground A also ground

F.   The dog believes that I propelled a ball through the air with a movement of my hand and arm.

Diva cannot make the discriminations necessary to differentiate a hand from an arm, nor does she have the concept of propelling. But if so, how can it be determinately true that the dog thinks that I threw a ball, as opposed to propelling a ball with a movement of my hand and arm?

In response: I argued above, in effect, that sentence A could be understood in two ways: as ascribing to Diva a belief in a content with a structure more or less isomorphic to the syntactic structure

A'. $[[_{DP} I] [_{VP} threw [_{DP} a ball]]]$,

or as ascribing to her a belief in a content with a structure isomorphic to something like

A''. $[[_{DP} I] [_{VP} threw\text{-}a\text{ -}ball]]$.

And surely something analogous is true of F. Using F in the relevant way is ascribing to the dog a belief with a content more or less isomorphic to something like

A'''. $[[_{DP} I] [_{VP} propelled\text{-}a\text{-}ball\text{-}through\text{-}the air\text{-}with\text{-}a\text{-}movement\text{-}of\text{-}my\text{-}hand\text{-}and\text{-}arm]]$.

If the dog has a content with A'', it has one with the content A''', for these are the same content. So there is, in my opinion, no question that one could use F to say something true if one could use A to do so. There is a question, of course, of why one would do this, if one were not making a joke and did not mean to ascribe to the dog abilities rather unusual in the canine world.

There is still the objection that even ascribing a content with this little structure to the dog is undermotivated, given the slack between Diva's states, considered by themselves or in tandem with her everyday interactions with the world, and ascription of one or another concept of ball propulsion to her. But that seems as much an objection to the idea that the content of her belief is given by the set of worlds that validate the structured content that I threw the ball as it is to the idea that the structured content itself is its content. In any case, it is hard to see why one would think that this is an objection to the idea that it is determinately true that Diva believes the structured content that I threw a ball. I would say that it is determinately true that Boswell and Johnson believed that water is wet. But I would not say that there is something about them and the relations they had to their environment and society in the seventeenth century that determine that the content of one of their beliefs is that water is wet. There is a certain amount of courtesy involved in the ascription—which does not mean that the ascription is not determinately true. Why is it that we cannot say the same thing about the dog?

2. Conventional Meaning, Belief, and Assertion

To utter the sentence, 'Selina believes that Horselover Fat is a writer' is to use the sentence, 'Horselover Fat is a writer' to characterize one of Selina's beliefs. It seems a short step from *My use of 'S' characterizes one of Selina's beliefs* to *The meaning of 'S' (and perhaps whatever my use of 'S' adds thereto) characterizes one of Selina's beliefs*. But the terrain here is treacherous, and we must step lightly.

The standard view in philosophy of language in the twentieth century was (speaking roughly and not worrying about words like 'I' and 'those') as follows. Convention associates with each sentence of a language a meaning. That meaning in turn determines what a use of the sentence 'strictly and literally says'. What a sentence use strictly and literally says is the determinant of truth and modal properties, what one must grasp in understanding its use, what serious use asserts, and what belief is expressed when it is expressive of belief. I have suggested several times that this view runs distinct notions of meaning together in an unhelpful, even pernicious way.

But I do think, as I said in Chapter 3, that there is a useful notion of 'what is said' on which what's said is in part determined by linguistic convention and which in some sense is more than merely a reflection of truth conditions. What is said in this sense by a sentence's use is a fusion of the (truth theoretic) semantic properties of the utterance with the ICG of the expressions used. What is so said by Donald's utterance of 'Sean has resigned' relative to a group G is a reification of what a member of G does when—given that the ICG of 'Sean' and 'has resigned' in G is d and r—he takes himself to have been invited to think of Sean and resignation in terms of d and r and to take the first to have done the second. What is said in this sense is what the competent interpreter brings to the table in trying to understand what another is doing in speaking. It is the default interpretation, the interpretation that the competent speaker expects the auditor to begin with (if nothing signals that another interpretation should be sought) and that the competent auditor begins by assigning (again, if nothing signals that another interpretation is to be sought). 'What is said' in this sense is a reification of what one entertains if asked, outside of particular contexts of use, to think about what a sentence says. If there is such a thing as literal meaning, this is it.

Given the conclusions of the last section, it's clear that if this is what is associated by convention with a sentence S's use, there is no intrinsic connection between what is conventionally meant by S's use and what I might correctly report with *X said that S*. There is no intrinsic connection between what is conventionally meant by S's use and a mental state correctly ascribed with *X thinks that S*. In uttering *X said that S* or *X thinks that S* I may intend a match between the ICG of my words and the ICG of X's, but I may instead intend my words to represent an utterance or thought of X's that has a relatively idiosyncratic property unrelated to the conventional meaning of T. That this is so is part of the point of the examples—of the Sumerians, of Bob and Ray, of Diva the dog—in the last section. For that matter, I may be indifferent to anything but a match of referential properties between my words and whatever realizes X's thought or assertion.

Perhaps you think that at the least there must be a tight relation between what S means/conventionally expresses as I use it, and what I think if I use S in thought, expressing to myself one of my beliefs. How, you might ask, could there not be, at least given that I know what S means? Suppose S, conventionally or otherwise, means that p when I use it and I am aware that this is what S means—my use doesn't stand to what I mean as Mrs. Malaprop's use of 'allegory' stands to what she means.[10] Then surely (at least if I am not being ironic, sarcastic, linguistically inventive, or the like), when I think to myself 'Indeed, S', I think p. As I say, you might think this. But you would—at least on a natural understanding of what it is to believe the thought conventionally associated with S—be wrong, as there is no particularly tight relation between a sentence's conventional meaning and what one thinks when one uses that sentence in thought.

To know what S conventionally means is to know how users generally expect to be understood when using it. To know, for example, what 'Bulls are dangerous' conventionally means is to associate the conventional wisdom ('wisdom', really, as it may be inaccurate) associated with 'bull' and 'are dangerous' and to be cognizant of the fact that it's common knowledge that when someone utters the sentence they are (assuming no signal to the contrary) inviting their audience to use the conventional wisdom to think about bulls and being dangerous and, while doing so, generically predicate the latter of the former.

What is it to believe the thought conventionally associated with 'Bulls are dangerous'? The most natural thing to say, I take it, is that to think this thought is (a) to think of

---

[10] In Act 3, Scene 3 of *The Rivals*, Mrs. Malaprop tells Captain Absolute that Lydia is 'as headstrong as an allegory on the banks of the Nile'.

bulls and danger in the ways determined by the ICG associated with 'bulls' and 'are dangerous' and (b) while doing this generically predicate the latter of the former. But I can naturally sincerely and believingly think, 'Hey, bulls are dangerous' without doing either of these. 'Everybody knows' that waving something red at a bull angers the bull; indeed, everybody knows that everybody knows this. In fact, speakers who use 'bull' (arguably) expect their audience to know that they presuppose this when they use it. So (arguably) that bulls are inflamed by red is part of the ICG of 'bull'. Now I may know all this and thus grasp the conventional meaning of 'bulls are dangerous' while also knowing that it's a lot of hooey that bulls are inflamed by red: they do not register red as a different color from many others and are emotionally indifferent to the display of red as opposed to blue as opposed to yellow. When I believingly think, 'Bulls are dangerous' I don't presuppose or otherwise accept all of the ICG of its words.

I'm happy to say that there is sense of 'think'—the sense in which to think p is something one does if one believes, doubts, denies, or hopes against hope that p—in which if one thinks, 'Bulls are dangerous', one thinks the thought conventionally associated with it. In this sense of thinking, one thinks the thought simply by using the sentence, 'Bulls are dangerous' in thought—expressing belief, doubt, puzzlement, whatever—while aware that people are aware of the fact that speakers tend to have certain expectations about their audience when they use the sentence. But to think the thought in this sense, one needn't believe in any sense whatsoever that bulls are inflamed by red, or any other part of the ICG of 'bull'. Indeed, one can, in this sense of 'think', think the thought conventionally associated with the sentence when assertively uttering it without even expecting one's audience to think one expects them to be participating in the (first-order) ICG involved in the thought, as would be the case if I said, 'As you and I know perfectly well, bulls do not react aggressively to the display of particular colors—it's just that they tend to react aggressively to sudden movement. And this is why bulls are dangerous'.

The natural account of what it is to think the thought conventionally associated in G with sentence S is one on which one makes the relevant presuppositions (those in the ICG of the words in S) and, while doing so, ascribes properties and relations to objects in the way dictated by the sentence's structure. But to know how people in my culture expect to be interpreted does not require that I endorse the presuppositions involved in that expectation. And I can use S in thought—or speech, for that matter—without making all the presuppositions in its ICG; such use, while it may depart from the norm, does not involve anything like a linguistic error.[11]

---

[11] Furthermore, I will typically be a member of *many* groups whose language I speak (and which overlap on the truth conditions of S). Given a group G whose talk I can interpret, there will be many other groups, some which contain it, some which it contains, and some which but partially overlap it, all of whom use the same syntax as G, associate the same truth-conditional contributions to the phrases of that syntax, and whom I can interpret. Insofar as languages are defined by circles of individuals in actual and potential communication, normal adults speak many, many languages. Relative to each such group, there is some proposition 'conventionally associated' with S relative to the group; my competence in the group idiom is a matter of being able to recognize, once I identify a speaker as a member of the group, an invitation to think

Of course, there is some connection between the meaning of S and the state of mind characterized by *Selina thinks that S*. Semantic values, which determine truth conditions by determining the sorts of things Russell thought were the constituents of propositions, are a kind of meaning. To use 'Horselover Fat is a writer' to characterize Selina's mind is to characterize it in part in terms of the truth conditions determined by the semantic values of the sentence's constituents. Thus, to use the sentence to characterize her belief is to use the sentence's meaning (and whatever my use contributes to fixing semantic values of its constituents) to characterize Selina's mind. But this is not to say that when I utter something of the form *Selina believes that S*, I am invariably or even very often using S's meaning-cum-ICG to characterize her mental state. This shouldn't be terribly surprising. What words we use to characterize another's wants or wishes is of course responsive to what words the other does or might use to express them. But it is also responsive to what we think facilitates comprehension on the part of the audience, and this will often be utterly independent of whatever ways the subject of the ascription has of thinking about the objects of her beliefs.

The idea that in ascribing attitudes we use the meaning of a sentence in a fairly rich sense of 'meaning' to characterize the minds of others was a mainstay of twentieth-century philosophy of language; that idea lay behind the idea that there is an important distinction to be drawn between two sorts of attitude reports. Some reports—de re reports—are ones in which some expression can be replaced with another with the same semantic value without changing the report's truth value. A use of 'Odile thinks that Twain yet lives', if it is understood to imply things of the form *if t is the same person as Twain, then Odile thinks that t yet lives*, t a name, demonstrative, or indexical, is de re in this sense.[12] A report that is not de re (with respect to any occurrence of its embedded expressions) is said to be de dicto. Many thought that the distinction is important because: (a) true de dicto, but not true de re, attitude ascriptions reveal the 'real content' of another's attitudes; (b) this is because de dicto ascriptions ascribe belief in something straightforwardly determined by 'the' meaning of the sentence in the

---

about things in a particular way. There will generally be no reason to think that one of these conventionally associated propositions is more definitive of what I think when I think with S than any other.

I used 'linguistic error' in the paragraph to which this note is annexed. Though I used it, frankly I do not much like the phrase. Error is first and foremost infringing a rule; linguistic errors would thus be first and foremost infringements of linguistic rules. But there aren't, to my way of thinking, linguistic rules; what there are are various more or less entrenched, less and more widespread regularities of use. Better, I think, to speak of competent use of phrases, where a phrase p is used competently relative to a community C if: user and audience are members of C; the user is cognizant of how P is used in C; it reasonable for the user to think that the audience will grasp how the user intends to depart from the regularities of p's use in C, should the user intend to so depart.

This makes competent use a matter of degree, since it can be more or less or reasonable to think that the audience will grasp one's intentions. It's perhaps worth observing that there is a difference between saying that competent *use* is a matter of degree and saying that *competence* is a matter of degree. While the latter is naturally (and I think correctly) taken to something that can be projected on to one or another scale (and so can be said to be a matter of degree), the way one would measure degrees of competence in a use is quite different from the ways in which one might measure the user's competence.

[12] Clearly we should speak of a report as being de re with respect to particular occurrences of expressions.

ascription's complement clause; (c) since behavior motivates via its content, it is only de dicto ascriptions that can play a role in explaining how the beliefs and desires of the agent motivate her behavior.

(a) through (c) seem to me fundamentally confused. First of all, the idea that (because attitudes motivate via their content) we must duplicate the content of motivating attitudes if we are to explain behavior via attitude ascription is surely wrong. Recall the example of Bob, Ray, and Eleanor Jane. Imagine that I said, 'Bob and Ray saw Jane leave, but only Ray realized that it was Jane who left' as an answer to your question, Why did Ray run out of the room while Bob stayed here? Assuming that Ray's running was the result of his realizing that Jane had left, this is a perfectly good explanation of his behavior. But we have already agreed that there is no match of non-referential content between Ray's belief state and the sentence that I use.

Truth be told, I'm suspicious of the claim that 'attitudes motivate via their content', as well. Attitudes do motivate and they do have content. There is usually a quasi-formal connection between the attitudes that motivate us and the syntactic forms of the sentences in attitude ascriptions that explain our behavior in terms of those attitudes. If Jerry is moved to leave the room by his belief that Jennifer is the next room and his desire to speak to her, that is presumably because the way Jennifer is represented in the belief is in some sense identical with the way she is represented in the desire; ascriptions that explain Jerry's behavior by reference to the belief and the desire such as

Jerry left the room because he wanted to speak to Mrs. Egan and thought that she/Mrs. Egan was in the next room

will use the same linguistic representation of Egan (or use anaphora), achieving a certain level of isomorphism between the relations between parts of Jerry's mentality and the structure of the sentences used to explain how the mentality drove the behavior. But this sort of connection has nothing to do with some sort of identity or overlap of (non-referential) content between Jerry's representations and those used in the ascription: Jerry need not know that Jennifer is married or named Egan; the ascriber need not know that Mrs. Egan is named Jennifer. Attitudes, it seems to me, motivate in good part simply in virtue of their formal properties. If this is all that's meant by 'attitudes motivate via content', well and good. But the slogan has misleading connotations: it's the coordination between the things that realize Jerry's attitudes that is the mechanism of motivation, not their content.[13]

It's not clear that the distinction between de dicto and de re ascriptions, at least on the above way of drawing the distinction, is pointing to anything of fundamental importance. There is, of course, a way of using the de dicto/de re terminology on which it does point to something of some importance: this is the distinction between ascriptions in which a variable or pronoun in a complement is controlled by something

---

[13] This idea is a leading theme of some of the essays in the first half of Richard (2013). Pryor (2017) gives a useful discussion of the issues this paragraph raises.

quantificational (or via anaphora) that is outside of the complement (these are de re in a sense distinct from the sense marked above) and ascriptions in which this is not the case (de dicto). The contrast here is between understandings of

Selina thinks that a French man wrote the novel

regimented

Thinks (Selina, that ∃x(x is a French man and x wrote the novel)) (de dicto)

and ones regimented

∃x(x is a French man and Thinks (Selina, that x wrote the novel)) (de re).

This is a genuine, truth-conditional difference. But it is a different difference than the first one: to draw this distinction, one does not even have to endorse the idea that there is such a thing as an attitude's non-referential content, much less the idea that there is a distinctive sort of attitude ascription which ascribes such content.

3. A Puzzle about Speech Reports

Chapter 4 discussed puzzles about reference and reports about what people mean and say with their words. One such puzzle uses a sequence of utterance pairs, each pair separated by a minute:

Time	Sally	Fred
t0	(silence)	(silence)
t1	I like salad	Sally said nothing a minute ago
t2	I like salad	Sally said she likes salad a minute ago
t3	I like salad	Sally said she likes salad a minute ago
...		
ti	I like salad	Sally said she likes salad a minute ago

Given the right interval, the reference of 'salad' as Sally and Fred use it will shift at some tj. But if the reference of 'salad' shifts from tj to tj + 1, Fred's contribution to this piece of performance art at tj + 1 will not be true, for something of the form *x said that* S is true only if the truth conditions of S match the truth conditions of (the sentence used in) an utterance of x's. But it seems implausible that any of the reports are false: given the presumably gradual nature of semantic shift, how could a minute ever make any difference to the truth of one of Fred's reports?

Now that we have a specific proposal on the table for the truth conditions of attitude ascriptions, we should return to Chapter 3's discussion. I propose to do this by considering the discussion of Cian Dorr and John Hawthorne—CJ, henceforth—of a modal variant of this puzzle (Dorr and Hawthorne 2014). In particular, I want to discuss whether CJ's critical remarks about some purported solutions to their version of the puzzle make trouble for the proposal I made in Chapter 3.

Here's a version of CJ's modal puzzle.[14] There seems to be a continuum of possible meanings for '(green) salad', each of which is very close to its actual meaning. To see why, suppose that given the actual meaning of 'salad', something the volume of which is less than 75 percent greens is (definitely) not a salad, but this is not true of percentages of greens greater than 75 percent. Then in some sense x's consisting of 75 percent greens by volume marks a cutoff for being a salad, and so for 'salad' applying to x. But there are (uncountably!) many cutoffs that differ from this one by no more than a percentage point, one for each real number within an integer of 75. All of these are possible meanings for 'salad', and for each such meaning m, if the world had been (very) minimally different than the actual world (if people had had slightly different dispositions undergirding their use of 'salad'), 'salad' would have meant not what it actually means, but m instead.

Now suppose we were to take Sally to lunch, but she canceled. If we'd lunched, she would have had salad, and, Sally being Sally, she would at some point have said, 'My salad is very good'. This should make

C: If we'd gone to lunch with Sally, she would have said that her salad was good

true; indeed, given nothing more than our knowledge of Sally, we should have every reason to be confident that C is true. But, CJ point out, it would seem that confidence in C's truth is misplaced, given the mammoth number of meanings 'salad' can take on. For very small variations in the physical facts will occasion a change in the semantics of 'salad' from its actual meaning to one of the meanings just considered, in which the cutoff for being a salad differs by less than a silly little millimeter. But then it is hard to see why we should think that 'the closest worlds' in which we go to lunch with Sally will all be ones in which 'salad' has exactly the semantics it actually has. Indeed, given the mammoth number of possible meanings of 'salad' that are very close to the actual one, the set of worlds in which the word has one of these meanings instead of another will be vanishingly small. But the consequent of C is true at world w only if Sally there asserts whatever proposition 'My salad is good' actually expresses. As CJ put it, counterfactuals like C are

> disturbingly analogous to utterly unassertable counterfactuals like
> D: If I had a thrown a dart at this dartboard, it would have hit the exact geometrical center.
> (Dorr and Hawthorne 2014, 301)

The argument begins by assuming that there is such a thing as **the** meaning-cum-possible-worlds-intension of 'salad' as it's actually used—call it s—and that many microscopic shifts in such things as dispositions to apply the word must result in a shift of meaning of 'salad' from s to some meaning distinct from but very much like s. It's in fact assumed that there is an enormous collection of meanings all distinct from s but

---

[14] I simplify in various ways. In particular, I do not explain how to understand *vanishingly small set of worlds* since that would require a detour through the use of measure theory to make comparisons of infinite sets.

clustered around it, none of which we could (without divine help) distinguish from s. And for each meaning in this cluster, some relatively small variation from the actual physical situation would make 'salad' have that meaning. Things go awry, I think, right at the beginning. Fix the physical facts relative to which an interpretation-cum-assignment-of-intensions to our actual uses of words is to be judged. There is no reason to assume that there is a particular intension for 'salad' that provides a better (relative to the facts) interpretation of it than many, many others that vary only by deciding a bit differently what volume of greens a salad doth make. The idea that there is a particular intension s which is **the** actual (determinate) meaning (at this moment) of 'salad' is not only gratuitous, it's just wrong. Ditto for our counterfactual uses of words. There will be a range of 'best interpretations' we can give of these, interpretations that are good enough and such that there are none better.

I argued in Chapter 3 that if, abstracting from whatever special interests we bring to the task of interpretation, it's not determinate whether the other's use of a phrase p shares semantics with our use of the phrase p', then it is felicitous and perfectly correct to interpret the other's use of p with our uses of p'. This, after all, is what we do all the time: we interpret our parents and grandparents as talking about pasta when they wrote or spoke the word 'pasta' twenty-five, fifty, or a hundred years back. And why shouldn't we? When we interpret another we are ... well, we are interpreting them. We find an adequate way to recast their idiom in ours. Too much variance between the physical properties and relations of their uses and ours (they use 'pasta' when picking up prunes) means that certain interpretations are verboten. But a tenth of a millimeter's variance in what counts as fettuccini—that doesn't rule out our interpreting their 'fettuccini' as meaning fettuccini. If this is correct, then there is no puzzle at all about why we should be confident of the truth of claims like C.

Suppose that the story about Sally—we were to go to lunch, we didn't, but had we, she would have uttered the relevant sentence—is factual, and that I uttered C. My intention in uttering it was in part to comment on how we would and should have understood her speech had we lunched—she would have spoken in a way that was well understood by understanding her words as I actually understand them. Surely there is no better way for me to understand Sally's utterances in very close counterfactual worlds. So relative to my context it is correct to so interpret Sally. So (assuming that in these worlds Sally utters, 'My salad is good', or words to that effect), my use of C is true. When I utter C, I say (something that entails) that Sally asserted a certain claim—that her salad was good. And this is correct in the context of my speech. Uttering C is not like trying to position a dart in an indiscernible point on a plane; it's like looking at someone from across town and recognizing correctly that he is, after all, a lot like us.

Note that I am not claiming that it is indeterminate whether my utterance of C was true. Whether a claim—in particular, whether a claim that x said p—is true, false, or indeterminate is a context-relative affair. Speaking from a context in which counter-factual Sally is interpreted, the suggestion I am making is not that it is a vague matter as to what Sally said, or as to whether the content of her counterfactual utterance matches that of my actual utterance; what was vague before interpretation is resolved in interpretation, just as the vagueness of whether eighteen-year-olds are adults (for such and such a purpose) is resolved in stipulating that (for those purposes) eighteen-year-olds are not adults.[15]

CJ criticize a proposal for resolving their puzzle that might seem very much like the view about attitudes and their ascription that I was pushing in the first section of this chapter. The proposal CJ criticize—call it BP—assumes that in reporting another's attitudes a speaker can focus on the other's use of a word with the intention to use the word in a report's complement with the semantics it has when the other uses it. The proposal is that when a speaker does this, then, all else being equal, the speaker's use of the word has, as it occurs in the complement of an attitude ascription to the other, the semantics it has as used by the other. So, for example, I might intend that, when reporting Johnson's utterance, 'I wanted a glass of water' with 'Johnson said that he wanted a glass of water', my use of 'water' has whatever semantic properties Johnson's utterance of the word had. Given this, we are pretty much guaranteed that when I echo Johnson's words in saying what he said I speak truly. If so, it is not implausible to think that if a speaker has the intention that his use of 'salad' reproduce the semantics of 'salad' as used counterfactually by Sally, his use of C is true.

I'll discuss CJ's primary criticism of BP anon. But I must first point out that they miss what's most obviously wrong with it. Suppose that Sally's use of 'salad' is different enough from mine that it is (definitely) true of some things of which mine is not. In particular, her use of the term is true of the quinoa-drenched concoction she had for lunch yesterday, the one of which she spoke when she said, 'I had a salad with a lot of quinoa in it'. But my use of 'salad' is false of the spotulism she had for lunch; whatever it was she ate, it definitely wasn't a salad. According to the proposal we're calling BP, so long as I have the intention that my words reflect her semantics when I say, 'Sally said that she had a salad with quinoa in it', I speak truly, as I ascribe to her a saying of what she in fact said. Since the concoction had quinoa in it, Sally asserted something true. So I should be able to say not just that she said she had a salad with quinoa, but that she truly said that she had a salad with quinoa. But ex hypothesi, she didn't have a salad—'salad' as I use it is not true of the concoction. So the proposal on the table seems to commit us to the impossibility that Sally truly says that she had a salad, though she did not have a salad.

BP gets what's going on in attitude ascription completely backwards. It says that in such ascriptions we can suck the semantics of the words of the person whose attitude we report onto our words. But that is not what is happening when I report Sally as having spoken about salad. Rather I am, in interpreting her with my words, projecting the semantics of my words onto hers. This, at any rate, is (part of) the point of the

---

[15] Since the proposal is one on which (in the relevant contexts) it is not a vague matter as to what Sally said or whether her utterance shares semantics with mine, the proposal is not, I think, subject to the sorts of worries CJ express (Dorr and Hawthorne 2014, section 4.3) about invoking vagueness in an attempt to defuse the puzzle.

proposal about the semantics of attitude ascription outlined at the beginning of this chapter. That proposal does not imply that Sally can truly say that she had a salad when she had none.

As I said, CJ criticize BP. Since it may seem that any good objection to BP would also be a good objection to the account sketched in Section 1, I'll close this chapter by discussing whether CJ's objections to BP are relevant to that account.

CJ observe that as it stands, BP does not explain why (in a case in which there is a semantic shift between lunchtime and report time) we are entitled to be confident that

E: Everyone I took to lunch said her salad was delicious

is correct, given that everyone I took to lunch uttered 'my salad is delicious'. They observe that one might posit variables that attach to words embedded in attitude ascriptions, so that E is (partially) regimented as

E':   (For every person x whom I took to lunch) x said that her salad$_y$ was delicious.

The semantics of E' is as follows: for each person t and person u, there is an interpretation of E' on which the material after the restriction in E' ascribes to t the assertion of what's expressed by 'x's salad was delicious' when t is assigned to 'x' and u's semantics for 'salad' is assigned to it.[16] We can then say that one understanding of E' is one on which it is true just in case whenever T is someone I took to lunch, the result of assigning T to both 'x' and 'y' in 'x said that her salad$_y$ was delicious' is true. Presumably the variables attached to the words in ascriptions like E' are not mandatorily bound by the sentence's subject; one reading of E will be obtained by assigning the person uttering it to 'y'. In this case—one thinks it should have something like the status of a default— E ascribes to each lunch partner x the assertion of what the speaker expresses, referring to x, with 'her salad was delicious'.

So far, so good. But, CJ observe, if this is what's going on in sentences like E, there should be a reading of

F: No one has ever said any salad is delicious

that is true. We simply pick someone who has never used 'salad is delicious' assertively and who means something a bit different from what everyone else means and assign him to the variable carried by the embedded words. More generally, CJ argue, unlike sentences like 'all my friends will be in a local bar tonight' which we recognize as

---

[16] The model here is the behavior of 'local', which seems in sentences like 'everyone went to a local bar' to produce an ambiguity well explained by positing that the 'local' in such sentences is to be regimented with the phrase 'local to x'. Sometimes the 'x' is bound by 'everyone', so the sentence's use says *everyone went to a bar local to him or her*; sometimes the 'x' is assigned to the speaker, so the sentence's use by u says what is said when u utters 'everyone went to a bar local to me'. To get the obvious reading of 'Bert went to Granville Island last month. I'm sure he had a great time; the local bars are fun' we need to understand 'local' as meaning something like 'local to Bert at the time he was in Granville Island'. The proposal in the text is a way of achieving this.

ambiguous, we do not take sentences like E and F to display the sort of ambiguity that the proposal on the table ascribes to them.

Like the proposal CJ criticize, the view I sketched at the beginning of the chapter allows that sentences like E and F can vary in truth value across simultaneous contexts. But this is not in virtue of anything like an ability of speakers to manipulate the interpretation of words in a complement clause. Rather, that view takes intentions and linguistic behavior of speakers, which vary across contexts, to affect the truth conditions of token reports. They do this in two ways. First, the speaker adopts a particular way of interpreting the semantics of the other's linguistic or mental states. I say, when Diva sees me throw a ball and runs after it, that she knew I'd thrown a ball; in doing this, I interpret a state of Diva's using words of mine as I mean them. A persnickety philosopher may balk at saying Diva knows any such thing, thinking it an error to identify Sheltie semantics with human semantics. In this disagreement, neither I nor the philosopher uses 'throw a ball' in a way that's novel: each of us is using 'throw a ball' in the way we always use it. My use of the phrase in the attitude ascription has the semantics it has when I say, 'I threw a ball'; likewise for Mr. Persnickety.

The second contextual sensitivity that sentences like E and F enjoy involves the use of certain of one's words as 'translations' of certain representations of the subject of the ascription, as when I say, 'The Sumerians didn't believe that Hesperus is Phosphorus', intending that 'Hesperus' represent the Sumerian word it translates, not the Sumerian word 'Phosphorus' translates. Given that I can, in ascribing an attitude, use 'Hesperus' as a translation of x's representation only when r (relative to my interpretation of x) has the same referential properties as my use of 'Hesperus' has, this second sort of context sensitivity does not involve my use of a term having (as I interpret the other) a semantics different from the semantics it has when I use it outside of attitude ascription.

Does any of this lead to objectionable predictions of readings of sentences like F? Consider first a case somewhat different from those CJ consider. Imagine we are discussing pasta through the ages. Showing off my culinary knowledge, I say:

> You know, today we think of pasta as something that can be made out of agar and various weird vegetable matters. But in Cosgrove's 1897 book *Cooking the Italian Way* we read 'Pasta must be made from wheat, water, and salt, though it may be colored with vegetable or ink'. Of course, he is not saying that agar pasta is not pasta, because he had a different concept of pasta than we do.

It's a lot of work to say this. That's because the overwhelmingly natural way of interpreting Cosgrove's use of 'pasta' is with 'pasta'. But it is possible to stamp one's foot and disavow homophonic interpretation, insisting that one will not understand another as meaning what one means with one's words.

Now consider sentence F, 'no one has ever said that salad is delicious'. CJ's objection to BP is that according to it, 'salad' as it occurs in F can carry the semantics of 'salad' as used by absolutely any English speaker, and so F has a 'true reading'. There is a grain of truth in the idea that I can impose pretty much any speaker's semantics for 'salad' on my use of 'salad' when it lies under an attitude verb: with elaborate stage setting—essentially by saying explicitly that one doesn't want one's words to have their normal interpretation—one can untie the complement of an attitude ascription from (what is in one's idiom) its normal semantics. This is what happens in the tolerably natural

> Siobhan's salads—well, the things she calls 'salads'—are so gross. For her, something that's more than 10 percent vegetables isn't a salad. It has to be mostly jello and something spicy—gochugaru, or Szechuan peppercorns, or chili peppers—on top. If we thought of salad that way, no one would think that salads are edible, much less delicious!

But to allow that one can speak in this way is not to allow that without fanfare or contextual cueing one can utter, 'No one ever said that salads are delicious' and, because one (without notifying the audience) intends 'salad' to carry Siobhan's semantics, speak truly. There is not, for each English speaker x, a 'reading' (in any sensible sense of 'reading') of this sentence on which it says that no one ever said that salad-in-x's-sense-of-'salad' is delicious. I don't see that the sort of objection CJ give to BP has any force against the account of attitude ascription sketched in this chapter.

6

Sex and Conversation

I say, linguistic entities are analogous to biological ones. You say, yeah, yeah, language evolves; so what?

In earlier chapters I suggested a philosophical payoff. Seeing that meanings are indeed species-like helps dissolve philosophical puzzles. Quine is right about analyticity; that doesn't mean that our intuitions that there is something like analyticity are tracking nothing. Just as a species can exist for many generations in stasis, with a reliable morphology and ecological niche, so the meaning of 'cousin' can remain in equilibrium over generations or even centuries. Seeing that the kind of meaning that philosophical analysis tries to uncover is something that is spread over a population, something that accumulates, as Austin puts it, the wisdom of generations, helps us understand what it is that philosophical analysis can, and cannot, do. It is also a corrective to over a century's obsession with those aspects of meaning that are reflected by truth conditions. What is in interpretive common ground (ICG) is often relevant to reference and truth—the fact that we all apply 'just' to these sorts of acts and not those and expect others to recognize this can hardly be irrelevant to what acts the term is true of. The fact that we use 'just' to commend an act and expect others to recognize that is not determinative of the term's reference, but it is a fact about what the term means, one that is at least as important as the fact that 'just' is true of an act iff the act is just.

Perhaps the most significant aspect of recognizing that meanings are species-like is that it suggests a range of questions that seem worth exploring. Meanings, like species, do seem relatively static in the short to medium term. It is certainly worth asking to what extent the appearance is reality, and, if it is, why it's so. Meaning also does change. 'Skyline' once meant, roughly, any line demarcating the earth and what is on it from the atmosphere; now it seems to mean, to most of us anyway, the line that demarcates the cityscape from the sky. 'Water' seems to have once had a (single) meaning that applied to both what one found in the Thames and to urine; this is no longer true. 'Marry' once meant, inter alia, a relation in which only those of different sexes could stand; this is changing. The mechanisms in these examples are presumably quite different. It is worth asking about the extent to which there is some relatively small set of processes that describe or even explain how such changes occur.

In some cases—'skyline' is perhaps an example—change may be driven by particular events (populations moving from the country to the city) and relatively simple learning processes. In other cases—'marriage' is perhaps an example—the processes driving meaning change may be in a certain sense Darwinian: one can (perhaps) look at the individuals which constitute a meaning at a particular time as reproducing, and see the change in the distribution of meaning-relevant properties in succeeding generations as determined in part by the advantages of one's lexicon embedding one such property instead of an alternative. Whether such changes are Darwinian or not, one can ask to what extent the processes underlying such changes are, like biological evolution, essentially arational. There is a suite of tools used in population biology, economics, and game theory to model the dynamics of change in the distribution of properties in populations. These may turn out to be useful to describing or even helping to explain the processes by which the meanings realized in the minds of a population change or remain in stasis as the members of the population interact with their non-linguistic environment and with each other.

This chapter discusses some of the questions about the processes that drive change of meaning. I don't try so much to answer questions as to illustrate and examine ways we might think about sharpening them enough so that we have interesting questions to which we might actually find answers.

1. A Simple Model of Meaning Change

There are surely semantic changes that result from the operation of straightforward learning mechanisms within populations; it is not difficult to develop models of how such mechanisms operate. It may even be possible to confirm or refute the claim that a particular model describes a semantic change of which we are aware. This section sketches a speculative example.

The word 'skyline' came into use as a term for the line in a visually perceivable scene that demarcates the terrestrial from the sky. These days, at least in my neck of the linguistic woods, no one uses it in quite so general a way; its use is confined to describing the line where a cityscape meets the sky.[1] People do not presuppose that bucolic skylines are skylines. How did this happen?

It seems that the best we can do is hypothesize. But what occurs to one immediately is that over time two things happened: for whatever reasons, the proportion of applications of the term to bucolic situations declined; this led 'in succeeding generations' to fewer and fewer individuals acquiring the word with its original semantics.

To say more, one needs to supply at least two things: a model of how the meaning of a word like 'skyline' is realized at a time within a population and a proposal about (how to represent in a diachronic model) the mechanisms that maintain or alter such realizations over time. We already have the germ of a proposal about meaning

---

[1] Claims about historical usage are, unless otherwise noted, based on the OED. In the case of 'skyline', the OED in fact reports two meanings: the more general meaning (any old sky–earth line); and 'The outline or silhouette of a building or number of buildings or other objects seen against the sky'. The examples of the first meaning are from the period from 1823 to 1897; those for the second range from 1896 to 1971.

realization: associated with each of an individual's lexical entries is a set of claims that the individual 'holds at the ready' for use in interpreting the use of the word by others and supposes that others likewise hold at the ready. These presuppositions about ICG are, to a first approximation, what realize the meanings of vocabulary items at a time; the meanings of those items, to a first approximation, are the ICG they determine. If we think of presuppositions as being, or being very much like, dispositions to behave in certain ways in certain situations, we can appropriate one or another psychological model of how behavioral dispositions are instilled, reinforced, and extinguished to satisfy the second need.[2]

If we embed these elements in a hypothesis about how the relevant presuppositions are realized, we can generate an idealized description of a possible mechanism of 'linguistic evolution'. Suppose that when an individual has a vocabulary item applied to visually observable scenes, she associates a prototype and/or an exemplar structure with it, and that these structures influence the way in which she applies the item. Given this, a crude first guess about what (in part) determines the interpretive presuppositions that are associated with such vocabulary might be that prototypes and exemplars do. This would be so if we are wired in such a way that (a) when we take something as stunningly obvious, then absent indications to the contrary, we assume everyone else does, and (b) when a certain application has particular relations to an exemplar or prototype structure—it is an overwhelmingly natural projection from the set of exemplars, or rates very high in terms of prototypicality—we take it to be stunningly obvious. Assume in addition: (c) prototype and exemplar structures are affected by applications of others we are aware of, so that (for example) how prototypical a feature is changes in proportion to the number of times it is salient (or taken to be salient to the speaker) in an application; (d) nothing other than prototype and exemplar structure generates interpretive presuppositions.[3] Now we have a description of a mechanism which in the right environment—one in which applications of 'skyline' begin for whatever reason to be primarily to cityscape lines—will tend to produce the observed change in the use of 'skyline'.

Such an explanation leaves some questions unanswered—for example, why the initial shift from general application of 'skyline' in bucolic and urban situations to one in which it is predominantly used in urban ones? We might be able to make a reasonable guess about the answer to such questions: Migration or certain uses in print becoming widely known and in some sense paradigmatic, for example. We might not. Not everything that has an explanation has an explanation that we can give in its entirety.

The mechanism just invoked is that of creation and extinction of behavioral dispositions within a diachronic population as a result of its interactions with the environment. The interactions are ones in which someone utters some words and is interpreted by an

---

[2] A certain sort of behaviorist might shrink from calling the sort of thing that happens in the mind when interpretation occurs 'behavior'. Of such a behaviorist, we might ask: How's that working out for you?

[3] Of course this last is implausible. The project here is to point to how, by idealizing, we can generate models of meaning change that can in some sense be tested by things like computer modeling.

audience—conversations, for short. In conversation, participants behave in certain ways as a result of the behavioral dispositions they bring to the table—they have certain communicative and interpretive strategies. As a result of the interaction, there may be changes in what grounds those strategies. Over time, these changes may change the individual's strategy. Since the communicative strategies of the members of a population at t are in the main what determine those of the next generation—the individuals who enter the population at or shortly after t—these changes can have a more or less profound impact on the strategies of the population over time.

This picture is not novel. Versions of it—on which behavior or other 'heritable traits' manifested in the environment are modified in virtue of the way their manifestation interacts with the environment—are common in population genetics, economics, and other fields.[4] Bryan Skyrms and others have investigated abstract versions of this picture, arguing (for example) that models based on such pictures explain how behavior that carries information can arise over generations with no preceding intentionality.[5] Often the picture is limned in game theoretic terms: we think of individual strategies as having 'payoffs' for those who use them, the payoff depending on the environment and what strategy one's 'opponent' is using; the encounters ('games') in which strategies are deployed occur repeatedly: we posit one or another mechanism that changes the strategy an individual uses, change occurring, for example, when one's neighbors are using a strategy that has given them a larger payoff than one's own in the immediate past.

What does this last bit come to? Let's borrow from the literature on signaling games.[6] Think of the use of a word in a sentence as a move in a game. The game is one of coordination: the hope is that the interpreter assigns to the word the meaning that the user expects her to assign. The operational measure of whether coordination is achieved is speaker and hearer feeling that understanding was achieved without anything like speaker intervention ('no, I mean bucolic skyline') or retroactive reinterpretation ('oh, she must use "skyline" so that only city skylines count as such') being necessary. Call a feeling-of-understanding-without-need-of-correction-or-reinterpretatoin a 104, pronounced ten four. If an utterance results in 104, everybody gets a positive payoff; otherwise, everybody gets a non-positive one. These games happen again and again. Players can be expected, every once in a while (every ten games, say), to reassess their strategies—that is, their presuppositions about what is ICG. What strategy for

---

[4] In the picture above, the heritable traits are interpretive strategies, the populations collections of interpretive strategies as they are realized at a time in a group of coordinated lexicons. My-lexicon-as-it-is-at-t will be one member of a diachronic population of coordinated lexicons, my-lexicon-as-it-is-at-t+n will be (if n>0) another. This way of conceptualizing things is discussed in the next section.

[5] See for instance Skyrms (2010) and references therein. My debt in this section to Skyrms' work is large indeed.

[6] This literature is rooted in Lewis (1969). An accessible introduction to it—one that makes important contributions—is the work of Skyrms, in particular Skyrms (2010).

Lewis was, of course, interested in giving an account of (linguistic and non-linguistic) convention. One doesn't need to be committed to the idea that linguistic meaning is 'set by convention' to think that some aspects of it can be modeled using ideas from Lewis.

strategy-change speakers use is an empirical matter. But for the sake of illustration, suppose that speakers uniformly adopt the following: for each lexical item, they assess their last interchanges (whether as speaker or interpreter) involving the word and decide how often 104 was achieved; if the speaker finds that she is not achieving 104 at least two-thirds of the time, she switches strategies so long as she sees an alternative strategy for interpreting the word that does better.[7]

Given these assumptions, we can look at what happens over time given various initial distributions of presuppositions among speakers. 'Looking' is a matter of computer simulation, though in an example this simple one can also just look at what statistics tells us about the likelihood of various distributions of presuppositions in succeeding generations. For example, we might assume that conversations occur randomly in the population, and that in our initial population, confining attention to conversations in which 'skyline' is used, an individual converses with six who mean *urban skyline* with the word for every four who mean *urban or bucolic skyline*. Suppose as well that when there is not a match of presuppositions associated with 'skyline', 104 is not achieved; if there is, it is.[8] If you spend some time with an app that calculates probability distributions, you will find that it doesn't take very long for it to be highly probable that the narrower meaning becomes fixed in the population.

Do I seriously suggest that this is the correct explanation of how the meaning of 'skyline' changed? Of course not. Even setting the absurd idealizations of the last paragraph aside, this model ignores all kinds of factors that may well have had a part in the process. For example, some users may have 'prestige' of one sort or another, and if so, their use—especially if it is widely broadcast—may speed up (or slow down) the process.[9] For another, it ignores the possibility that the uses of a word one encounters may have a more subtle effect on meaning than the simple 'if things aren't working well, jump ship' mechanism just invoked. This would be the case if the assumptions at the beginning of this illustration were correct and (a) the word usage one encounters can affect what one takes to be prototypical, and (b) prototypicality, in turn, may affect the way a word is transmitted. (How often, after all, does one show a child a picture of an emu in teaching 'bird'?) Conceivably this sort of thing might do a great deal of work in the sort of case we're considering, since 'skyline' is not an everyday vocabulary term.

2. Meaning Change and Evolution via Natural Selection

In one sense of 'evolves', pretty much any change over time in the characteristics of a population is evolution. So there is certainly a sense in which semantic change is a

---

[7] 'Seeing strategy s' here is most simply understood as a matter of there being someone using s in one's 'neighborhood'.

[8] This is certainly the most unreasonable idealization here. Models in which it is not made are discussed in the next section.

[9] Levy (2011) trenchantly argues that many 'evolutionary' models of social phenomena neglect 'non-Darwinian' causes of change in social behavior.

process of evolution. But when biologists say that it is evolution that has over four billion years generated the varieties of life on earth, they have a specific process in mind, one whose driving force is natural selection. A standard gloss of natural selection is that it is change in the distribution of heritable characteristics in a population that is caused by an advantage that some of those characteristics give to their possessors. In the Darwinian paradigm, the advantage has to do with survival and reproduction: selection occurs when those with a characteristic C are more likely to survive long enough to have offspring—and to have more offspring—than those with alternatives to C, and this likelihood translates over generations to an increase in the percentage of Cs in the population.

I have not said that any of the processes that change meanings are analogous to natural selection, but I haven't denied it either. The way I described the toy example of the last section—as one in which interpretive strategies are 'heritable traits' that may 'give rise' to strategies identical to them in the 'next generation'—certainly suggests that the example was one of Darwinian natural selection. This section and the next are devoted to discussing whether (some) processes of semantic change are well thought of as cases of evolution via natural selection—ENS, for short.[10]

Peter Godfrey-Smith observes that there are three overlapping ways of thinking about, modeling, and explaining change across time in populations. A population is a (diachronic) collection of 'individual things that have some degree of autonomy and a significant number of properties in common'.[11] Some populations—call them M-populations in honor of the biologist Ernst Mayr—are ones in which some common properties come in families of variants (in the way that, for example, genes have alleles) and in which there is variation across time in the distribution of such variants, variation that is determined by earlier distributions of variants and the interaction of the population with its environment. The set of English speakers (or the set of time slices of English speakers' lexicons) in the skyline example of the last section forms an M-population in this sense.

Change in the distribution of variants in an M-population may be due to ENS; it may not. To the extent that it is due to natural selection, the population is a D (for Darwinian) population.[12] Some of the diachronic variation in a D-population may involve processes of selection on variants that tend to reproduce themselves in 'high-fidelity' ways, so that their structure tends to be preserved over many generations. Genes are the poster children for such units of selection. Such a D-population is one whose evolution is (in part, at least) driven by (selection on) replicators. I'll defer discussion of the idea

---

[10] There are processes responsible for change in the forms of life on earth besides evolution—genetic drift (chance changes in the distribution of alleles), for example. To say that a diachronic process of reproduction is one of ENS is to say that ENS is (among) the most significant force(s) that explain the process's dynamics.

[11] Godfrey-Smith (2009, 149). I depart somewhat from Godfrey-Smith's characterization of (what I call) M-populations; whatever departure there might be is in part inspired by Sober (1980).

[12] As Godfrey-Smith observes, some change in an M-population may be Darwinian, some may not be. Processes of change may also be more or less Darwinian, as we will see below.

that meanings (or the words to which they are attached) are replicators to Section 5, concentrating for now on the question of whether various examples are best thought of as ones involving D-populations, M- but not D-populations, or aren't really well thought of in terms of population dynamics.[13]

Common sorts of meaning change are ones that involve narrowing or expansion of application: the skyline example is an example of the former; the change in the application of 'tall' in the sixteenth century that extended it from a predicate applied only to tall men to one applied to tall men, women, buildings, trees, and so forth is an example of the latter. Let's look again at the skyline example, asking whether it is in fact Darwinian.

That example presumably involves (at least) two sorts of meaning-relevant change: (i) a shift in the basis of the ICG of 'skyline' in which the claim

W: skylines are those lines where the sky meets the earth

is replaced with the claim

N: skylines are those lines where the sky meets the cityscape;

(ii) a shift in the prototype structure associated by most of the population with 'skyline' from one in which bucolic and urban lines are equally prototypical to one in which only the latter is.[14] Are either of these changes aptly described as changes brought about by natural selection in the biologist's sense of natural selection?

In part, this is a question about how we choose to describe the players in the process. Who are the individuals, what events are events of individuals reproducing, what traits are we to take as heritable variants? In the last section, the individuals were taken to be time slices of lexical entries; reproduction was the event of an individual revising her interpretive strategy (which could be thought of as associating a particular set of presuppositions with a lexical item) every ten conversations; the variant traits were associating W with 'skyline' and associating N with 'skyline'. We assumed that the strategies that conversants were using were 'visible' to everyone—in revising an entry, a player knew what presuppositions those who used the word were employing.[15] Under this assumption, the 'parents' of a new time slice of a lexical entry would be (the time slice of the entry that immediately precedes it and) whatever time slices are imitated. The way we described the example suggested that something like natural selection was

---

[13] Frankly, when I say that we should think of meanings as species, what I mean is that we should think of meanings as forming M-populations: though some meaning change looks to involve something very much like ENS, other processes of change aren't so obviously ones in which anything like natural selection is involved. The title of this book probably ought to be something like *Meanings as Populations in Something Like the Sense That People Have in Mind When Discussing the Turn in Biology Occasioned by Darwin-as-Synthesized-with-Mendelian-Genetics*. Peter Momtchiloff tells me that so titling it might detract from sales.

[14] Take prototype structures here to be representatives of the various cognitive structures that directly determine application in speech.

[15] This because speakers were assumed, if they were failing to understand others enough of the time, to adopt that strategy—i.e., that set of presuppositions—of their 'neighbors' that was most successful.

going on, since change in strategy was driven by a benefit (smooth conversation) that one strategy gave that the other did not.

You might reasonably observe that this is not a very plausible model of how the change in question occurred. If you and I are talking in an urban environment, there needn't be any situation in which the difference between playing the W strategy and playing the N strategy is perceptible, since the only skylines we discuss may be the ambient ones. In fact, one imagines that the switch from W constituting the meaning of the word to N's doing so might be achieved almost entirely through attrition of bucolic applications, which leads to learners of the word simply assuming that it means *lines like those urban lines Mom and Dad use it to talk about.* Something similar may well be true of changes in paradigms. Many words that are primarily applied on the basis of observable traits will, in the course of acquisition, be associated with paradigmatic instances, particularly 'good examples' which serve as a basis for projection to new cases. We can expect that what is paradigmatic for an individual can and sometimes does change simply because the frequency of certain sorts of applications fluctuates.

The problem is that in a realistic description of the process of change of the meaning of 'skyline', the characteristics, *meaning W by 'skyline'* and *meaning N by the word,* do not look to be heritable traits during all periods in which the change occurs. Whether a time slice of a speaker means W or N by the word is unlikely to vary systematically with what 'the parents' of that time slice mean, simply because it is unlikely, at crucial times in the process of meaning change, that the difference between meaning W and meaning N is 'visible' in a way that would lead to differential reproduction. The environment and the distribution of the properties in the population of speakers at one time produces behavior that has a (fairly) systematic effect on the distribution of those properties at a later time. But as far as finding a framework in which to describe and explain changes in distribution goes, it doesn't look like the population is profitably described as a D-population.

Those who think of cultural items like canoes and concepts, rituals and rulers as memes—units of information or ways of doing things that replicate themselves in the mental and social lives of people who build, think, or practice them—may insist that examples like the 'skyline' example are indeed cases of ENS. I'll take up this view in Section 5.

3. Semantic Ecology

Biological evolution occurs when phenotypic differences—differences in shape, behavior, internal constitution, and the like—that are caused by heritable genetic differences result in differences in longevity and reproduction, with a consequent change in the distribution of the genetic differences. So biological evolution is a product of how varying phenotypes interact with the environment. When speaking of it we tend to use dramatic language—individuals compete; only the fittest survive. But 'winning the competition' needn't be a matter of 'doing' anything. Suppose there are three varieties of a fish species in a pond, one with bright-green stripes on a brown background, one with violet stripes on a brown background, and one with muted-blue stripes on a brown background. The fish mate randomly so far as striping is concerned. Suppose (absurdly, but simply to have a manageable example) that the variation is caused by pair of alleles A and a: fish that have a pair of as are striped green, those with a pair of As are striped violet, and aAs are striped blue. If the pond is murky, differences in color may be irrelevant to survival and number of progeny. But if the pond changes from murky to transparent, or the murk is replaced by green (or blue or violet) weeds, the change in habitat may make one variety fitter than the others, which will result in a different distribution of alleles a and A. The change in gene and phenotype frequency is not due to anything that fish are doing in any normal sense of 'do'; they're just swimmin' around as usual, munchin' minnows. What's changed is the environment in which their phenotypes have effects. Much the same, of course, could be said of a case in which we start with a pond with only aa fish and throw in a collection of AA or aA fish, introducing a 'competitor' to the a-allele.

One way to probe for selection effects in semantic change begins by asking, With what should we identify the environment of a natural-language meaning? An answer begins by observing that linguistic meanings are, well, linguistic: they are 'embodied' by being associated by speakers with relatively easy-to-copy and -remember forms individuated by morphology, phonetics, and syntax. Call such morphophonetic/syntactic forms phones. Part of a meaning's environment is constituted by herds of phones—individual lexicons made up of phones paired with meanings-cum-presuppositions-held-at-the-ready-for-interpretation.

Call such pairings i-phones.[16] I-phones are used to give expression to our thoughts, hopes, and fears; thoughts, fears, and the rest both reflect and help determine individual behavior and social practices. This gives our words' meanings roles in both individual cognitive economies and the society at large. The meaning of 'marriage'—what it means to society as a whole, to be married—has a particular role in such things as determining who is allowed to marry whom, what duties and privileges are associated with being married, etc. The meaning of 'marriage'—what it means to an individual—has a particular role in an individual's mentality—for example, it determines the associations the word prompts and its contribution to inferential roles.

Animals and plants tend to be found in particular ecological niches; those niches can have a marked effect on how they develop. Words are of course capable of ranging widely, since they can in principle be used in any situation whatsoever. That said, a word may have something like a natural habitat: words and phrases are often standardly used in certain sorts of situations and contexts while avoiding others. 'Hello' is for the most part used at the beginning of an encounter; 'y'all' mostly addresses people

---

[16] Sorry. It was an accident, honest. 'I' for interpreted. Didn't plan the pun, it just sort of happened. Dan Dennett pointed out to me that my characterization of i-phones is much like Ray Jackendoff's (2002) characterization of lexical items.

already known; 'fuck' tends to avoid high tea with the Queen; 'polyploid' is rarely observed in kindergarten.

We have three things, then, that can be analogized to play for meanings a role like the ecosystem plays in biological evolution: the linguistic world, populated with (other) embodied meanings; the individual and social roles meanings take on in virtue of commonly held beliefs, laws, institutions, regulations, and so forth; the patterns of use that associate a meaning or a word that expresses it with some sorts of situations and keep it away from others. Are there interactions between meanings and this semantic ecosystem that are examples of meanings undergoing selection, changes in frequency of one sort or another in virtue of some environmental advantage that one meaning has over another?

Phones often have several meanings—'bank' is homophonous; 'smoke' is polysemous. Homophony often involves meanings that are unrelated in any intuitive sense, as with 'bank'. Polysemous words are phones (or collections of phones that don't differ in phonetics) with multiple, closely related meanings, typically with some of the phone's meanings incorporating others. 'Smoke', for example, can mean: floating particulate resulting from burning (smoke 1); to inhale smoke 1 using a cigarette or pipe; to treat food by exposing it to smoke 1.[17] Homophony and polysemy are often stable states. There's no reason—at least no reason having to do with communicative efficiency or the role of the various meanings of 'bank' in finance or potamology—for 'bank' to shed one of its meanings; as long as syntax and morphology with the help of context allow us to identify which sense of 'smoke' a use carries, what harm is there in the polysemy of 'smoke'?

But there is under certain conditions something that looks a lot like 'competition' to occupy a particular morphophonetic niche: different meanings duking it out to determine who will have a home on a particular shape and sound.

'Gay' once had as its primary meanings *lighthearted, carefree; bright, showy; dissolute, promiscuous*. Its current primary meaning gained currency in the late 1930s or early 1940s. The term is shedding its former meanings in the sense that there are relatively few uses of the term today with any of the old meanings; the overwhelming majority of (non-middle school) uses of the term are ones that apply to someone in virtue of being homosexual or to an object or kind in virtue of its being associated with homosexuals. It is plausible that once gay people began using the term to describe themselves, the general populace became reluctant to use the word to mean 'lighthearted' in good part because simply using the term, no matter what one meant by it, in one way or another conjured up the meaning *homosexual*. That this was the case, in turn, disinclined (non-gay) users to use the term, presumably sometimes out of embarrassment, sometimes because of fear of offending or upsetting the audience, sometimes because the topic of homosexuality was taboo, sometimes simply out of fear that one would be misunderstood as speaking of matters homosexual. (That one didn't mean to be talking about

---

[17] And several other things; see the interesting discussion in Jackendoff (2002).

homosexuality in speaking about someone's gay attire is neither here nor there; to use the word is to point to the big pink elephant in the room.) At this point in linguistic history, using the word with one of the original meanings sounds archaic, arch, or insidiously bigoted.[18]

This looks to be a process quite like ENS. The reproducing individuals are certain 'meaning tokens'—meanings as realized in the lexicon of a particular speaker. When, for example, Noel Coward wrote in 1929, 'Art is our inspiration, And as we are the reason for the "Nineties" being gay, We all wear a green carnation' and readers recognized his (relatively novel) use of 'gay' to mean gay, the part of Coward's lexical entry for the phone that paired it with that meaning 'reproduced itself' in the lexicons of readers.[19] Once this use of the word became established, so that the linguistic landscape was littered with tokens of 'gay' meaning homosexual, (relational) properties of the old meanings of the term made it more difficult for those meanings to reproduce, reproduction on this way of thinking of matters being achieved by audible or written tokens with the relevant meaning being recognized as so meant, and thereby causing new lexical entries to be formed. As both the absolute and relative number of tokens with the old meanings decrease, reproduction of those meanings becomes more difficult.

I should here stress that I really am thinking of meanings as things that are constituted by population lineages. The meaning of 'gay' manifested by its use to pick out homosexuals or things associated with homosexuality is literally a lineage: its founders were the lexicons of users like Gertrude Stein and Noel Coward; its members are the descendent lexical entries that are ancestrally related to the original uses. The meaning of the term in the relevant population is constituted by objects that stretch across time and space, the overwhelming majority of which have among their properties the property of being lexical entries for the phone 'gay'. There is a use of 'synonymous' on which 'gay' (used to refer to homosexuals) is synonymous with 'homosexual'. But on the view of meaning I'm developing, tokens of 'gay' and 'homosexual' do not share a meaning in what I take to be the fundamental sense of 'share a meaning', since sharing a meaning requires being part of the same 'meaning lineage'.[20]

My speculative history of various i-phones inscribed as 'gay' hypothesizes that two factors were important in the selection effects I've discussed. One is that uses of the word with one meaning would be mistaken for, or at least conjure up in the audience's mind, another meaning; the other is that this second meaning carried in the population at large a certain negative valence—that is, its use tended to bring about a particular negative affective reaction in either the user or her audience. I hypothesize[21] that there

[18] Actually, trying to use the word to mean *degenerate* is hopeless, as few people seem to be aware today that the word ever had this meaning.

[19] Coward's is the second example of this use of the word in the OED; the first is one by Gertrude Stein in 1922.

[20] This is not to say that there isn't a sense of 'synonymous' on which the two words could share a meaning. Most straightforwardly, they might have strongly overlapping ICGs, ones that are, abstracting from each word's involvement in its own ICG, more or less identical.

[21] A five-dollar phone for the fifty-cent 'guess'.

will be a general tendency, when a word is homophonous in a way that allows for it to be applied with either meaning to (much) the same objects and one of the meanings has pronounced valence, for selection in favor of the valenced meaning. The hypothesis is that once people are aware of the existence of a valenced meaning for a term, in everyday situations in which a use of the term can be taken to have either the valenced or the unvalenced meaning, auditors will tend to interpret the use as carrying the valenced meaning. Speakers will be dimly aware of this and thus tend to eschew using the term with the unvalenced meaning simply to avoid misunderstanding.

'Awesome' perhaps provides an example of the hypothesis. One hundred or so years ago, its primary meanings were *full of awe; inspiring awe; dreadful*. The use of the term to mean 'dreadful' seems to have died out for whatever reason some time back—I certainly wasn't aware of it as a child or an undergraduate. It is sometimes used in the first two ways today, but my sense is that many people aren't even aware that it has these meanings; it's often used to mean *overwhelming, remarkable*; surely its most common use is what the OED charmingly describes so: 'In trivial use…an enthusiastic term of commendation'.[22] Once the latter two uses are common, the hypothesis just proposed leads one to expect the sort of decline in other uses that seems to be occurring. If this is in fact what's happening, it is another example of semantic selection.

Don't get me wrong: One would have to do considerable empirical work to validate both the hypothesis about affect and meaning change, as well as the suggestion that it contributes to an explanation of changes in the use and meaning of 'awesome'. All that I have been trying to do here is to point to reasons for thinking that something like ENS is sometimes involved in semantic change.

4. Contested Meanings and Competition

Many changes explained by selection don't involve much we'd describe as literal combat between the more fit and the less. Those fish that were just doing their thing as the environment changed were duking it out in only a metaphorical sense. Some selection looks more like combat, or at least active competition. An often-cited study by Peter and Rosemary Grant traced rapid evolution in the average beak size of finches when a drought caused plants that produced small seeds to die: with only large seeds to feed on, finches with larger beaks (which were better at breaking the large seeds open) were much more viable than those with smaller beaks, so much so that over very few generations there was a significant change in the average beak size in the population studied. Here is selection driven by competition for a life-sustaining resource.[23]

In many examples of semantic change meanings compete to occupy a particular niche in the semantic landscape. An obvious example is the battle over the institution

---

[22] Which is, of course, a pretty awesome putdown.

[23] Pretty much any introductory textbook on evolution discusses the Grants' work; my source is Zimmer and Emlen (2012, 220–3). Several years after the drought, heavy rain changed the climate on the island and produced, by causing smaller seeds to proliferate, another change in average beak size.

of marriage and the meaning of 'marry'. Over the past thirty or so years two different understandings—two different conceptions or ways of thinking—of marriage have been competing with one another, not only for a particular legal and social role but for the role of dominant understanding in the public mind. Such examples raise descriptive, explanatory, and practical questions. One wonders how to describe such cases: was 'marry' as used in the US in 2008 ambiguous? Did the average speaker have two (or more) concepts of marriage, a public concept and a private concept? One wonders how the forces that drive change are to be characterized: When the concept of marriage as (necessarily) a relation that unites only those of different sexes is driven to extinction, is this in some more than metaphorical sense a case of evolution via natural selection? And just as one might wonder whether we might control biological evolution, one might wonder whether we can control conceptual evolution, and if so, how.

The next sections discuss these questions, starting with the descriptive one. It's good to focus discussion with examples; this section focuses on feminist attempts in nineteenth-century America to change the way that both law and society thought of rape. The historical details I draw from an article by Jill Hasaday.

The nineteenth-century American legal understanding of rape—and surely its dominant social understanding for at least the first two-thirds of the century—was that it occurred when a man had intercourse with a woman who was not his wife without her consent.[24] The nineteenth-century feminist movement in America began arguing publicly in favor of the idea that a women 'has a right to her own person'—and thus has a right to refuse her husband's demands for sex—in the mid-1850s; the radical 'Free Love' movement at about this time went so far as to apply the terms 'rape' and 'sexual slavery' to much of what happened in the marital bed (Hasaday 2000, 1415ff). These ideas were pressed fairly vigorously for the balance of the nineteenth century, but had little effect beyond making sexual abuse in some states a ground for divorce. That the idea that women have a right to their bodies was a cornerstone of the feminist movement in the US in the 1800s seems to have been pretty much forgotten for much of the twentieth century.

The legal and cultural surround of the official definition of rape here is of some interest. The idea that a man could not rape his wife was tied to two things. The first was a legal view of marriage as involving a status that was permanent and non-negotiable. The state set certain parameters for the rights and duties of marriage partners that were not optional. Hasady quotes the author of 'one of the most influential family law treatises' of the time as writing:

[T]he idea, that any government could, consistently with the general weal, permit this institution to become merely [a] matter of bargain between men and women and not regulate it by its own power is…too absurd to require a word of refutation.[25]

---

[24] Throughout what follows I simplify the presuppositions that articulate concepts.

[25] Joel Bishop in *Commentaries on the Law of Marriage and Divorce 11* (Little, Brown, 1864); cited at Hasaday (2000, 1387).

Secondly, assumptions about marital rape depended on the idea that in agreeing to marry one gave irrevocable consent to having sex whenever one's partner requested it—an idea that, as is well known, traces back to the British jurist Matthew Hale, who wrote that marital rape was impossible 'for by their mutual matrimonial consent and contract the wife hath given herself up in this kind [i.e., sexually] unto her husband, which she cannot retract'.[26] If you don't question the bizarre view of consent in Hale's doctrine, the idea that marital rape is impossible might well seem correct.

At the beginning of the nineteenth century, there was an official notion—ON, call it—of rape, the notion of the moral and legal infraction of sexual intercourse forced upon a woman without her consent by someone other than her husband. Everyone would have recognized that ON was just that: it was the notion of rape that (it was commonly known) played a certain role in law and society so that for legal and most social purposes all and only those things described by its articulation counted as rape. By the mid-1860s there was a competitor notion, CN, that of sexual intercourse forced upon any woman without her consent. Though ON continued throughout the nineteenth and much of the twentieth century to be the 'official' notion of rape, it seems that by about 1875 it was commonly known—at least among the well educated who paid attention to these things—that ON had in some sense acquired a competitor—there were people who were pushing to have CN play the role of 'the official notion' of rape.

What did the word 'rape' as used by tolerably educated adults in the US in 1875 mean? The question could be construed in several ways. Thinking that reference is determined by meaning, one might take it as a question whose answer needs to tell us something about reference and truth conditions. Thinking that 'what is strictly and literally said' is determined by meaning, one might take it as a question whose answer needs to tell us something about 'the propositions expressed by sentences in which "rape" is used'. Thinking that meaning is a handy substantive for whatever it is whose grasp makes one a competent speaker, one might want the answer to the question to tell us what it was about the relations of the minds of adults who understood 'rape' to the linguistic and social world that constituted their competence. I take the question in this last sense.

In trying to answer it, I will make some assumptions. In line with the view that I have been developing, I assume that facts about meaning are in a fairly strong sense determined by the presuppositions that speakers make in speech, in particular by those they expect their auditors to bring to the task of interpretation. Many of these presuppositions will be part of what I've been calling ICG—they are the norm, so far as what speakers presuppose in speaking, and their normality is common knowledge. But not all such assumptions need be the norm in this way. In particular, some of what nineteenth-century feminists presupposed about rape were things that most people didn't presuppose, and feminists would have been painfully aware of this fact. What feminists could and (I think) did assume was that educated speakers were aware that a fair number of

---

[26] Matthew Hale, *The History of the Pleas of the Crown* (1736), quoted at Hasaday (2000, 1397).

people used 'rape' presupposing that all forced intercourse is rape; they could and did presuppose that when they spoke publicly of rape, their audience would recognize that they were making this presupposition. Certainly speech in which activities in the marital bed were called rape would be accompanied by this presupposition—if the audience didn't recognize that it was expected to recognize the presupposition, what the feminist said would appear more or less unintelligible.

I think there are five likely answers to our question, What did the word mean in 1875? (a) It meant what it meant in 1800, ON. (b) It meant CN, or something very much like CN, which in turn is close to the modern meaning of the word. (c) It was ambiguous: in some mouths it expressed something like ON; in others, one or another variant of CN. (d) At least as it was used by the educated, it had a meaning that in a sense (which I will explain presently) combined both ON and CN. (e) The question is misconceived: in times in which a word threatens to undergo semantic change, it will often be impossible to come up with an account of what it means. In the case at hand, there was a distribution of variant uses of 'rape' in the population, much as there was a distribution of alleles that, in the normal course of things, led to brown or blue or green or grey eyes. In such a case, there is no more such a thing as the meaning of the word than there is such a thing as the eye color of the population.

(d) needs to be clarified. To do this, we need the notion of competing ways of using a phone in a population. Recall that an i-phone is a phone (a linguistic form, individuated in terms of morphology, phonology, and syntax) paired by a speaker with a meaning(-cum-presuppositions-taken-to-be-held-at-the-ready-for-interpretation). An i-phone is, or at least can be used to represent, a particular way of using a phone in a population.[27] Speakers often have multiple i-phones involving the same phone; homophony and polysemy are examples. Even abstracting from population-wide homophony and polysemy, for many phones p, speakers' lexicons often contain i-phones that encode distinct common ways of using a term in a population. If you've spent time in Alberta, you interpret the natives' use of 'toboggan' differently from American uses of the word. Someone who travels between Boston and New York and likes soup knows that what the speaker expects if she asks for clam chowder in Boston is very different from what the speaker expects if she asks for it in New York. Someone who knows me and knows my daughter knows that I assume that a concoction involving vodka and various liquors is not and could not be a 'martini'; not so my daughter.[28]

---

[27] 'Use' in a broad sense, on which interpretation is use. Aunt Tillie presumably includes in her lexicon an i-phone that helps her interpret others' uses of 'muddafucka', though she herself would never utter it. Her i-phone records what others presuppose in use, but not presuppositions she herself need make.

[28] As will become clear, in asking the question, What did such and such a word in such and such a population mean?, we are asking a question that could in part be construed as one about how we ought, when looking at a lexicon, to count i-phones: if we decide (for some theoretical purpose) that we should think that each adult lexicon in 1875 contained a single i-phone for the noun 'rape' that the user used to both produce and interpret utterances with the term, that will (tend to) make it natural to say that the term had a single meaning in the population.

I-phones—IPs, for short—populate a social and linguistic landscape constituted in part by the mentalities of individual users, in part by the roles that IPs play in legal, religious, and other social structures. IPs realized by a particular individual's use of a word carry such things as inferential connections, behavioral dispositions cued to beliefs, and particular presuppositions. Social structures are more or less enduring ways people behave, ones involving standardized patterns of behavior in particular situations, expectations about such behavior, behavioral norms, and publicly recognized ways of labeling such behaviors and norms. Information about such structures is typically carried by the (token) IPs used to describe and think about them.

A token IP—the understanding Vice President Schuyler Colfax or the feminist Elizabeth Cady Stanton voiced in 1870 with 'rape', for example—has a particular role, determined by its role in a particular individual's lexicon, and the connections it has to the social structures it describes and is used to think about. There can be, and often is, a kind of competition between kinds of IPs that results from this. In the case at hand, the competition is (idealizing only a bit) one between ON and CN to occupy the niche in the population of English speakers defined by (a) the functional roles associated by users with the phone and (b) the legal and social role that the notion of rape had in the society. And this really is a competition: One can't, in using 'rape', presuppose both that marital intercourse is never rape and that it sometimes is; legally, forced intercourse in marriage can't be and not be rape.

That said, there is a way that the understanding one assigns to the word 'rape' can be constituted by both ON and CN, a way not altogether unlike the way a heterozygote combines two variants of a particular gene. It's common for someone to associate several overlapping sets of presuppositions with a phone; 'toboggan', 'clam chowder', and 'martini' are examples. This is not like standard cases of homophony or polysemy. If Jane says, 'I went to the bank yesterday to make a deposit' and Jim says, 'I went to the bank yesterday to collect reeds', one cannot say things like 'Jane and Jim each went to a bank yesterday' or 'Jane and Jim both said that they went to a bank yesterday'. If Jim says, 'Let's smoke a blunt' and Jane says, 'Let's smoke the salmon', one cannot say, 'Jim and Jane each wants to smoke something'. But if Jane says, 'May I have a vodka, Chambord, and pineapple martini' and Jim says, 'Gimme a dirty Hendricks martini', I can and (to expedite communication) will say, 'Jane and Jim asked for a martini' or 'Jane and Jim had martinis', even though I reject Jane's presuppositions about martinis. I take it this indicates that, however reluctantly in the case of Jane, I interpret the IPs that lie behind Jane and Jim's utterances with the IP that I use when I speak of martinis, even though

---

In what follows I will for the most part ignore issues having to do with individuating phones within an individual lexicon, though such issues obviously overlap with our present concerns. You are from Nebraska, I am from Neu Yawk; you say 'cah-fee', I say 'cough-fee'. You understand me, I understand you. Does your lexicon have one i-phone for 'coffee', one that represents us assigning the same phonology to the word, or does it have two? I'm inclined toward the view that this is a question that different theories might reasonably differ on; I won't argue for that here.

I got the example of 'martini' from Ted Sider, who tells me that he got it from Karen Bennett.

I am aware of a difference in the meaning-cum-endorsed-presuppositions that Jane and I assign to the phone 'martini'.[29] Something similar will be true of Jane's interpretation of me if she knows my feelings about what counts as a martini: If I ask for a martini, she will interpret me as having asked for the same sort of drink as she did— she'll think I asked for a martini—though she knows that there is a difference in meaning-cum-endorsed-presuppositions between us. All this suggests that Jane's and my uses of 'martini' stand in a relation of coordination; though we knowingly differ in the presuppositions we endorse, we discount that difference in communication.[30]

In this situation there are two ways of using the phone 'martini', ways defined by sets of presuppositions made by a user and expected by her to be recognized as being made. Furthermore, it is common knowledge that there are these two ways of using the phone: those who use the phone in one of the ways know that others use it in the other way. And these ways of using the phone stand in a curious relation. On the one hand, embedded in a single individual they are in some sense inconsistent; they are distinct concepts whose presuppositions aren't consistent. One can't (without hypocrisy, at least) adopt a policy of using the word in full voice sometimes in one way, sometimes in another.[31] On the other hand, the two ways of using the term are treated socially as if they expressed the same concept. My daughter and I interpret each other as speaking about 'the same thing' with 'martini', as evidenced (for example) by our practices of reporting each other's thinkings and sayings.

The structure of the 'rape' example is much the same as that of the 'martini' example. A feminist and a conservative in the 1880s who recognized that they differed as to whether marital rape was possible would of course interpret uses of 'rape' in a way that indicated their lexical entries for the word were coordinated with one another and with those of other members of the society: They would report one another as disagreeing about rape, which suggests that their lexical entries for the phone are coordinated.

We are finally in a position to clarify the idea that 'rape' in late nineteenth-century America had a meaning that in some sense combined ON and CN. I take it that in the population we are discussing, the lexical entries—particular IPs—involved in uses of the word to pick out sexual violation were coordinated in the way just mentioned. This network of IPs was associated with a certain kind of individual functional role (everyone, for example, expected all to take rape to be a serious crime) and a particular social role (it was a felony). We call such a network of coordinated IPs with a tolerably

---

[29] Whether I will say Jane had a martini actually depends in part on my audience.

[30] There is another difference between the martini example and standard examples of homophony and polysemy. There is a sort of tension between Jane's and my uses of 'martini'—I can't endorse both uses in full voice. But I feel no tension in my uses of 'smoke' with its various transitive meanings—as something one does to a cigarette or a salmon fillet or to another person. Those meanings do not strike me as being— they are not—in the kind of competition that differing uses of 'martini' are. Likewise for 'bank'.

[31] This needs qualification. I could, of course, adopt a policy of using the word in different ways as the way it is used by my audience shifts. The point in the text is that there is something odd about a person who willfully (and without fairly elaborate signaling) uses the word now one way and several sentences down the conversation the other.

well-defined common individual and social role a p- (for public) word in the population. Note that a p-word need not be used with the same first-order presuppositions by those who share it: Jane assumes a martini can be made from vanilla vodka; I don't. And that this is so may be common knowledge within a population: People in 2005 knew that there was a way of using 'marriage' on which the user presupposed that marriage between those of the same sex is impossible (and expected their audience to recognize this), and another way of using it on which the user presupposed that same-sex marriage is possible (and expected their audience to recognize this).

When it is common knowledge among users in the network that constitutes a p-word that a particular kind S of IP accompanies (some) uses of a p-word w, S is a p-sense of w in the population. The set of presuppositions about rape made by feminists that they expected their audience to recognize was one p-sense of 'rape' in 1875; the set of corresponding conservative presuppositions another. When there are multiple p-senses of w in a population, we say (with a nod to Gallie 1956) that the sense (sometimes I will say 'the meaning') of w is contested in the population.[32] The meanings of 'martini', 'rape', and 'marriage' are all contested in the relevant populations.

The idea of a word's having a contested meaning is a fairly straightforward generalization of the idea of a word's meaning being its ICG. When a word's meaning is contested, each competent user uses it with one of its p-senses: the user makes the presuppositions that are the basis of that sense, expects auditors to recognize that, and makes whatever higher-order assumptions make the fact that w is used with this p-sense common knowledge. And for each way of using the term—for each of its p-senses—it is common knowledge that that is a way the term is used in the population.[33] If one insists on synchronic stand-ins for word meaning, the meaning of a word, when its meaning is contested, is the collection of its p-senses. This collection, after all, is something that competent speakers are in cognitive contact with. They know that its member senses are ones that other users employ in communication: each constituent sense is known to include the assumptions that some subset of the population makes and expects its audience to recognize. The collection of p-senses associated with the relevant word are publicly acknowledged/known to be senses that are in a certain sense 'co-interpretable'. If Colfax presupposes the basis of ON and Susan Anthony that of

---

[32] Gallie assumed that only words whose meaning was in some sense normative could express what he called contested concepts—his idea, as I understand it, was that it was essential to the phenomenon he was interested in that differences in conception resulted from the way one's values or other broadly normative commitments influenced one's conceptualizing. One might agree with Gallie about this by arguing that *every* concept has a normative element.

George Lakoff, influenced by the work of his student Alan Schwartz, has made much of the notion of contested concepts. For a summary of Lakoff's take on the notion, see chapter 12 of Lakoff (2008); see also the (remarkable) senior thesis of Schwartz (1992).

[33] This is oversimplified, since there are different ways to be competent—one can make all the presuppositions involved in a way of using a word, just the first-order ones, or just the second-order ones; see the discussion in Chapter 3. We might also want to allow that one can be a competent user of a word whose meaning is contested without knowing all its p-senses. I'm going to leave that issue for someone else to straighten out.

CN in joint conversation, they will, even though they know this, interpret one another as 'talking about the same thing' when they use 'rape'; each will say things like 'well, you and I just disagree as to whether that is a case of rape'.

I think this is the best way to think of meaning in the case at hand. Compare it to the nihilistic view that in 1875 there was no more such a thing as the public meaning of 'rape' than there was such a thing as the eye color of human beings. The nihilist, it seems to me, has got ahold of the wrong analogy. True, there's no such thing as the eye color of human beings. But there is such a thing as the human eye. Its realization varies from individual to individual, but there are commonalities that make it sensible to talk of the human eye, a reification of what's common to all normal eyes. There is variation across tokens of the human eye in such things as color and pupil size, but the variation is relatively constrained. In describing the human eye, one describes both the commonalities—rods and cones are always present—and the variations—one finds a range of pigmentations. Likewise, there was a common structure—a common set of first-order presuppositions—to conservative and feminist views of rape in 1875, as well as something like allelic variation. Both the common structure and the variations can be read off of the (contested) meaning of the term 'rape', and it justifies the reification involved in speaking of the meaning of the term at the time.

The human eye is a biological object that has a history. While its structure is currently stable, it's nonetheless a historical entity. New eyes tend to resemble the eyes of those responsible for the body in which they are situated; future distribution of properties like eye colors is determined by the way current eye owners and their progeny interact with each other and the environment; the eye is in principle liable to historical change due to changes in genomes, selective pressures, and drift. All of this is mirrored in the semantic case: meaning structure is heritable; variant distribution is determined by such things as interaction of variants with one another and the environment, along with forces analogous to drift and mutation. The nihilist's view, refusing to think of meaning in population terms, misses just the sort of thing we miss if we refuse to speak of the human eye—or, for that matter, the human species.

What was said above about coordination and reported speech gives us reason to reject the view that in 1875 'rape' was ambiguous, as people like Stanton meant one thing, CN, with it while people like Colfax meant something else, ON. This is really a version of the nihilistic view that there was no such thing as **the** meaning of the term. Agreed, there is clearly a sense in which it is correct to say that different people meant different things in using the term, this sort of difference in meaning residing in the differences in presuppositions speakers made and expected the audience to recognize as being made. But from the fact that people mean different things in this sense with a word, it doesn't follow that there isn't such a thing as the meaning of the word as it is used by everyone. First of all, there is of course a good deal that the various ways of using the term had in common; each way of using the term involved in a clear sense an 'extension' of a 'common core' of presuppositions. Second of all, I take it to be an upshot of the sort of interpretive coordination of uses mentioned above that in interpreting the use of 'rape', speakers proceeded in the way one proceeds when one takes another to mean what one does with a term, though differing on some of the 'theory' associated with it. Speakers proceeded as would speakers with at least some commitment to reaching a common understanding of how the term was to be used—they co-interpreted but reserved the right to insist that their own conception was the one that all should adopt. That they proceeded in this way, I would say, means that they understood one another as sharing a word which meant the same, whoever used it. We, I would say, should understand them this way as well.

The drift of the last few pages is that we are best off if we take the word to be univocal as Stanton and Colfax use it, and that this scuttles the idea that it is just the presuppositions involved in ON or in CN that constitute the word's meaning. I imagine that some will agree with the claim about univocality, but say that what the word meant in 1875 is pretty much what it means today. The argument is simple: When Stanton and Colfax used the word, they were talking about, they were referring to, what we're talking about when we use the word. For suppose Colfax uttered

(R)   It's impossible for a man to rape his wife.

Stanton would probably have asserted both

(1) When Colfax uttered 'it's impossible for a man to rape his wife', he said that it was impossible for a man to rape his wife.
(2) If Colfax said that it was impossible for a man to rape his wife, he was wrong.

All of us will say these things. The truth of (1) and (2) when uttered by Stanton and endorsed by us suggests identity of reference of 'rape' as used by Stanton, Colfax, and us.

Reference supervenes on meaning. So, whatever the word meant in 1875 has to be pretty closely related to what the word means today, close enough so that the reference of the word then is (more or less) what it is now. The simplest account is that the word's meaning is what it contributed and still contributes to what is said when the word is used. But this is what's determined by an articulation of CN—it's an extension, or (structured) intension, or something of the sort.

This kind of argument—in particular, the premise that meaning determines reference—was discussed at the end of Chapter 3. I don't propose to repeat that discussion here, but I will say this. We can agree, for the sake of argument, with the sequence of dialectical steps—that the nineteenth- and twenty-first-century references were the same, that reference supervenes on meaning (and environmental relations), that this means there has to be a pretty significant similarity in meaning across the centuries—up to the last one. Why should we suppose it to be 'simpler' (in some sense of simplicity that governs choice of theory) to identify the meaning of the word with its reference than to say that there are a number of notions of meaning and that what the word meant—in the sense of meaning on which word meaning is what the user grasps in understanding public use—is something that is constituted by the evolving practice of speakers and auditors to describe, think about, condemn, and regulate certain aspects of the social world? We need a notion of meaning that is tied closely to what enables understanding and communication, allows meaning to be shared by people who differ on details (even fairly significant ones), reflects the idea that meaning can in some significant way persist through cultural shifts in belief, and allows for persistence in what we are talking about across these shifts. The idea that a word's meaning is species-like—constituted by the mental states of users across time—does quite well in all these ways. In particular, if that's what a meaning or concept is, there is nothing particularly odd about the idea that all of those who think with a concept at a particular time are completely misconceiving what they are thinking about, even if we suppose that the semantic properties of a concept supervene on nothing beyond the articulations of the concept its users would on reflection give.[34] The concept's users are spread across time and cultural space; the articulations users give today may well be quite different from those users (even those same users) will give in the future. Reference of a use of a term at one time need not invariably be determined by how users of the term at that time conceive of what they are referring to. Neither is there any particular problem, if we think of concepts in this way, with thinking that both (1) and (2) are true—this, after all, was the burden of much of the argument of Chapter 4. The suggestion that there is some gain in theoretically relevant 'simplicity' in saying that the predicate's meaning is simply a property or relation, or function from contexts or worlds or situations to extensions, strikes me as a cry of despair, prompted probably by the fact that the tools we've developed for 'the theory of meaning' (aka formal semantics) aren't really up to the descriptive task of describing (every kind of) meaning.[35]

5. Meanings, Memes, and Species

There was a kind of competition between the concepts ON and CN to occupy a particular niche in the late 1800s; ON carried the day then, but went on to be driven more or less to extinction (in the US at least) about 100 years later. Was the competition Darwinian? Was ON's transient victory a matter of natural selection?

Not every populational dynamism is Darwinian. Recall the 'skyline' example. Does it provide something that much resembles differential selection of a meaning because the meaning is able 'to do better reproducing itself' in the conceptual ecosphere? I suggested in Section 2 that this is a poor way of thinking about matters: The 'selection' of the meaning *line where the cityscape meets the sky* is not caused by that meaning's being 'better suited' to the conceptual ecosystem. The change in the meaning of 'skyline'— that is, the process by which pretty much everyone comes to mean *line where the cityscape meets the sky* with the word—is simultaneous with a change in the 'habitat'—the

---

[34] Not that I would endorse this idea.

[35] Don't get me wrong; as I said at the end of Chapter 4, I'm not suggesting abandoning the project of formal, truth-conditional semantics. I'm simply suggesting that what we're doing when we do formal semantics has much less to do with understanding use and communication than some seem to suppose.

linguistic community—in which the meaning exists. The process of the new meaning becoming established is also a process of the environment changing in a way that is progressively more favorable to that meaning. The final meaning is thus a better fit with the final mind-set of the linguistic community. But this does not imply that the 'fitness' of the meaning helped cause the transformation of the former into the final meaning.[36]

So, at least, one might say. But some seem to take such examples to be more or less paradigms of (cultural) evolution by natural selection. If one is attracted to Richard Dawkins' idea of 'memes'—units of information or ways of behaving that reproduce themselves in the soup of culture—one may take the example to be one in which a variant of a particular meme—a word or meaning—is introduced into the 'meme-pool' and triumphs in virtue of selection pressures. Some discussion of this view is in order.

Biologists and the philosophers who read them argue over whether the individuals natural selection selects—the units of selection—are genes, organisms, or something larger like communities or species. Dawkins allows that there is a process of evolution via natural selection in which the things that reproduce and are in some sense in competition with one another are organisms. But according to Dawkins, this process is not fundamental: the fundamental players in evolution aren't things like bison, rattlesnakes, or fungi, but those things that natural selection selects over generations—versions of genes (Dawkins 1976, 1999). Selection is a process in which copies of certain 'things' proliferate at the cost of copies of other things; the units of selection are the things copies of which proliferate or dwindle. Organisms like copperheads and beagles aren't copied, though; their genetic material is. The right way for biology to think about matters, according to Dawkins, is to see the traits on which selection acts as belonging to genes.[37] It is genes that are literally reproduced when one generation of organisms gives rise to the next, since genes make more or less exact, 'high-fidelity' copies of

---

[36] There is controversy as to whether ENS, thought of as a biological process, is best thought of as a causal process. Some say it's only a 'statistical process in which selection emerges only from a host of events'; Matthen and Ariew (2002) and Dan Dennett (personal communication, from which the quotation here is lifted) are examples. Others say it is a causal process, with the relata individuals (see, for example, Bouchard and Rosenberg 2004) or populations realizing properties, as when the relative frequency of genotypes in a population at one time is responsible for a change in such frequency in descendent populations. Millstein (2006) defends this last view. I recognize that those who think that natural selection is 'just' a statistical process will be less impressed with the worry in the text than those who think it a causal process. The arguments for its being a causal, population-level process do seem to me pretty compelling, but it would be a long detour to argue for that here. Thanks to Dan Dennett for comments that sparked this note.

[37] The reader might well wonder what on Dawkins' view genes are. Higher organisms typically reproduce by a sort of cut-and-paste method in which what the biology textbook has in mind when it speaks of genes are always at risk of being obliterated. If genes are things that (save for mutations) faithfully replicate their structure, they must be units much smaller than the genes of the textbook. Dawkins' official definition of 'gene' is that a gene is any arbitrary sequence of DNA (Dawkins 1982, 87), as any such sequence has the potential of being replicated. As has been frequently pointed out, this makes it questionable that genes can be seen as carriers of phenotypical traits, and thus questionable that selection, which acts in the first instance on such traits, could be said to be selecting genes.

This is an essay in the philosophy of language, not the philosophy of biology. And so it is not the place for an extended discussion of Dawkinsesque views about the nature of biological selection. Useful discussions of Dawkins' views are part II of Sterelny and Griffiths (1999) and Lloyd (2017).

themselves. Genes are the replicators; organisms are simply vehicles for their genes; in David Hull's term, an organism is an interactor—something that 'interacts with its environment as a cohesive whole in such a way that replication [of the replicators that inhabit it] is differential' (Hull 1980, 318).

Dawkins famously suggested that cultural items—'tunes, ideas, catch-phrases, clothes, fashions, ways of making pots or building arches' (Dawkins 1976, 192)—are just as much replicators as are genes. *Meme* is Dawkins' term for such; he says that they are 'cultural units of information in the brain' (Dawkins 1982, 109). Memes have a structure; thus, it makes sense to speak of them reproducing themselves more or less faithfully; like a gene, a meme has phenotypical effects which 'may be in the form of words, music, visual images...They may be perceived...and they may so imprint themselves on the brains...that a copy (not necessarily exact) of the original meme is graven in the receiving brain' (Dawkins 1982, 110). Such units of information are subject to selection pressure in something like the way that genes are: 'Meme survival, like gene survival, depends on what else is in the meme/gene pool and environment, and will vary with variations therein' (Dawkins 1982, 112). For example, ideas that cohere with the dominant ideology of a society will be more likely to hop from host to host than will ones that run counter to it.

Dawkins' *The Selfish Gene* gives various examples of memes: the song 'Auld Lang Syne', the ideas of God and eternal damnation, Darwin's theory of evolution, 'the meme-complexes of Socrates, Leonardo, Copernicus and Marconi'. These things exhibit fecundity—they produce many copies of themselves—and some of them persist through many generations. But to be replicators, they must (tend to) produce 'high-fidelity' copies of themselves. 'I must admit that I am on shaky ground', Dawkins (1976, 194) writes, in suggesting that they do so. Having admitted that, he goes on to speculate that if we look closely enough—perhaps breaking down cultural items into 'smaller parts', as we might divide a symphony into movements, themes, and such—we will find things that indeed replicate themselves (more or less) precisely.

The author of *The Extended Phenotype* is more cautious. Of memes, he writes that:

It not clear they occupy and compete for distinct 'loci', or...have...'alleles'...The copying process is probably much less precise...Memes may partially blend with each other in ways that genes do not...[replication may involve] 'Lamarckian' causal arrows leading from phenotype to replicator, as well as the other way around. These differences may prove sufficient to render the analogy with genetic natural selection worthless or even positively misleading. My own feeling is that its main value may lie not so much in helping us to understand human culture as in sharpening our perception of genetic natural selection.   (Dawkins 1982, 112)

Though Dawkins seems to have backed off the idea that there is a worthwhile analogy between the biological and the social, Daniel Dennett ringingly endorses it.

Dennett identifies memes with 'semantic information', 'prescriptions for ways of doing things'.[38] He takes words (qua combinations of sound, syntax, and meaning) to

---

[38] Unless otherwise noted, citations here and in the next paragraphs are from Dennett (2017, chapter 10).

be memes par excellence; other examples are songs, ways of making a boat, and ways of being in the world (e.g., getting a college education). Dennett endorses the idea that the transmission of words, meanings, practices, and so on involves 'high-fidelity copying'. He holds further that to label cultural items as memes in Dawkins' sense is to endorse the claims that:

1. The complexity of cultural items needn't be in any way due to design or intelligent authorship. We know full well from the biological case that a flabbergasting complexity and adaptation to a particular niche may arise over many generations with no design, no understanding on the part of the organisms that embody the complexity.
2. Cultural items qua things that replicate themselves in the soup of culture will 'have their own reproductive fitness just like viruses'; what is good for a cultural item (that is, what contributes to its differential reproductive success) need not be good for the users of the item (i.e., it need not contribute to their differential success).
3. Cultural items are 'informational things' that can be stored, transmitted, and so forth without being 'executed or expressed'.

Dennett and I are both pushing biological analogies. I want to point to ways in which the analogy I am most interested in—that meanings are species-like—differs from Dennett's—that cultural items are replicators.

What is striking about the cultural-items-are-memes idea—and what seems insightful about it—is that many cultural items do seem to be transmitted in a virus-like fashion. Someone who knew something about trees and who surfed described a wave as gnarly and... well, it sounded pretty cool and waves *are* sort of gnarly and nothing like an in-group use to separate the in-group from others and... Dude! The term spread among the surfing community like an STD at an orgy. What one might worry is missing in this analogy, if one is interested in lexical meaning, is recognition of a sort of ontogenetical change in token cultural items that occurs because they are part of a larger, species-like whole.

Consider the earworm 'Uptown Funk'.[39] If you are infected with this confection, it almost certainly took some time for it to take hold. You heard someone playing it, or your children singing it, perhaps ten times before it began haunting your cranium. ('Don't believe me, just watch...') You probably had to adjust your register of the lyrics over time ('Oh: 'Uptown *Funk* you up...'); repeated listening may have brought new insight to your memory of the horn line; etc. Cultural items like songs, ways of tying a knot, the meaning of 'chucks' (as in 'Got chucks on with my St. Laurent')—these are gradually absorbed from the Kultursuppe, and their token realizations often fluctuate more or less in time with it. The idea of cultural items becoming initially established in ways that resemble those in which small strands of RNA infect us—that idea has

---

[39] Listen at your peril: https://www.youtube.com/watch?v=OPf0YbXqDm0.

something going for it. But the ontogenesis of a token way of flirting, or of thinking about marriage, or of taking a right on red can't be predicted or even reliably sketched simply from the original intake from the cultural pool. The point of suggesting that meanings are like species is at least partially to point to the inherently social, inherently dynamic nature of the meanings of our words, something that I fear is, if not left out, at least obscured if one simply says that meanings are memes.

Because the origin of the notion of memes lies in Dawkins' *The Selfish Gene*, it is hard not to hear 'meme' as meaning something that is reproduced in a 'particulate, all-or-none' manner, a thing whose transmission is not 'subject to continuous mutation, and also to blending' (Dawkins 1982, 195). Like a gene, a meme's tokens are subject to mutation, but mutation is not the norm. A meme's being gene-like, one thinks— Dawkins surely thinks—requires that in reproduction it literally be copied.

As noted above, Dennett says that memes are high-fidelity reproducers; words qua phonemic structures are his poster children for the idea that (quite generally) memes are involved in high-fidelity replication (Dennett 2017, 190–204). Arguably we do see gene-like fidelity in replication in the propagation of phonemic information, at least once the child has acquired the ambient phonemic categories: Assuming that speakers of a language share such categories—something I would not want to deny—when one acquires a word one generally acquires the phonemic structure one's teachers associate with the word. I am less sanguine that this is true of the transmission of the sort of meaning I've been discussing for the last 200 or so pages.

In part this is because meaning acquisition is very much a process in which the learner is supposed to make inferences that he may not (and need not for success) make. The child probably gets that everybody knows that you can see yourself in a mirror right away. It is only after some time (if ever) that he cottons on to the fact that everybody (else) knows that mirrors are made of glass, even though that fact is (argu-ably) part of the ICG of 'mirror'. Even if he never cottons on to this fact, he may still be credited with knowing what 'mirror' means. Likewise, the token meanings that the learner has at the end of word acquisition may involve presuppositions, ones the learner expects the world to grasp that she makes in using the word, that are quite idio-syncratic. Having been raised on the farm, Bea thinks, and thinks that everyone thinks, and thinks everyone expects everyone to agree, that dogs and horses quite generally are animals that are raised for farm work.

My differences with Dennett may be more semantic than substantial. Dennett does not have a fixed picture of how words or meanings reproduce themselves; he allows that one model that one could reasonably adopt considers 'words, and memes more generally, to be the result of variable, temporally extended processes of reproduction (as if father's contribution was not made "at conception" but at some later time after mother had already given birth), an imaginable variation on our normal mode of sexual reproduction' (Dennett 2017, 246). This picture is not so far removed from the picture I've been painting, though I'm not sure I see why this would be a picture on which memes generally 'faithfully reproduce themselves'—it sounds rather like a picture on which there is 'continuous mutation, and also ... blending' of memes.

Memesists have this right: we tend to overestimate the amount of rational control we have over what we mean and what we think. We acquire much of what fills our heads—the thought that large waves are gnarly, the notion of global warming, the disposition to assent to any instance of *it's true that S iff S*, an earworm of Benjamin Clementine singing *it's my home, home, home, home*—automatically, without conscious supervision, pretty much without being able to resist or override.

Of course, we are not in semantic chains. What our words mean and what thoughts we express with them can change; part of the point of saying that meanings are species is to stress the fact that what we and Stanton and Schuyler said in tokening 'marital rape occurs' is the same even though the meaning of the phrase we token has changed. The meaning of the sentence is like Theseus' ship—replacing the planks or presupposition that make up the ship or meaning needn't destroy it. But a good part of this semantic dynamic is simply outside of our control; of much of it we aren't even aware.

I started this section by wondering whether the transition, from a contested meaning for rape to the dominance of ON in its meaning to the eventual fixation of something like CN, was Darwinian. Frankly, I don't know. To some extent, this seems to me a question about how to describe the populations in which meanings are found. Do we want to think of the individuals in the population as enduring lexical entries that acquire characteristics that they then pass on to lexical entries of those who acquire the language from them, or should we take the individuals to be time slices of such that 'give birth' to later time slices? Each way of thinking of things may be apt for certain purposes, much as a view of evolution as involving selfish genes may be apt for some purposes, a view of the units of selection as organisms or groups apt for others.

6. Conceptual Engineering

Saying that meanings are species-like is in part saying that meanings are molded by forces independent and out of the control of the organisms whose acts have meaning, be those forces Darwinian or 'merely' populational. To say this may seem to call into question currently popular views about the what philosophy can or should be doing—views on which its task is or should be to contribute to 'ameliorative engineering' of our concepts. I'll end this chapter with some discussion of this issue, focusing on recent work of Sally Haslanger's.

In a number of papers, Haslanger has pursued what she calls an ameliorative project. This is a kind of conceptual analysis in which you begin by looking at the purposes behind the use of a concept—you ask what people are actually doing when they apply the concept and why they are doing it—and then go on to evaluate those purposes: you ask if those purposes are ones we ought to have, or if there are different ones that should be assigned to the concept. One then considers whether some modification of the concept is called for, given the purposes it ought to have, and, if so, what they are. If the analyst thinks new purposes ought to be assigned to the concept, she may well propose a revisionary account of the concept, one on which it is suited for the purposes it ought to have.[40]

An ameliorative account of a concept is potentially quite different from other sorts of accounts one might give. It is not an attempt at conventional conceptual analysis, in which one 'seek[s] an articulation' of a concept (employing, perhaps, a method of reflective equilibrium to arrive at an all-things-considered definition)—it is not, to borrow Haslanger's terminology, an attempt to uncover the manifest concept associated with a term. Neither is it the quasi-empirical (descriptive, as Haslanger calls it) project of looking for a natural, physical, or social kind that (is the most plausible candidate for what) our applications of the concept are in fact tracking (Haslanger 2012a, 223). Nor is it the attempt to limn the set of things that it is our practice to apply the concept— to characterize what Haslanger calls the operative concept.[41] But while different, these three sorts of accounts of concept as well as ameliorative accounts all seem to involve reference and extension. Conventional conceptual analysis seeks to identify, via conceptual articulation, what we on our best reflection take ourselves to be talking about when we apply a concept. A descriptive account identifies what (kind of) objects our practice 'tracks', and thus what (kind of) objects we should take the concept to contribute to truth conditions; an account of an operative concept computes a concept's 'practical extension'. And an ameliorative account aims, put roughly, to tell us what objects we should (given our 'proper purposes') be talking about when we use the concept.

---

[40] Haslanger writes:

> The task is not simply to explicate the normal concept of X; nor is it to discover what things we normally take to fall under the concept have in common; instead we ask what purpose is served in having the concept of X, whether this purpose is well-conceived and what concept (or concepts) would serve our well-conceived purpose(s)...best...this approach [to conceptual analysis] is quite comfortable with the result that we must revise—perhaps even radically—our ordinary concepts.   (Haslanger 2012b, 352)

> ...we begin by considering more fully the pragmatics of our talk employing the terms in question. What is the point of having these concepts? What cognitive or practical task do they (or should they) enable us to accomplish?...In the limit case [of the project] the concept in question is introduced by stipulating the meaning of a new term...But if we allow that our everyday vocabularies serve both cognitive and practical purposes, purposes that might also be served by our theorizing, then a theory offering an improved understanding of our (legitimate) purposes and/or improved conceptual resources for the tasks at hand might reasonably represent itself as providing a (possibly) revisionary account of the everyday concepts [that are the subject of ameliorative analysis].   (Haslanger 2012a, 223–4)

Page references here and below are to reprintings of articles in Haslanger (2012d). I should note that in Haslanger (2012a), she uses the phrase 'analytic account of a concept' instead of 'ameliorative analysis'.

[41] The distinctions and terminology here are something of a mash-up of the discussions in Haslanger (2012a), (2012b), and (2012c).

A descriptive account of a concept is not an account of an operative account—we might clearly be tracking a natural kind with a word but widen or narrow its application due to theoretical confusion. That said, for simplicity in what follows I ignore whatever differences there might be in a descriptive account of a concept and an attempt to find an operative concept.

Haslanger herself offers 'ameliorative analyses' of the concepts of woman, man, and (roughly speaking) racial group. She begins by asking 'what work the concepts of gender and race might do for us in a critical... social theory' (Haslanger 2000, 36–7). Her answer, put generally, is that what is needed are 'accounts of gender and race that will be effective tools in the fight against injustice'. As I understand her, in the case of the concept *woman* she reasons as follows. The, or an important, purpose of the concept *woman* is to subordinate people on the basis of their (perceived) female properties. We shouldn't be subordinating people on this basis; indeed, we should be fighting against such subordination. One way to do this is to reformulate the concept so that, so to speak, its noxious purpose is part of its definition. This will put the purposes for which the concept is actually being used front and center, allowing us to fight gender subordination. We should therefore understand what it is to be a woman as being someone who is systematically subordinated on the basis of (perceived) female properties. This makes the concept *woman* determine a response-dependent property: women are people who are perceived in a particular way, and as a result are treated in a particular way.

Since the behavioral response arises only in certain kinds of societies, on this account women exist only in societies whose ideology marks certain groups for oppression. The concept man is taken to be analogous, though men are privileged, not subordinated, on the basis of their perceived properties. Of course these analyses are strikingly out of synch with the accounts most philosophers and non-philosophers would give of the concepts.[42]

I will call a project of offering and trying to get others to accept revisionary ameliorative analyses an A-project. An A-project is something that is carried out in a particular social situation at a particular time. It is undertaken as a reaction to a particular social and historical situation as conceptualized in a particular way with a particular vocabulary. It is focused on a particular concept C, expressed by particular vocabulary W, and the way that concept functions in its historical milieu. It will be successfully carried off only if a large number of those who think about the world using C, expressing those thoughts with W, come to do something we might call 'changing their concept C' in ways that reflect the revisionary analysis while continuing to use W to express their (revised) concept C. It will be successful only if these uses of W are

---

[42] The text oversimplifies Haslanger's proposal. Her (penultimate) definition is:

> S is a woman iff i) S is regularly and for the most part observed or imagined to have certain bodily features presumed to be evidence of a female's biological role in reproduction; ii) that S has these features marks S within the dominant ideology of S's society as someone who ought to occupy certain kinds of social position that are in fact subordinate (and so motivates and justifies S's occupying such a position); and iii) the fact that S satisfies (i) and (ii) plays a role in S's systematic subordination, i.e., along some dimension, S's social position is oppressive, and S's satisfying (i) and (ii) plays a role in that dimension of subordination.

And this requires Chisholming in light of the fact that one's real or imagined traits may trigger in different contexts and countries quite different patterns of ideologically inspired behavior.

accompanied by the intention that they should be understood as having the relevant meaning, and are indeed so understood.[43]

It is obvious, I think, that the A-project is often worthwhile. But there are cases— Haslanger's own version of the A-project is one—in which it can at least seem downright odd. Her project, after all, would be successfully carried off only if a large number of those who theorize about gender and race were to come to use 'woman', 'Latino', and so on with the conscious intention that they should be understood as using the words with the relevant meanings, and indeed are so understood.[44] But why should we want to pull this off, as opposed to the seemingly simpler task—the B-project—of getting theorists to agree that (most of) the relevant classes—females, those of Hispanic descent—are indeed systematically subordinated on the basis of being members of those classes?

The answer, I take it, is that our (legitimate) purposes for having concepts of gender and race are much better served by pulling off the A-project than the B-project. These purposes, I take it, are ones like trying to get rid of the subordination of females and Latinos by theorizing about it in a fruitful way, a way that 'cuts at the social joints'—that is, that displays social kinds and social forces that explain why the social world is as it is.

But this answer invites the question, Why should we think that these purposes are better served by the A-project than the B-project? A reason one might have for thinking this is that the notion *group identified in terms of marks M and subordinated on the basis of having M* is of considerable explanatory utility: unless and until you see the relevant groups in that way, you will be unable to perceive or explain various social facts. I agree with the thought, but it doesn't seem to be a reason for preferring the A-project to the B-project. Why think that we are more likely to get people to recognize and be able to explain subordination by conceptual reformation than by…getting them to recognize social structures for what they are? Doesn't the A-project require fighting two battles—overcoming resistance to recognizing such things as implicit bias and overcoming resistance to using a word in a counter-intuitive way? Wouldn't the project's goals be achieved by fighting and winning just the first battle? For that matter, doesn't the A-project as Haslanger executes it cross the line between conceptual therapy and stipulative rebranding? Isn't the fact that people perceive it in just this way a reason to think that in this case we are better off pursuing a B-project instead of an A-project?

These sound like rhetorical questions, I know. But I don't intend them that way. After all, there are versions of the A-project that involve revisions that look similar to those Haslanger proposes, but don't seem to involve anything like changing the

---

[43] Actually, this is not quite right as it stands. An A-project will be directed at a particular audience, and that audience may be considerably smaller than the set of all those (in the relevant historical milieu) who use C, expressing it with W. So the text needs to be restricted: success requires that a large number of those at whom the project is directed who think about the world using C etc., etc.

[44] The concept *Latino* is a tricky case, as it is arguably an ethnic and not racial term. It's clear that Haslanger's intention is that her proposal should generalize to such concepts.

subject—ones that in fact seem like natural, though hardly inevitable, examples of conceptual evolution. This might be said of the conceptual transformation inherent in the appropriation of racial or sexual epithets by their targets; of proposals to rework the notion of gender so that it is a (choppy) continuum, not a binary division (Fausto-Sterling 2000); of the campaign by nineteenth- and twentieth-century feminists to get the legal and social world to reconceptualize rape; and of the ongoing attempt to drag the social world toward a concept of marriage on which it is a bond between persons of any sex. In retrospect, none of these seem odd or perverse conceptual turns—indeed, they seem to many of us in some sense the way the relevant concepts ought to have evolved. Noticing this, one might wonder whether resistance to Haslanger's version of the A-project isn't just unwarranted theoretical conservatism, something that stands to philosophy of language as a horror of government-mandated health insurance stands to practical politics.

This thought is bolstered, I think, by the idea that meanings are something like species or populations, historical ensembles of connected ways of thinking whose members display something very much like allelic variation. The A-theorist introduces a novel allele into the conceptual gene pool with the hope that it will be driven to fixation by social and intellectual forces, its competitors driven, if not to extinction, then at least to the status of marginal conceptual alternatives. Under what conditions does such a project have any chance of success? A preliminary to giving an answer is considering concrete cases.

The nineteenth-century feminist A-project is not an example of a completely successful A-project. Insofar as the audience addressed was not simply women willing to listen to feminist arguments, but the society as a whole, the project failed; witness that it was necessary to launch the whole thing again seventy years later. But it succeeded in the sense that a significant number of people accepted the competitor notion CN, as opposed to the official notion ON, as 'the correct' way to think about the topic.

Why is this? Well, for one thing, the feminist project was conceptually, though not socially, rather conservative. The purposes the feminists in effect were assigning to the concept of rape would likely appear to the target audience to be more or less continuous with the cognitive and social purposes the concept already served, even at the beginning of the nineteenth century. Even then, to call something rape was, first and foremost, to identify it as a sexual, not a property, violation, and to condemn it for that reason. One did not, after all, need to be married to be raped. Insisting that marital rape is possible preserves this aspect of the concept of rape, while attempting to undermine an ideology that constrained the way in which the concept could be applied. Arguing for the understanding of rape embodied in CN is in good part a matter of straightforward ideological critique of ideas that are in some sense independent of the concept rape: once one rejects the view of consent underlying Hale's doctrine and the quasi-legal doctrine that the state has an interest in preventing marriage from being treated as an ordinary contract, it is natural (though not inevitable) that the legal and cultural understanding of rape would be transformed from ON into something like CN.

A consequence is that it would not feel like false advertising—it would not have been false advertising—for feminists to represent themselves as pointing out that the best way to understand the existing practice of labeling and prosecuting things as rape is as a practice whose rationale—rationale, not practical upshot—is to condemn sexual violation of women, no matter who the agent is.

Consider, next, the example of that brilliant provocateur who began using 'queer' as a badge, if not of honor, then at least of defiance and pride. There is a sense in which his or her 'proposal' for reworking the concept expressed by the word is also conceptually conservative. For the proposal to express approval or at least neutrality toward gay people in applying the word 'queer' is not a proposal to change what we might call the 'practical extension' of the term—that is, it is not a proposal, the upshot of which is to add or subtract from the collection of those to whom the term would commonly be taken to apply. The 'proposal', as I see it, is to change the affective, expressive component in the concept—its common, mutually recognized pragmatic trappings, if you will. Classification itself—the circumscribing of a particular (albeit fuzzily defined) group of objects—remains the same.

Consider now Haslanger's own version of the A-project. As noted above, when one reads her proposed analyses of concepts like woman and Latino, one has a strong feeling that she is engaged in persuasive definition or some other subject-changing maneuver. It is not difficult to see why one might feel this way.

Haslanger's idea seems to be something like this: The application of a concept like *Latino* is the first step in a systematic (though partially non-conscious) process of discrimination against the group to which the term is applied. Latinos are so classified in good part in order to discriminate against them; indeed, Latinos are people with a certain ethnic heritage who are discriminated against on the basis of that heritage. It is important to recognize this social fact. One way to do this is to revise our understanding of 'Latino' to reflect this fact.

One feels that, unlike the two examples of 'concept engineering' just mentioned, Haslanger's proposal imposes understandings of and purposes upon talk and thought involving the concept *Latino* that are quite foreign to the ways such thought and talk can be understood and the purposes it in fact serves. The proposal is certainly not classificatorily conservative in the way the feminist or the appropriative projects are. The new concept doesn't arise simply by removing ideological accretions from something that could be said to be a notion that was there all along. We do not hold constant the classification the concept effects in practice while flipping its emotive valence. Nor do we claim that there was a kind users of the word in some sense meant to be talking about with the term, a kind that is more clearly conceptualized once the alternative analysis is adopted. One feels that the proposal's analysans is pretty much discontinuous with the analysandum on all relevant dimensions.

Now, it is not altogether clear whether this feeling is correct. There are any number of stories one might tell about 'the' purpose or purposes of our gender and race concepts. Focus on the concept *Latino*. My suspicion is that the story most people would on reflection tell about the meaning of 'Latino'—and thus the core of the presuppositions most people make and expect to be recognized as making in using the term—is something like:

> P1:   The concept *Latino* is the concept of a person whose heritage includes (a significant number of) ancestors from Latin American countries who were themselves of Hispanic descent. Thus, to think of someone as a Latino is to think of them in this way.

Certainly the way we actually proceed in classification seems to be captured by something like this. Because of this convergence of presupposition and practical application, one is inclined to say that the best way to understand our existing practice of classifying people as Latino is given by P1. And so, one might argue, an account of the concept *Latino* like Haslanger's that incorporates a notion of subordination that is absent from both what's presupposed and from classificatory behavior is simply changing the subject.

But one might also say that, whether we are conscious of it or not, the following is true:

> P2:   An important function of the concept *Latino* is that it facilitates classifying people whose heritage includes (a significant number of) ancestors from Latin American countries who were Hispanic as having such a heritage so that they can be discriminated against and otherwise subordinated. Thus, 'the', or a, point of having the concept is to facilitate discrimination on the basis of ethnicity.

Let us agree that a good part of the upshot of classifying people as Latinos is captured by P2. Because of this, one might say, a good part of the purpose of the concept is to conceptualize people ethnically so as to subordinate them on that basis. And so an account of the concept like Haslanger's, an account that incorporates a notion of subordination, is one that simply brings the concept's 'point' into focus. So it can't be said to be an account that is 'changing the subject'.

I have doubts about this argument. There is a difference between what a thing is and what it gets used for: a screwdriver doesn't become a can opener by being used almost exclusively to prise the lids off paint cans. I worry that the argument just given blurs this sort of difference. To agree that the upshot of ethnic classification is subordination is not to agree that in classifying ethnically we are classifying (in part) on the basis of subordination.

The A-project is a project that seeks to change the meaning of a term. There are at least two things that are naturally labeled as changing the meaning of a predicate, a change in its ex- or possible worlds intension—r-change—and a change in the presuppositions that constitute the predicate's ICG—c-change. The version of the A-project we are discussing looks to involve both, since it is a matter of giving an extension-shifting meaning to terms like 'woman', 'Latino', and the like and a matter of getting a group to take a certain way of thinking of the extensions for granted.[45] Insofar as this particular

---

[45] 'Way of thinking' has unfortunate Fregean connotations; Fregean ways of thinking (senses) are reference determining. I mean here ways of thinking in a more or less colloquial sense, on which (for example)

version of the project involves extension shifting, it strikes me that it was never likely to be successful. Haslanger tells us that she wants to answer such questions as: What is it to be a man? What is it to be a Latino? The answers are to be 'critical analytical' ones, in the sense that the search for answers is to be guided by considering 'what work the concepts of gender and race might do for us in a critical...social theory' (Haslanger 2000, 226). But of course we begin by using the concepts *man* and *Latino* in delimiting the project. An extension-shifting answer strikes me as one very difficult to make stick—as very difficult to get people to accept—if it is not grounded in something about prior usage that can be adduced to make plausible that the answer 'simply reveals what we were talking about all along', or that the answer is an apt response to an ambiguity or confusion in prior use.

It is worth observing that r-change is in this regard quite different from c-change. Suppose, addressing feminists and race theorists, that I point long and loudly to the facts that women and people of color as classes are subordinated, and that this subordination is achieved on the basis of a classification in terms of 'observed or imagined bodily features presumed to be evidence of their role in reproduction (women) or ancestral links to a certain geographic region (racial groups)'. Suppose I make it clear that the fact that I am pointing to is a fact about history and culture—it is a fact about women and minorities in particular historical and cultural contexts, significant in part because the relevant sort of subordination occurred and occurs in a startlingly wide swath of history. Suppose I go on to say that this fact about females and people who have the relevant racial heritage is significant enough that it should be at the forefront of our theorizing about gender and class, and that I am heard: people accept what I say, recognize that others do, and come to expect others to know these facts. As a result, generics like *women are subordinated on the basis of observed or imagined bodily features presumed to be evidence of their role in reproduction* become part of the ICG of the term 'woman' (and so in a tolerably clear sense of the concept *woman*), and such generics come to play a role in thought and theory about women and minorities.

All of this would effect a change in the meaning of 'women', 'Latino', and so on—not an r-change, but a c-change. It is not a change in what people think they are talking about with those terms; rather, it is a change in the way they think about them—in the assumptions and presuppositions they make about them—when they use the terms. It is a change that is relatively easy to effect—indeed, it's plausible that progress has already been made in getting people in general, not just activists and academic theorists, to think of the relevant groups in this way. Effecting this sort of change, it seems to me, achieves much, perhaps most, of what Haslanger's project was meant to achieve. And it does this without having to take on the burden of shifting the reference

---

stereotypes associated with racial and gender terms are ways of thinking of their references associated with the terms.

of anything. For changing what everyone takes for granted in using a word is not, in itself, shifting what anyone is talking about with a word.

Bringing about what I've been calling c-change is a sort of 'conceptual engineering'. One might engage in it with the intention that it will lead to r-change. But there's no need to have such an intention in order to try to change what is common ground about what users of a (term expressing a) concept presuppose. And of course this sort of 'conceptual engineering' is not particularly the province of philosophy or of the academy in general. It happens all the time.

Conceptual engineers and ameliorists often describe their projects in ways that imply that they will be successful only if the reference of the concept under their scalpel shifts.[46] That seems to me a pretty narrow vision of what it could be to ameliorate our thinking. Certainly the arch conceptual engineers—propagandists, advertising copy writers, spinmeisters, cagey politicians—don't think of what they are doing in such terms. The minions of the Tea Party have pretty much succeeded in getting the generic idea that illegal immigrants are bad hombres into the common ground of certain groups. Doing this, I would say, clearly changed the meaning of 'illegal immigrant' in those groups, but of course it didn't change its reference. Pretty obviously the goal was never to change the reference of the phrase: shifting the reference would have been the wrong outcome, since the goal was obviously to get people to think of illegal immigrants, not of just illegal immigrants who are bad hombres, as rapists and murders.

We ought to think of conceptual amelioration and engineering as an attempt to foster a kind of evolution within a population. The revisionary analyst drops a mutation into a population, hoping that it will 'reproduce' and in one way or another establish itself, even replace all of its alternatives over time. The goal might be referential shift, but often enough such shift will be unnecessary for the project to achieve whatever goals are driving it. In order to think fruitfully about the prospects of success for such a project, we need to think about the questions raised in this chapter: In what sense do meanings and concepts reproduce? Given a population into which a new use of the word is introduced, under what conditions can we expect the new use to establish itself? What sorts of conversational encounters make people adopt a new interpretive strategy, one that involves coming to a conversation with the presupposition that others do or may presuppose that the interpreter will understand them in a particular way? Do new meanings reproduce fastest if they are first firmly entrenched in small groups, or do they naturally spread like the flu? Etc., etc.

If you think of the A-project not as an ivory tower exercise—an ex cathedra philosophical pronouncement of what the little people should be meaning with their words, but as a genuine attempt to effect social change—you should be thinking about these sorts of questions. You should be asking questions like: What are reasonable, what unreasonable, models of how conceptual change occurs in a population? Given that we think a model reasonable, which of its variables are open to manipulation by the

---

[46] See, for example, the essays in Burgess, Cappelen, and Plunkett (forthcoming).

revisionary analyst? How do we change the strategies that people bring to the game—that is, to the project of interpreting others?

These are the sorts of questions that we ought to be asking, not only about versions of the A-project, but about conceptual analysis in general. Conceptual analysis is generally not just descriptive but normative. In interesting cases—the analysis of knowledge, of free action, of truth—what we tend to find is evidence not of a single underlying albeit vague concept, but a profusion of more or less mutual, not altogether consistent, presuppositions and patterns of application that with a bit of the philosopher's art can be resolved into a collection of candidates for what we might mean by the terms we use. To arbitrate amongst them is at least in part a matter of asking not what natural or gerrymandered kind we are trying to pick out, but asking what is the point or points of having and applying the concept under study. Philosophical analysis is pretty much always a (thinly veiled) version of the A-project. So, at least, I find myself tempted to claim. Philosophical analysis is not simply theory; it is practice. And as practice, it demands that its practitioners be practical.

Coda

One kind of meaning is constituted by what we need to grasp about usage in order to be competent participants in the linguistic practices of a community. What we need to grasp first and foremost is how those with whom we communicate normally expect us to understand them, and how those interlocutors assume we are normally to be understood. I've argued that we should think of this sort of meaning as a population-level, process-like phenomenon. It's population-level since what needs to be grasped is determined by a rough equilibrium of assumptions across speakers: the competent speaker needs to track certain bits of *common* knowledge that she is *commonly* assumed to know are presupposed. It's a process-like affair since what needs to be grasped is a dynamic property of a *practice*, of something that occurs and evolves: the competent speaker needs to track how what's taken for granted about a community's words fluctuates, as speakers join and leave the community and as the environment changes what is salient to all.

Thinking of meaning in this way has a number of payoffs. It reconciles Quine's skepticism about an epistemically interesting sort of analyticity—one that could ground a priori knowledge—with the belief that everyday talk about meaning is tracking something real, something about which we can and should theorize. It helps ground a sensible way of thinking about philosophical analysis and the role of our intuitions therein, philosophical analysis being in part an attempt to get at the real but unarticulated presuppositions that undergird our use of philosophically interesting terms. It helps ground a sensible way of thinking about our practices of ascribing content to others: once we recognize that identity of meaning and reference across individuals is to some extent a matter of how we choose to interpret them, and that such interpretive choices are heavily influenced by overlap of what I've called inter-pretive common ground (ICG), we are able to make sense of how words as we use them can mean the same as they did when our forebears used them, even if we and they are not using those words to talk about exactly the same things. It helps provide an understanding of 'conceptual engineering'—as an attempt to add or subtract from ICG but not (necessarily) to shift reference—that makes such engineering look like a sensible, conceivably successful project.

I have argued that we ought to think about meaning in a particular way, as being a population-level, process-like thing. Thinking of meaning in this way is something that can be done in many ways, just as there are many ways of thinking of species as population-level and process-like. As should be clear from Chapter 6, I do not have a detailed picture of the mechanisms of meaning evolution to give you. But it should be clear that in saying that meanings are species-like, I intend in the first instance that there are significant analogies between species, characterized as something like reproductively isolated lineages that produce fertile progeny via combinations of parental genetic material, and lineages of lexical entries established and maintained through language learning and conversation.

I do not say that there could not be a linguistic lineage that resembled, say, a lineage of replicators that reproduce by fission. But I am inclined to say that such things should be expected to be rare, language being on this planet a social, socially inculcated art. Neither, in saying that there is an important analogy between Mayrian biological species and things linguistic, do I mean to rule out a place in theory for sorting linguistic lineages in the way we sort biological ones when we think of them paraphyletically or even monophyletically. The idea that there are linguistic phylogenies—language families—is a staple of historical linguistics. In pointing to ways in which sex and conversation have parallel roles among zebras and French speakers, I am suggesting not that one should grab ahold of one analogy and run with it; my thought is that the semanticist or philosopher of language interested in meaning should steep herself in evolutionary theory and use it as a source for generating models of meaning and the processes that shape it.

This book is a baby step in the process of reflecting on evolutionary theory in order to generate such models. I am quite aware that it is only a baby step. To settle in any detail on a picture of the mechanisms that govern semantic-change-cum-change-in-ICG, we need a way to generate, codify, and evaluate judgments about what things are and are not in a community's ICG on the basis of accessible evidence—its newspapers, talk radio, Netflix series, subreddits, graffiti, and so on. The difficulty here is not (so much) making reasonable judgments about this sort of thing. More or less accurately making such judgments is what constitutes our ability to navigate the sea of language; we are in some sense already experts in making these judgments. The problem is articulating and codifying the judgments, a matter—given that we are thinking of presuppositions as things that often are embedded in a Bourdieuian *habitus*—which often requires discerning 'principle[s] . . . immanent in practice, which should be called implicit rather than unconscious, simply to indicate that [they exist] in a practical state in agents' practice' (Bourdieu 1977, 29). Once we have the ability to codify the data, we can start to develop a range of models that do something like describe how a speaker's understanding of ICG is likely to change when we add environmental cues about usage to a speaker's understanding of what speakers generally presuppose. One thinks that since we do manage to coordinate our expectations, there is an account that describes how we do it. How tractable is the problem of giving such an account is a matter for investigation.

I have argued that we ought to think about meaning in a particular way, as being a population-level, process-like thing, something that resembles in certain ways biological species. I have advertised this way of thinking as a way of avoiding a kind of despair about meaning associated with Quine. Some may find the analogy unhelpful, the notion of a species itself being something of a mess. Trying to interpret everyday judgments—or even the judgments of biologists—with extant attempts to elucidate the notion of species is a mug's game. If we say that species are reproductively isolated population lineages whose members are able to interbreed, or which have mate recognition systems, or something of the sort, we look either to be saying nothing about which paths on the tree of life correspond to species (because we don't mean for the biological criterion to be a diachronic criterion of conspecificity), or to be running counter to our judgments about species persistence, since we seem to think that a species can endure through evolution of the mechanisms of reproduction and potential mate recognition. If we take something like the clade as the paradigm of a species, we have a notion of species on which, for all we know, (many) dinosaurs and birds are members of a single species. It's not really clear that species talk—talk, that is, that is first and foremost responsible to colloquial judgments about species—is tracking anything biologically real. So if we accept the analogy *meanings are like species*, don't we run the risk of ending up saying that meanings, thought of as something that our meaning talk is tracking, are a sham?

I think the worry here is overdone. Even species skeptics agree that our talk about species tracks a real phenomenon. Marc Ereshefsky, to take an example, complains that the species concept is empty, arguing so: There are various coherent notions of species, in particular ones characterized in terms of reproductive mechanisms or employing phylogenetic criteria. But these notions not only cross-classify the biological world, many fail to even apply to large swathes of it.[1] Furthermore, the different, coherent notions simply don't have anything significant in common—the processes and structures that give reproductive species evolutionary coherence are altogether different from those that give phylogenetic ones coherence. It thus seems that if the concept *species* picks out anything, it does so because it's disjunctive. Now, disjunctively defining species may suffice to characterize our linguistic practice but, without some unity across the disjuncts, the possibility of such a definition does not show that *species* is a concept with any ontological heft. So since there are species only if they are important units in biological explanation (and thus are packing ontological heft), the concept *species* is empty (Ereshefsky 1998).

Suppose we buy in to this skepticism. It doesn't mean that our talk of *Canis familiaris* doesn't pick out something genuine and biologically significant. According to Ereshefsky, his

argument...is merely against the existence of the species category. Nothing I have said casts doubt on the existence of those taxa we call 'species'. We can remain confident that there are such taxa as *Homo sapiens* and *Canis familiaris*...The important point here is that the non-existence of the species category does not imply that the taxa we call 'species' are mere artifacts. (Ereshefsky 1998, 117)

---

[1] For example, species concepts that apply only to sexually reproducing lineages don't apply to all plants or many single-celled animals. For enlightening discussion see Ereshefsky (2010).

Taxa are well-trodden paths on the tree of life. Species talk is a means, in part, to discuss and theorize about such taxa. If species talk is talk about (say) four or five or fifteen different but well-trodden sorts of paths on the tree of life, well, then, species talk tracks something genuinely significant.

There is something even stronger to be said here. Someone like Ereshefsky is in fact—and rightly, in my opinion—not at all skeptical about some individual candidates for '*the* concept *species*' being notions that track things that are biologically real; his skepticism is simply about the existence of a single concept that can do all the work in biology that species talk does. Ereshefsky is a species pluralist. We philosophers of language should not be surprised if an analogous pluralism about the kinds of pathways of semantic evolution is appropriate. Let a hundred theoretical models bloom, a hundred stories about meaning change contend.

Bibliography

Austin, J.L. 1957. A Plea for Excuses. In Austin, J.L. (1979). *Philosophical Papers*, 3rd edition. Oxford University Press.

Boghossian, P. 1996. Analyticity Reconsidered. *Nous* 30, 360–91.

Boghossian, P. 1997. Analyticity. In Wright, C. and Hale, B., eds. *A Companion to the Philosophy of Language*. Blackwell.

Bouchard, F. and Rosenberg, A. 2004. Fitness, Probability, and the Principles of Natural Selection. *British Journal for the Philosophy of Science* 55, 693–712.

Bourdieu, P. 1977. *Outline of a Theory of Practice*. Cambridge University Press.

Brandom, R. 2000. *Articulating Reasons*. Harvard University Press.

Burge, T. 1986. Intellectual Norms and Foundations of Mind. *Journal of Philosophy* 83, 697–720.

Burgess, A., Cappelen, H., and Plunkett, D. Forthcoming. *Conceptual Engineering*. Oxford University Press.

Camp, Elizabeth. 2018. Slurs as Dual-Act Expressions. In Sosa, D., ed. *Bad Words*. Oxford University Press.

Cappelen, H. 2012. *Philosophy Without Intuitions*. Oxford University Press.

Carey, S. 2009. *The Origin of Concepts*. Oxford: Oxford University Press.

Carnap, R. 1956a. *Meaning and Reference*. Chicago University Press.

Carnap, R. 1956b. Meaning and Synonymy in Natural Language. In Carnap, R. *Meaning and Reference*. Chicago University Press.

Chalmers, D. 2011. Revisability and Conceptual Change in 'Two Dogmas of Empiricism'. *The Journal of Philosophy* 108, 387–416.

Chalmers, D. 2012. *Constructing the World*. Oxford University Press.

Chomsky, N. 1980. *Rules and Representations*. Columbia University Press.

Chomsky, N. 2000. *New Horizons in the Study of Language and Mind*. Cambridge University Press.

Claridge, M. et al. 1997. *Species: The Units of Biodiversity*. Chapman and Hall.

Darwin, C. 2003. *The Origin of the Species: 150th Anniversary Edition*. Signet Books.

Davidson, D. 1967. Truth and Meaning. In Davidson, D. (1984). *Essays on Truth and Interpretation*. Oxford University Press.

Davidson, D. 1973. Radical Interpretation. In Davidson, D. (1984). *Essays on Truth and Interpretation*. Oxford University Press.

Davidson, D. 1984. *Essays on Truth and Interpretation*. Oxford University Press.

Davidson, D. 1986. A Nice Derangement of Epitaphs. In Grandy, R. and Warner, R., eds. *Philosophical Grounds of Rationality*. Oxford University Press.

Dawkins, R. 1976. *The Selfish Gene*. Oxford University Press.

Dawkins, R. 1982. *The Extended Phenotype*. Oxford University Press.

Dennett, D. 1971. Intentional Systems. *Journal of Philosophy* 68, 87–106.

Dennett, D. 2017. *From Bacteria to Bach and Back*. W.W. Norton & Company.

De Queiroz, K. 1998. The General Lineage Concept of Species, Species Critria, and the Process of Speciation. In Howard, D. and Berlocher, S., eds. *Endless Forms*. Oxford University Press.

Devitt, M. 2006. *Ignorance of Language*. Oxford University Press.

Dorr, C. and Hawthorne, J. 2014. Semantic Plasticity and Speech Reports. *The Philosophical Review* 123, 281–338.

Dummett, M. 1973. *Frege: Philosophy of Language*. Harvard University Press.

Ereshefsky, M. 1998. Species Pluralism and Anti-Realism. *Philosophy of Science* 65, 103–20.

Ereshefsky, M. 1999. Species and the Linnaean Hierarchy. In Wilson, R., ed. *Species: New Interdisciplinary Essays*. MIT Press.

Ereshefsky, M. 2010. Microbiology and the Species Problem. *Biology and Philosophy* 25, 67–79.

Fausto-Sterling, Anne. 2000. *Sexing the Body: Gender Politics and the Construction of Sexuality*, revised edition. Basic Books.

Field, H. 1994. Deflationist Views of Meaning and Content. *Mind* 103, 249–85.

Field, H. 2005. Reply to Barry Loewer. *Philosophical Studies* 124, 110–18.

Foster, J. 1976. Meaning and Truth Theory. In Evans, G. and McDowell, J., eds. *Truth and Meaning: Essays in Semantics*. Oxford University Press.

Gallie, W.B. 1956. Essentially Contested Concepts. *Proceedings of the Aristotelian Society New Series* 56 (1955–6), 167–98.

Gluer, K. and Pagin, P. 2003. Meaning Theory and Autistic Speakers. *Mind and Language* 18, 23–51.

Godfrey-Smith, P. 2009. *Darwinian Populations and Natural Selection*. Oxford University Press.

Goldman, A. 1976. Discrimination and Perceptual Knowledge. *Journal of Philosophy* 73, 771–91.

Graff, D. 2000. Shifting Sands: An Interest-Relative Theory of Vagueness. *Philosophical Topics*, 45–81.

Grice, P. and Strawson, P. 1956. In Defense of a Dogma. *The Philosophical Review* 65, 141–58.

Hajek, A. 2003. What Conditional Probability Could Not Be. *Synthese* 137, 273–323.

Hampton, J. 1982. A Demonstration of the Intransitivity of Natural Categories. *Cognition* 12, 151–64.

Harman, Gilbert. 1996. Analyticity Regained? *Nous* 30, 392–400.

Hasaday, J. 2000. Contest and Consent: A Legal History of Marital Rape. *California Law Review* 88, 1373–505.

Haslanger, S. 2012a. Race and Gender: (What) Are They? (What) Do We Want Them to Be? In Haslanger, S. *Resisting Reality*. Oxford University Press.

Haslanger, S. 2012b. What Are We Talking About? The Semantics and Politics of Social Kinds. In Haslanger, S. *Resisting Reality*. Oxford University Press.

Haslanger, S. 2012c. What Good Are Our Intuitions? Philosophical Analysis and Social Kinds. In Haslanger, S. *Resisting Reality*. Oxford University Press.

Haslanger, S. 2012d. *Resisting Reality*. Oxford University Press.

Higginbotham, H. 1992. Truth and Understanding. *Philosophical Studies* 65, 1–18.

Higginbotham, J. 1989. Knowledge of Reference. In George, A., ed. *Reflections on Chomsky*. Blackwell.

Hom, C. and May, R. 2018. Pejoratives as Fiction. In Sosa, D., ed. *Bad Words*. Oxford University Press.

Hull, D. 1980. Individuality and Selection. *Annual Review of Ecology and Systematics* 11, 311–32.

Hull, D. 1997. The Ideal Species Concept—and Why We Can't Get It. In Claridge, M. et al. *Species: The Units of Biodiversity*. Chapman and Hall.

Jackendoff, R. 2002. *Foundations of Language*. Oxford University Press.

Joseph, B. and Janda, R. 2003. *The Handbook of Historical Linguistics*. Blackwell.

Kahneman, D. 2013. *Thinking, Fast and Slow*. Farrar, Straus, and Giroux.

Kaplan, D. 1989. Demonstratives. In Almog, J. et al. *Themes from Kaplan*. Oxford University Press.

Kaplan, D. 1990. Words. *Proceedings of the Aristotelian Society Supplementary Volumes* 64, 93–119.

Kaplan, D. ms. *The Meaning of Ouch and Oops*.

Lakoff, G. 2008. *The Political Mind*. Penguin Books.

LaPorte, J. 2004. *Natural Kinds and Conceptual Change*. Cambridge University Press.

Levy, A. 2011. Game Theory, Indirect Modelling and the Origin of Morality. *Journal of Philosophy* 108, 171–87.

Lewis, D. 1969. *Convention*. Harvard University Press.

Lewis, D. 1979. Scorekeeping in a Language Game. *Journal of Philosophical Logic* 8, 339–59.

Lightfoot, D. 1999. *The Development of Language: Acquisition, Change, and Evolution*. Blackwell.

Lloyd, E. 2017. Units and Levels of Selection. *Stanford Encyclopedia of Philosophy*. https://plato.stanford.edu.

Machery, Edouard. 2009. *Doing Without Concepts*. Oxford University Press.

Malmgren, A.S. 2011. Rationalism and the Content of Intuitive Judgements. *Mind* 120, 263–327.

Margolis, E. and Laurence, S., eds. 1999. *Concepts: Core Readings*. MIT Press.

Matthen, M. and Ariew, A. 2002. Two Ways of Thinking about Fitness and Natural Selection. *Journal of Philosophy* 99, 55–83.

Mayden, R. 1997. A Hierarchy of Species Concepts: The Denouement in the Saga of the Species Problem. In Claridge, M. et al. *Species: The Units of Biodiversity*. Chapman and Hall.

Millstein, R. 2006. Natural Selection as a Population-Level Causal Process. *British Journal for the Philosophy of Science* 57, 627–53.

Murphy, G. 2002. *The Big Book of Concepts*. MIT Press.

Nickel, B. 2016. *Between Logic and the World*. Oxford University Press.

Perry, J. 2000. *The Problem of the Essential Indexical and Other Essays*. CSLI Publishing.

Pinker, S. 1989. *Words and Rules*. Basic Books.

Pryor, J. 2017. *De Jure* Codesignation. In Hale, B., Wright, C. et al. *A Companion to the Philosophy of Language*. Wiley-Blackwell.

Putnam, H. 1962. It Ain't Necessarily So. *Journal of Philosophy* 59, 658–71.

Putnam, H. 1975. The Meaning of 'Meaning'. *Minnesota Studies in the Philosophy of Science* 7, 131–93.

Putnam, H. 1986. Meaning Holism. In Hahn, P. and Schlipp, P., eds. *The Philosophy of W.V. Quine*. Open Court.

Quine, W.V. 1951. Two Dogmas of Empiricism. *The Philosophical Review* 60. Reprinted in Quine, W.V. 1981. *From a Logical Point of View*, second edition, revised. Harvard University Press. (Page references to the reprinted version.)

Quine, W.V. 1960a. Carnap and Logical Truth. In Quine, W.V. *The Ways of Paradox and Other Essays*. Harvard University Press.

Quine, W.V. 1960b. *Word and Object*. MIT Press.

Quine, W.V. 1969a. *Ontological Relativity and Other Essays*. Columbia University Press.

Quine, W.V. 1969b. Speaking of Objects. In Quine, W.V. *Ontological Relativity and Other Essays*. Columbia University Press.

Quine, W.V. 1969c. Ontological Relativity. In Quine, W.V. *Ontological Relativity and Other Essays*. Columbia University Press.

Quine, W.V. 1981. *From a Logical Point of View*, second edition, revised. Harvard University Press.

Quine, W.V. 1992. *Pursuit of Truth*, revised edition. Harvard University Press.

Raffman, D. 1994. Vagueness without Paradox. *The Philosophical Review* 103, 41–74.

Reinhart, Tanya. 1979. Syntactic Domains for Semantic Rules. In Guenthner, F. and Schmidt, S.J., eds. *Formal Semantics and Pragmatic for Natural Language*. Reidel.

Richard, M. 1990. *Propositional Attitudes*. Cambridge University Press.

Richard, M., ed. 2003. *Meaning*. Blackwell.

Richard, M. 2008. *When Truth Gives Out*. Oxford University Press.

Richard, M. 2013. *Meaning in Context, Volume I*. Oxford University Press.

Richard, M. 2015. *Meaning in Context, Volume II*. Oxford University Press.

Richard, M. ms. Reference to Rabbits. Posted at https://markrichardphilosophy.wordpress.com/work-in-progress.

Richards, R. 2010. *The Species Problem: A Philosophical Analysis*. Cambridge University Press.

Russell, G. 2008. *Truth in Virtue of Meaning*. Oxford University Press.

Schwartz, A. 1992. *Contested Concepts in Cognitive Social Science*. Senior Thesis, University of California, Berkeley.

Skyrms, B. 2010. *Signals*. Oxford University Press.

Soames, S. 1989. Semantics and Semantic Competence. *Philosophical Perspectives* 3, 575–96.

Soames, S. 1999. *Understanding Truth*. Oxford University Press.

Soames, S. 2002. *Beyond Rigidity*. Oxford University Press.

Sober, E. 1980. *The Nature of Selection*. MIT Press.

Sosa, E. 2007. Experimental Philosophy and Philosophical Intuition. *Philosophical Studies* 132, 99–107.

Spencer, J. 2016. Disagreement and Attitudinal Relativism. *Mind* 125, 511–39.

Stalnaker, R. 1984. *Inquiry*. MIT Press.

Stalnaker, R. 2014. *Context*. Oxford University Press.

Steinmetz, Sol. 2008. *Semantic Antics*. Random House.

Sterelny, K. and Griffiths, P. 1999. *Sex and Death*. University of Chicago Press.

Szabolcsi, Anna. 2010. *Quantification*. Cambridge University Press.

Unger, P. 1984. *Philosophical Relativity*. University of Minnesota Press.

Williamson, T. 2008. *The Philosophy of Philosophy*. Wiley-Blackwell.

Wilson, M. 1982. Predicate Meets Property. *The Philosophical Review* 91, 549–89.

Wilson, M. 2006. *Wandering Significance*. Oxford University Press.

Wilson, R., ed. 1999. *Species: New Interdisciplinary Essays*. MIT Press.

Wright, C. and Hale, B. *A Companion to the Philosophy of Language*. Blackwell.

Zimmer, C. and Emlen, D. 2012. *Evolution: Making Sense of Life*. Roberts and Company Publishers.

Index